History of the Expedition
to Russia, 1812

Volume Two

Count Platoff

History of the Expedition to Russia, 1812

Volume Two

General Count Philippe de Ségur

Quamquam animus meminisse horret, luctuque refugit,
Incipiam.—   VIRGIL

NONSUCH

First published 1836
Copyright © in this edition 2005
Nonsuch Publishing Ltd

Nonsuch Publishing Limited
The Mill, Brimscombe Port, Stroud, Gloucestershire, GL5 2QG
www.nonsuch-publishing.com

British Library Cataloguing in Publication Data.
A catalogue record for this book is available from the British Library.

ISBN I-84588-022-6

Typesetting and origination by Nonsuch Publishing Limited
Printed in Great Britain by Oaklands Book Services Limited

CONTENTS

BOOK XI

BOOK XII

INTRODUCTION TO THE MODERN EDITION

From the Niemen to Vilna, I have seen nothing but ruined houses and abandoned carts and equipment. 10,000 horses have been killed already by the cold rains and eating unripe rye which they are not accustomed to. The smell of the dead horses on the road is perfectly horrible. But that is not so bad as the shortness of rations. Several of my Young Guard have already starved to death.

> From a letter of Marshal Adolphe Mortier,
> Commander of the Young Guard

On 23rd and 24th June 1812, Napoleon's Grande Armée of over 600,000 French, Austrian, German, Polish and Italian soldiers crossed the River Niemen unopposed and started the march to Moscow. However, from the start the army was plagued by problems with supply, disease and harsh weather conditions. The Russian campaign was to become one of Napoleon's greatest defeats, and was the beginning of a series of military losses which were to lead to his eventual exile to Elba in 1814.

In 1812 Russia was the last great mainland European threat to Napoleon's power. Traditionally one of Britain's strongest allies, Russia had been part of the Third Coalition which was formed to oppose Napoleon, along with Britain, Prussia, Austria and Sweden. However, after the French defeat of the Austrian forces at Ulm in 1805 and the Prussian army at Jena-Auerstadt in 1806, Russia was left to oppose Napoleon largely unaided. Confrontation was inevitable and after the bloody but indecisive Battle of Eylau in February 1807, Napoleon comprehensively defeated the Russian army at Friedland later that year, forcing Tsar Alexander I into signing a peace treaty with the

French at Tilsit. By the terms of this agreement the Russians left most of Europe under French control and became part of the Continental System, which entailed a complete trade embargo against Britain. However, this embargo seriously damaged the Russian economy and by 1810 Russian ports had once again been opened to British trade. This, along with worsening relations over Napoleon's German and Baltic campaign, led to a breakdown in relations and, as early as 1810, Napoleon began to plan his campaign to conquer Russia.

By the start of the 1812 campaign Napoleon faced strong opposition to his plans from his own generals. Not only would the plan denude France of her fighting population at a time when Wellington was steadily pushing back the French forces in Spain, but, if successful, it would also increase French-controlled territory to a size which would be almost impossible to maintain. Despite these objections the invasion went ahead and was meticulously planned by Napoleon himself. However, he envisaged a quick campaign, defeating the Russians in battle and forcing the Tsar's surrender. What he could not plan for was the 'scorched earth' policy of the Russians, who retreated before the massive Grande Armée, destroying any source of food, shelter and fodder which might serve the enemy as they went. This put a massive strain on the invaders from the outset, who were reliant on living off the lands they were passing through. Diseases like dysentery and typhus were soon rife, and the advent of winter, with its freezing conditions for which the army was totally unprepared, added to the casualties. Napoleon's assertion that on taking Moscow he would force the Tsar to surrender was soon proved to be incorrect and the Grande Armée was forced into ignominious retreat.

Only around 22,000 soldiers made it back across the River Niemen. The Russian Expedition was an unmitigated disaster for Napoleon; not only did it lead to a catastrophic loss of men, horses and artillery, but it also provided the rest of Europe with the first real evidence that the Emperor himself was not invincible.

EDITORIAL NOTE: The footnotes are from the 1836 edition.

BOOK VIII

CHAPTER I

THE RUSSIANS RETREAT TO MOSCOW

WE have seen that the emperor Alexander, surprised at Wilna amidst his preparations for defence, retreated with his disunited army, and was unable to rally it till it was at the distance of a hundred leagues from that city, between Witepsk and Smolensk. Hurried along in the precipitate retreat of Barclay, that prince sought refuge at Drissa, in a camp injudiciously chosen and intrenched at great expense; a mere point in the space, on so extensive a frontier, and which served only to indicate to the enemy the object of his manœuvres.

Alexander, however, encouraged by the sight of this camp, and of the Dwina, took breath behind that river. It was there that he first consented to receive an English agent, so important did he deem it to appear till the last moment faithful to his engagements with France. Whether he acted with real good faith, or merely made a show of doing so, we know not: so much is certain, that at Paris, after his success, he affirmed, on his honour, to Count Daru, that, "notwithstanding the accusations of Napoleon, this was his first infraction of the treaty of Tilsit."

At the same time he caused Barclay to issue addresses, designed to corrupt the French and their allies, similar to those which had so irritated Napoleon at Glubokoé:—attempts which the French regarded as contemptible, and the Germans as unseasonable.

In other respects, the emperor had given his enemies but a mean opinion of his military talents: this opinion was founded on his having neglected the Berezina, the only natural line of defence of Lithuania: on his eccentric retreat towards the north, when the rest of his army was fleeing southward; and lastly, on his ukase relative to recruiting, dated Drissa, which assigned to the recruits, for their places of rendezvous, several towns that were almost immediately occupied by the French. His departure from the army, as soon as it began to fight, was also a subject of remark.

As to his political measures in his new and in his old provinces, and his proclamations from Polotzk to his army, to Moscow, to his great nation, it was admitted that they were singularly well adapted to persons and places. It appears, in fact, that in the political means which he employed there was a very obvious gradation of energy.

In the recently acquired portion of Lithuania, the country, the houses, the inhabitants, in short, every thing had been spared, either from hurry or designedly. No contributions had been levied; only the most powerful of the nobles had been carried off: their defection might have set too dangerous an example, and had they still further committed themselves, their return in the sequel would have been more difficult; besides, they served as hostages.

In the provinces of Lithuania which had been of old incorporated with the empire, where a mild administration, favours judiciously bestowed, and a longer habit of subjection, had extinguished the recollection of independence, the inhabitants were hurried away with all they could carry with them. Still it was not deemed expedient to require of subjects professing a different religion, and a nascent patriotism, the destruction of property: a levy of five men only out of every five hundred males was ordered.

But in Russia Proper, where religion, superstition, ignorance, patriotism, all went hand in hand with the government, not only had the inhabitants been obliged to retreat with the army, but every thing that could not be removed had been destroyed.

Those who were not destined to recruit the regulars, joined the militia or the Cossacks.

The interior of the empire being then threatened, it was for Moscow to set an example. That capital, justly denominated by its poets, *"Moscow with the gilded cupolas,"* was a vast and whimsical assemblage of two hundred and ninety-five churches, and fifteen hundred mansions, with their gardens and dependencies. These palaces of brick, and their parks, intermixed with neat houses of wood, and even thatched cottages, were spread over several square leagues of irregular ground: they were grouped round a lofty triangular fortress; the vast double enclosure of which, half a league in circuit, contained, the first, several palaces, some churches, and rocky and uncultivated spots; the second, a prodigious bazaar, the town of the merchants and shopkeepers, where was displayed the collected wealth of the four quarters of the globe.

These edifices, these palaces, nay, the very shops themselves, were covered with polished and painted iron: the churches, each surmounted by a terrace and several steeples, terminating in golden balls, then the crescent, and lastly the cross, reminded the spectator of the history of this nation: it was Asia and its religion, at first victorious, subsequently vanquished, and finally the crescent of Mahomet surmounted by the cross of Christ.

A single ray of sunshine caused this splendid city to glisten with a thousand varied colours. At sight of it the traveller paused, delighted and astonished. It reminded him of the prodigies with which the eastern poets had amused his childhood. On entering it, a nearer view served but to heighten his astonishment: he recognised the nobles by the manners, the habits, and the different languages of modern Europe; and by the rich and airy elegance of their dress. He beheld, with surprise, the luxury and the Asiatic form of those of the traders; the Grecian costumes of the common people, and their long beards. He was struck by the same variety in the edifices: and yet all this was tinged with a local and sometimes harsh colour, such as befits the country of which Moscow was the ancient capital.

When, lastly, he observed the grandeur and magnificence of the numerous palaces, the wealth which they displayed, the luxury of the equipages, the multitude of slaves and obsequious servants, the splendour of those gorgeous spectacles, the noise of those sumptuous festivities, entertainments, and rejoicings which incessantly resounded within its walls, he fancied himself transported into a city of kings, into an assemblage of sovereigns, who had brought with them their manners, customs, and attendants from all parts of the world.

They were, nevertheless, only subjects; but opulent and powerful subjects; grandees, vain of their ancient nobility, strong in their collected numbers, and in the general ties of consanguinity contracted during the seven centuries which this capital had existed. They were landed proprietors, proud of their existence amidst their vast possessions; for almost the whole territory of the government of Moscow belongs to them, and they there reign over a million of serfs. Finally, they were nobles, resting with a patriotic and religious pride upon "the cradle and the tomb of their nobility"—for such is the appellation which they give to Moscow.

It seems right, in fact, that here the nobles of the most illustrious families should be born and educated; that hence they should launch into the career of honours and glory; and lastly, that hither, when satisfied, discontented, or undeceived, they should bring their disgust or their resentment to pour it forth; their reputation, in order to enjoy it, to exercise its influence on the young nobility; and to recruit, at a distance from power, of which they have nothing farther to expect, their pride, which has been too long bowed down near the throne.

Here their ambition, either satiated or disappointed, has assumed, amidst their own dependents, and, as it were, beyond the reach of the court, a greater freedom of speech: it is a sort of privilege which time has sanctioned, of which they are tenacious, and which their sovereign respects. They become worse courtiers, but better citizens. Hence the reluctance of their sovereigns to visit this vast repository of glory and of commerce, this city of nobles whom they have disgraced or disgusted, whom age or reputation have placed beyond their power, and whom they are obliged to be cautious of offending.

To this city necessity brought Alexander: he repaired thither from Polotzk, preceded by his proclamations, and looked for by the nobility and the mercantile class. His first appearance was amidst the assembled nobility. There every thing was great—the circumstance, the assembly, the speaker, and the resolutions which he inspired. His voice betrayed emotion. No sooner had he ceased, than one general, simultaneous, unanimous cry burst from all hearts:—"Ask what you please, sire! we offer you every thing! take our all!"

One of the nobles then proposed the levy of a militia; and in order to its formation, the gift of one peasant in twenty-five; but a hundred voices interrupted him, crying that "the country required a greater sacrifice; that it was necessary to grant one serf in ten, ready armed, equipped, and supplied with provisions for three months." This was offering, for the single government of Moscow, 80,000 men, and a great quantity of stores.

This sacrifice was immediately voted without deliberation—some say with enthusiasm, and that it was executed in like manner, so long as the danger was at hand. Others attributed the consent of this assembly to so extreme a proposition, to submission alone—a sentiment, indeed, which, in the presence of absolute power, absorbs every other.

They add, that, on the breaking up of the meeting, the principal nobles were heard to murmur among themselves against the extravagance of such a measure. "Was the danger, then, so pressing? Did, then, the Russian army, which, as they were told, still numbered 400,000 men, no longer exist? Why, then, deprive them of so many peasants? The service of these men would be, it was said, only temporary; but who could ever hope for their return? It was, on the contrary, an event to be dreaded. Would these serfs, habituated to the irregularities of war, bring back their former submission? Undoubtedly not: they would return full of new sentiments and new ideas, with which they would infect the villages; they would there propagate a refractory spirit, which would give infinite trouble to the master by spoiling the slave."

Be this as it may, the resolution of the assembly was generous, and worthy of so great a nation. The details are of little consequence. We well know that it is the same every where; that every thing in the world loses by being seen too near; and lastly, that nations ought to be judged by the general mass and by results.

Alexander then addressed the traders, but more briefly: he ordered that proclamation to be read to them, in which Napoleon was represented as "a perfidious wretch; a Moloch, who, with treachery in his heart and loyalty on his lips, was striving to blot out Russia from the face of the earth."

It is said that, at these words, the masculine and highly coloured faces of the auditors, to which long beards imparted a look at once antique, majestic, and wild, were inflamed with rage. Their eyes flashed fire; they were seized with a convulsive fury: their stiffened arms, their clenched fists, the gnashing of their teeth, and subdued execrations, expressed its vehemence. The effect was correspondent. Their chief, whom they elect themselves, proved himself worthy of his station: he put down his name the first for 50,000 rubles. It was two-thirds of his fortune, and he paid it the next day.

These traders were divided into three classes: it was proposed to fix the contribution for each; but one of the assembly, who was included in the lowest class, declared that his patriotism would not brook any limit, and he immediately subscribed a sum far surpassing the proposed standard: the others followed his example more or less closely. Advantage was taken of their first emotions. Every thing was at hand that was requisite to bind them irrevocably while they were yet together, excited by one another, and by the words of their sovereign.

This patriotic donation amounted, it is said, to two millions of rubles. The other governments repeated, like so many echoes, the national cry of Moscow. The emperor accepted all;

but all could not be given immediately: and when, in order to complete his work, he claimed the rest of the promised succours, he was obliged to have recourse to constraint; the danger which had alarmed some and inflamed others, having by that time ceased to exist.

CHAPTER II

EVACUATION OF MOSCOW

MEANWHILE Smolensk was reduced, Napoleon at Viazma, and consternation in Moscow. The great battle was not yet lost, and already people began to abandon that capital.

In his proclamations the governor-general, count Rostopchin, told the women, that "he should not detain *them,* as the less fear the less danger there would be; but that their brothers and husbands must stay, or they would cover themselves with infamy." He then added encouraging particulars concerning the hostile force, which consisted, according to his statement, of "one hundred and fifty thousand men, who were reduced to the necessity of feeding on horse-flesh. The emperor Alexander was about to return to his faithful capital; eighty-three thousand Russians, both recruits and militia, with eighty pieces of cannon, were marching towards Borodino, to join Kutusoff."

He thus concluded: "If these forces are not sufficient, I will say to you, 'Come, my Muscovite friends, let us march also! we will assemble one hundred thousand men: we will take the image of the Blessed Virgin, and one hundred and fifty pieces of cannon, and put an end to the business at once!'"

It has been remarked, as a purely local singularity, that most of these proclamations were in the scriptural style and in poetic prose.

At the same time a prodigious balloon was constructed, by command of Alexander, not far from Moscow, under the direction of a German artificer. The destination of this winged machine was to hover over the French army, to single out its chief, and destroy him by a shower of balls and fire. Several attempts were made to raise it, but without success, the springs by which the wings were to be worked having always broken.

Rostopchin, nevertheless, affecting to persevere, is said to have caused a great quantity of rockets and other combustibles to be prepared. Moscow itself was designed to be the great infernal machine, the sudden nocturnal explosion of which was to consume the emperor and his army. Should the enemy escape this danger, he would at least no longer have an asylum or resources; and the horror of so tremendous a calamity, which would be charged to his account, as had been done in regard to the disasters of Smolensk, Dorogobouje, Viazma, and Gjatsk, would not fail to rouse the whole of Russia.

Such was the terrible plan of this noble descendant of one of the greatest Asiatic conquerors.[1] It was conceived without effort, matured with care, and executed without hesitation. This Russian nobleman has since visited Paris. He is a man of correct habits, a good husband, an excellent father; he has a superior and cultivated mind, and in society his manners are mild and pleasing: but, like some of his countrymen, he combines an antique energy with the civilisation of modern times.

His name henceforth belongs to history: still he had only the largest share in the honour of this great sacrifice. It had been previously commenced at Smolensk, and it was he who completed it. This resolution, like every thing great and entire, was admirable; the motive sufficient and justified by success; the devotedness unparalleled, and so extraordinary, that the historian is obliged to pause in order to fathom, to comprehend, and to contemplate it.[2]

One single individual, amidst a vast empire nearly overthrown, surveys its dangers with a steady eye: he measures, he appreciates it, and ventures, perhaps uncommissioned, to devote all the public and private interests a sacrifice to it. Though but a subject, he decides the lot of the state, without the countenance of his sovereign; a noble, he decrees the destruction of the palaces of all the nobles, without their consent; the protector, from the post which he occupies, of a numerous population, of a multitude of opulent merchants and traders, of one of the largest capitals in Europe, he sacrifices their fortunes, their establishments, nay, the whole city; he himself consigns to the flames the finest and the richest of his palaces, and proud and satisfied, he quietly remains among the resentful sufferers who have been injured or utterly ruined by the measure.

What motive then could be so just and so powerful as to inspire him with such astonishing confidence? In deciding upon the destruction of Moscow, his principal aim was not to famish the enemy, since he had contrived to clear that great city of provisions; nor to deprive the French army of shelter, since it was impossible to suppose that out of eight thousand houses and churches, dispersed over so vast a space, there should not be left buildings enough to serve as barracks for one hundred and fifty thousand men.

He was no doubt aware also that by such a step he would counteract that very important point of what was supposed to be the plan of campaign formed by Alexander, whose object was thought to be to entice forward and to detain Napoleon, till winter should come upon him, seize him, and deliver him up defenceless to the whole incensed nation. For it was natural to presume that these flames would enlighten that conqueror; they would take from his invasion its end and aim. They would of course compel him to renounce it while it was yet time, and decide him to return to Lithuania, for the purpose of taking up winter quarters in that country—a determination which was likely to prepare for Russia a second campaign more dangerous than the first.

But in this important crisis Rostopchin perceived two great dangers: the one, which threatened the national honour, was that of a disgraceful peace dictated at Moscow, and forced upon his sovereign; the other was a political rather than a military danger, in which he feared the seductions of the enemy more than his arms, and a revolution more than a conquest.

Averse, therefore, to any treaty, this governor foresaw that in the populous capital, which the Russians themselves style the oracle, the example of the whole empire, Napoleon would have resource to the weapon of revolution, the only one that would be left him to accomplish his purpose.[3] For this reason he resolved to raise a barrier of fire between that great captain and all weaknesses, from whatever quarter they might proceed, whether from the throne or from his countrymen, either nobles or senators; and more especially between a population of serfs and the soldiers of a free nation; in short, between the latter and that mass of artisans and tradesmen, who form in Moscow the commencement of an intermediate class—a class for which the French revolution was especially brought about.

All the preparations were made in silence, without the knowledge either of the people, the proprietors of all classes, or perhaps of their emperor. The nation was ignorant that it was sacrificing itself. This is so strictly true, that, when the moment for execution arrived, we heard the inhabitants who had fled to the churches, execrating this destruction. Those who beheld it from a distance, the most opulent of the nobles, mistaken like their peasants, charged us with it; and in short, those by whom it was ordered threw the odium of it upon us, having engaged in the work of destruction in order to render us objects of detestation, and caring but little about the maledictions of so many unfortunate creatures, provided they could throw the weight of them upon us.

The silence of Alexander leaves room to doubt whether he approved this grand determination or not. What part he took in this catastrophe is still a mystery to the Russians: either they are ignorant on the subject, or they make a secret of the matter:—the effect of despotism, which enjoins ignorance or silence.

Some think that no individual in the whole empire, excepting the sovereign, would have dared to take on himself so heavy a responsibility. His subsequent conduct disavowed without disapproving it. Others are of opinion that this was one of the causes of his absence from the army, and that, not wishing to appear either to order or to forbid it, he would not stay to be a witness of the catastrophe.

As to the general abandonment of the houses, all the way from Smolensk, it was compulsory, the Russian army defending them till they were carried sword in hand, and describing us every where as destructive monsters. The country suffered but little from this emigration. The peasants residing near the high road escaped through by-ways to other villages belonging to their lords, where they found accommodation.

The forsaking of their huts made of trunks or trees laid one upon another, which a hatchet suffices for building, and of which a bench, a table, and an image constitute the whole furniture, was scarcely any sacrifice for serfs, who had nothing of their own, whose persons did not even belong to themselves, and whose masters were obliged to provide for them, since they were their property, and the source of all their income.

These peasants, moreover, in removing their carts, their implements, and their cattle, carried every thing with them, most of them being able to supply themselves with habitation, clothing, and all other necessaries: for these people are still in but the first stage of civilisation, and far from that division of labour which denotes the extension and high improvement of commerce and society.

But in the towns, and especially in the great capital, how could they be expected to quit so many establishments, to resign so many conveniences and enjoyments, so much wealth, moveable and immoveable? and yet it cost little or no more to obtain the total abandonment of Moscow than that of the meanest village. There, as at Vienna, Berlin, and Madrid, the principal nobles hesitated not to retire on our approach: for, with them, to remain would seem to be the same as to betray. But here, tradesmen, artisans, day-labourers, all thought it their duty to flee like the most powerful of the grandees. There was no occasion to command: these people have not yet ideas sufficient to judge for themselves, to distinguish and to discover differences; the example of the nobles was sufficient. The few foreigners who remained at Moscow might have enlightened them; some of these were exiled, and terror insulated the rest.

It was, besides, an easy task to excite apprehensions of profanation, pillage, and devastation in the minds of people so cut off from other nations, and in the inhabitants of a city which had been so often plundered and burnt by the Tartars. With these examples before their eyes, they could not await an impious and ferocious enemy but for the purpose of fighting him: the rest must necessarily shun his approach with horror, if they would save themselves in this life and in the next: obedience, honour, religion, fear, every thing in short enjoined them to flee, with all that they could carry off.

A fortnight before our arrival, the departure of the archives, the public chests and treasure, and that of the nobles and the principal merchants, together with their most valuable effects, indicated to the rest of the inhabitants what course to pursue. The governor, already impatient to see the city evacuated, appointed superintendents to expedite the emigration.

On the 3rd of September, a Frenchwoman, at the risk of being torn in pieces by the furious Muscovites, ventured to leave her hiding-place. She wandered a long time through extensive quarters, the solitude of which astonished her, when a distant and doleful sound thrilled her with terror. It was like the funeral dirge of this vast city; fixed in motionless suspense, she beheld an immense multitude of persons, of both sexes, in deep affliction, carrying their effects and their sacred images, and leading their children along with them. Their priests, laden with the sacred symbols of religion, headed the procession. They were invoking Heaven in hymns of lamentation, in which all of them joined with tears.

On reaching the gates of the city, this crowd of unfortunate creatures passed through them with painful hesitation: turning their eyes once more towards Moscow, they seemed to be bidding a last farewell to their holy city: but by degrees their sobs and the doleful tones of their hymns died away in the vast plains by which it is surrounded.

1. Count Rostopchin was the son of a steward of count Orloff. He was promoted by the emperor Paul, whose confidence he had possessed before that prince came to the throne.—*Ed.*

2. Count Rostopchin, we know, has written that he had no hand in that great event: but we cannot help following the opinion of the Russians and French, who were witnesses of and actors in this grand drama. All, without exception, persist in attributing to that nobleman the entire honour of that generous resolution. Several even seem to think, that if count Rostopchin, who is yet animated by the same noble spirit, which will render his name imperishable, still refuses the immortality of so great an action, it is that he may leave all the glory of it to the patriotism of the nation, of which he is become one of the most remarkable characters.

3. Napoleon was decidedly averse from employing "the weapon of revolution." Accordingly, he refused to listen to revolutionary plans, which were proposed to him by some of the Russians.—*Ed.*

CHAPTER III

PREPARATIONS
FOR ITS DESTRUCTION

THUS was this population dispersed in detail or in masses. The roads to Cazan, Wladimir, and Yaroslaff, were covered to the distance of forty leagues by fugitives on foot, and several unbroken files of vehicles of every kind. At the same time the measures of Rostopchin, to prevent dejection and to preserve order, detained many of these unfortunate people till the very last moment.

To this must be added the appointment of Kutusoff, which had revived their hopes, the false intelligence of a victory at Borodino, and, for the less affluent, the hesitation natural at the moment of abandoning the only home which they possessed; lastly, the inadequacy of the means of transport, notwithstanding the quantity of vehicles, which is peculiarly great in Russia; either because heavy requisitions for the exigencies of the army had reduced their number; or because they were too small, as it is customary to make them very light, on account of the sandy soil and the roads, which may be said to be rather marked out than constructed.

It was then that Kutusoff, though defeated at Borodino, sent letters to all quarters announcing that he was victorious. He deceived Moscow, Petersburgh, and even the commanders of the other Russian armies. Alexander communicated this false intelligence to his allies. In the first transports of his joy he hastened to the altars, loaded the army and the family of his general with honours and money, gave directions for rejoicings, returned thanks to Heaven, and appointed Kutusoff field-marshal for this defeat.

Most of the Russians affirm that their emperor was grossly imposed upon by this report. They are still unacquainted with the motive of such a deception, which at first procured Kutusoff unbounded favours, that were not withdrawn from him, and afterwards, it is said, dreadful menaces, that were not put in execution.

If we may credit several of his countrymen, who were perhaps his enemies, it would appear that he had two motives. In the first place, he wished not to shake, by disastrous intelligence, the little firmness which, in Russia, Alexander was generally, but erroneously, thought to possess. In the second, as he was anxious that his dispatch should arrive on the very name-day of his sovereign, it is added that his object was to obtain the rewards for which this kind of anniversaries furnishes occasion.

But at Moscow the erroneous impression was of short continuance. The rumour of the destruction of half his army was almost immediately propagated in that city, from the singular commotion of extraordinary events, which has been known to spread almost instantaneously to prodigious distances. Still, however, the language of the chiefs the only persons who durst speak, continued haughty and threatening; many of the inhabitants, trusting to it, remained; but they were every day more and more tormented by a painful anxiety. Nearly at one and the same moment, they were transported with rage, elevated with hope, and overwhelmed with fear.

At one of those moments when, either prostrate before the altars, or in their own houses before the images of their saints, they had no hope but in Heaven, shouts of joy suddenly resounded: the people instantly thronged the streets and public places to learn the cause. Intoxicated with joy, their eyes were fixed on the cross of the principal church. A vulture had entangled himself in the chains which supported it, and was held suspended by them. This was a certain presage to minds whose natural superstition was heightened by extraordinary anxiety; it was thus that their God would seize and deliver Napoleon into their power.[1]

Rostopchin took advantage of all these movements, which he excited or checked according as they were favourable to him or otherwise. He caused the most diminutive to be selected from the prisoners taken from the enemy, and exhibited to the people, that the latter might derive courage from the sight of their weakness:[2] and yet he emptied Moscow of every kind of supplies, in order to feed the vanquished, and to famish the conquerors. This measure was easily carried into effect, as Moscow was provisioned in spring and autumn by water only, and in winter by sledges.

He was still preserving with a remnant of hope the order that was necessary, especially in such a flight, when the effects of the disaster at Borodino appeared. The long train of wounded, their groans, their garments and linen dyed with gore; their most powerful nobles struck and overthrown like the others—all this was a novel and alarming sight to a city which had for such a length of time been exempt from the horrors of war. The police redoubled its activity; but the terror which it excited could not long make head against a still greater terror.

Rostopchin once more addressed the people. He declared that "he would defend Moscow to the last extremity; that the tribunals were already closed, but that was of no consequence; that there was no occasion for tribunals to try the guilty." He added that "in two days he would give the signal." He recommended to the people to "arm themselves with hatchets, and especially with three-pronged forks, as the French were not heavier than a sheaf of corn." As for the wounded, he said he should cause "masses to be said, and the water to be blessed, in order to their speedy recovery. Next day," he added, "he should repair to Kutusoff, to take final measures for exterminating the enemy. And then," said he, "we will send these guests to the devil; we will despatch the perfidious wretches, and fall to work to reduce them to powder."

Kutusoff had in fact never despaired of the salvation of the country. After employing the militia during the battle of Borodino to carry ammunition and to assist the wounded, he had just formed with them the third rank of his army. At Mojaisk, the good face which he had kept up had enabled him to gain sufficient time to make an orderly retreat, to select his wounded, and abandon such as were incurable, in order to embarrass the enemy's army with them. Subsequently at Zelkowo, a check had stopped the impetuous advance of Murat. At length, on the 13th of September, Moscow beheld the fires of the Russian bivouacs.

There the national pride, an advantageous position, and the works with which it was strengthened, all induced a belief that the general had determined to save the capital or to perish with it. He hesitated, however, and, whether from policy or prudence, he at length abandoned the governor of Moscow to his full responsibility.

The Russian army in this position of Fili, in front of Moscow, numbered ninety-one thousand men, six thousand of whom were Cossacks, sixty-five thousand veteran troops, (the relics of one hundred and twenty-one thousand engaged at the Moskwa,)[3] and twenty thousand recruits, armed half with muskets and half with pikes.

The French army, one hundred and thirty thousand strong the day before the great battle, had lost about forty thousand men at Borodino, and still consisted of ninety thousand. Some regiments on the march and the divisions of Laborde and Pino had just rejoined it: so that on its arrival before Moscow it still amounted to nearly one hundred thousand men. Its march was retarded by six hundred and seven pieces of cannon, two thousand five hundred artillery carriages, and five thousand baggage wagons; it had no more ammunition than would suffice for one engagement. Kutusoff perhaps calculated the disproportion between his effective force and ours. On this point, however, nothing but conjecture can be advanced, for he assigned purely military motives for his retreat.

So much is certain, that the old general deceived the governor to the very last moment. He even swore to him "by his grey hair that he would perish with him before Moscow," when all at once the governor was informed, that, in a council of war held at night in the camp, it had been determined to abandon the capital without a battle.

Rostopchin was incensed at this intelligence, but his resolution remained unshaken. There was now no time to be lost; no farther pains were taken to conceal from Moscow the fate that was destined for it; indeed it was not worth while to dissemble for the sake of the few inhabitants who were left; and besides it was necessary to induce them to seek their safety in flight.

At night, therefore, emissaries went round, knocking at every door and announcing the conflagration. Fuses were introduced at every favourable aperture, and especially into the shops covered with iron of the tradesmen's quarter. The fire engines were carried off: the desolation attained its highest pitch, and each individual, according to his disposition, was either overwhelmed with distress or urged to a decision. Most of those who were left formed groups in the public places; they crowded together, questioned each other, and reciprocally asked advice: many wandered about at random, some depressed with terror, others in a frightful state of exasperation. At length the army, the last hope of the people, deserted them: the troops began to traverse the city, and in their retreat they hurried along with them the still considerable remnant of its population.

They departed by the gate of Kolomna, surrounded by a multitude of women, children, and aged persons in deep affliction. The fields were covered with them. They fled in all directions, by every path across the country, without provisions, and laden with such of their effects as in their agitation they had first laid their hands on. Some, for want of horses, had harnessed themselves to carts, and in this manner dragged along their infant children, a sick wife, or an infirm father, in short, whatever they held most dear. The woods afforded them shelter, and they subsisted on the charity of their countrymen.

On that day, a terrific scene terminated this melancholy drama. This, the last day of Moscow, having arrived, Rostopchin collected together all whom he had been able to retain and arm. The prisons were thrown open. A squalid and disgusting crew tumultuously issued from them. These wretches rushed into the streets with a ferocious joy. Two men, a Russian and a Frenchman, the one accused of treason, the other of political indiscretion, were selected from among this horde, and dragged before Rostopchin, who reproached the Russian with his crime. The latter was the son of a tradesman: he had been apprehended while exciting the people to insurrection.[4] A circumstance which occasioned alarm was the discovery that he belonged to a sect of German illuminati, called Martinists, a society of superstitious independents. His audacity had never failed him in prison. It was imagined for a moment that the spirit of equality had penetrated into Russia. At any rate he did not impeach any accomplices.

At this crisis his father arrived. It was expected that he would intercede for his son: on the contrary, he insisted on his death. The governor granted him a few moments, that he might once more speak to and bless him. "What, I! I bless a traitor!" exclaimed the enraged Russian, and turning to his son, he, with a horrid voice and gesture, pronounced a curse upon him.

This was the signal for his execution. The poor wretch was struck down by an ill-directed blow of a sabre. He fell, but wounded only, and perhaps the arrival of the French might have saved him, had not the people perceived that he was yet alive. They forced the barrier, fell upon him, and tore him to pieces.

The Frenchman during this scene was petrified with terror. "As for thee," said Rostopchin, turning towards him, "being a Frenchman, thou canst not but wish for the arrival of the French army: be free, then, but go and tell thy countrymen, that Russia had but a single traitor, and that he is punished." Then addressing himself to the wretches who surrounded him, he called them sons of Russia, and exhorted them to make atonement for their crimes by serving their country. He was the last to quit that unfortunate city, and he then rejoined the Russian army.

From that moment the mighty Moscow belonged neither to the Russians nor to the French, but to that guilty horde, whose fury was directed by a few officers and soldiers of the police. They were organized, and each had his post allotted to him, in order that pillage, fire, and devastation might commence every where at once.

1. This entanglement of the vulture in the chains of the cross is supposed to have been a trick of count Rostopchin's, to excite the fanaticism of the people.—*Ed.*

2. He is accused of having ill-treated, stripped, and kept them without food for thirty-six hours previously, and then caused them to be led through the streets, exposed to the hooting and blows of the populace, after which they were thrown into prison, where the greatest part of them perished of hunger.—*Ed.*

3. This statement makes the Russian loss at Borodino only 30,000 men. According to the statement of Colonel Boutourlin, aide-de-camp to the emperor Alexander, the loss amounted to 50,000.—*Ed.*

4. The crime of the tradesman's son was his having translated a French bulletin. The statement with respect to his father is erroneous.—*Ed.*

CHAPTER IV

NAPOLEON ADVANCES ON MOSCOW

THAT very day (September the 14th), Napoleon, being at length satisfied that Kutusoff had not thrown himself on his right flank, rejoined his advanced-guard. He mounted his horse a few leagues from Moscow. He marched slowly and cautiously, sending scouts before him to examine the woods and the ravines, and to ascend all the eminences to look out for the enemy's army. A battle was expected: the ground favoured the opinion: works had been begun, but had all been abandoned, and we experienced not the slightest resistance.

At length the last eminence only remained to be passed: it is contiguous to Moscow, which it commands. It is called *The Hill of Salvation*, because, on its summit, the inhabitants, at sight of their holy city, cross and prostrate themselves. Our scouts soon gained the top of this hill. It was two o'clock: the sun caused this great city to glisten with a thousand colours. Struck with astonishment at the sight, they paused, exclaiming, "Moscow! Moscow!" Every one quickened his pace; the troops hurried on in disorder; and the whole army, clapping their hands, repeated with transport, "Moscow! Moscow!" just as sailors shout "Land! land!" at the conclusion of a long and toilsome voyage.

At the sight of this gilded city, of this brilliant knot uniting Asia and Europe, of this magnificent emporium of the luxury, the manners, and the arts of the two fairest divisions of the globe, we stood still in proud contemplation. What a glorious day had now arrived! It would furnish the grandest, the most brilliant recollection of our whole lives. We felt that at this moment all our actions would engage the attention of the astonished universe; and that every one of our movements, however trivial, would be recorded by history.

On this immense and imposing theatre we fancied ourselves marching, accompanied, as it were, by the acclamations of all nations: proud of exalting our grateful age above all preceding ages, we already beheld it great from our greatness, and completely irradiated by our glory.

At our return, already so ardently wished for, with what almost respectful consideration, with what enthusiasm should we be received by our wives, our countrymen, and even by our parents! We should form, during the rest of our lives, a particular class of beings, at whom they would never look but with astonishment, to whom they would listen with mingled curiosity and admiration! Crowds would throng about us wherever we passed; they would treasure up our most insignificant words. This miraculous conquest would surround us with a halo of glory: henceforward people would fancy that they breathed about us an air of prodigy and wonder.

When these proud thoughts gave place to more moderate sentiments, we said to ourselves, that this was the promised term of our labours; that at length we should pause, since we could no longer be surpassed by ourselves, after a noble expedition, the worthy parallel to that of Egypt, and the successful rival of all the great and glorious wars of antiquity.

At that moment, dangers and sufferings were all forgotten. Was it possible to purchase too dearly the proud felicity of being able to say, during the rest of life, "I belonged to the army of Moscow!"

Well, comrades, even now, amidst our abasement, and though it dates from that fatal city, is not this reflection of a noble exultation sufficiently powerful to console us, and to make us proudly hold up our heads, bowed down by misfortune?

Napoleon himself hastened up. He paused in transport: an exclamation of happiness escaped his lips. Ever since the great battle, the discontented marshals had shunned him: but at the sight of captive Moscow, at the intelligence of the arrival of a flag of truce, struck with so important a result, and intoxicated with all the enthusiasm of glory, they forgot their grievances. They pressed around the emperor, paying homage to his good fortune, and already tempted to attribute to the foresight of his genius the little pains he had taken on the 7th to complete his victory.

But in Napoleon first emotions were of short duration. He had too much to think of, to indulge his sensations for any length of time. His first exclamation was: "There, at last, is that famous city!" and the second: "It was high time!"

His eyes, fixed on this capital, already expressed nothing but impatience: in it he beheld in imagination the whole Russian empire. Its walls enclosed all his hopes,—peace, the expenses of the war, immortal glory: his eager looks therefore intently watched all its outlets. When would its gates at length open? When should he see that deputation come forth, which will place its wealth, its population, its senate, and the principal of the Russian nobility, at our disposal? Henceforth that enterprise in which he had so rashly engaged, brought to a successful termination by dint of boldness, would pass for the result of a deep combination; his imprudence for greatness: henceforth his victory at the Moskwa, incomplete as it was, would be deemed his greatest achievement. Thus all that might have turned to his ruin would contribute to his glory: that day would begin to decide whether he was the greatest man in the world, or the most rash; in short, whether he had raised himself an altar, or dug himself a grave.

Anxiety, however, soon began to take possession of his mind. On his left and right he already beheld Prince Eugene and Poniatowski approaching the hostile city; Murat, with his scouts, had already reached the entrance of the suburbs, and yet no deputation appeared: an officer, sent by Miloradowitch, merely came to declare that his general would set fire to the city, if his rear was not allowed time to evacuate it.

Napoleon granted every demand. The foremost troops of the two armies were, for a short time, intermingled. Murat was recognized by the Cossacks, who, familiar as the nomadic tribes, and expressive as the people of the south, thronged around him: then, by their gestures and exclamations, they extolled his valour and intoxicated him with their admiration. The king took the watches of his officers, and distributed them amongst these barbarous warriors. One of them called him his *hetman*.

Murat was for a moment tempted to believe that in these officers he should find a new Mazeppa, or that he himself should become one: he imagined that he had gained them over. This momentary armistice, under the actual circumstances, sustained the hopes of Napoleon, such need had he to delude himself. He was thus amused for two hours.

Meanwhile the day was declining, and Moscow continued dull, silent, and as it were inanimate. The anxiety of the emperor increased; the impatience of the soldiers became more difficult to be repressed. Some officers ventured within the walls of the city. "Moscow is deserted!"

At this intelligence, which he angrily refused to credit, Napoleon descended the Hill of Salvation, and approached the Moskwa and the Dorogomilow gate. He paused once more, but in vain, at the entry of that barrier. Murat urged him. "Well!" replied he, "let them enter then, since they wish it!" He recommended the strictest discipline; he still indulged hopes. "Perhaps these inhabitants do not even know how to surrender; for here every thing is new; they to us, and we to them."

Reports now began to succeed each other: they all agreed. Some Frenchmen, inhabitants of Moscow, ventured to quit the hiding-place which for some days had concealed them from the fury of the populace, and confirmed the fatal tidings. The emperor called Daru. "Moscow deserted!" exclaimed he: "what an improbable story! We must know the truth of it. Go and bring me the boyars." He imagined that those men, stiff with pride, or paralysed with terror, were fixed motionless in their houses: and he, who had hitherto been always met by the submission of the vanquished, provoked their confidence, and anticipated their prayers.

How, indeed, was it possible for him to persuade himself, that so many magnificent palaces, so many splendid temples, so many rich mercantile establishments, were forsaken by their owners, like the paltry hamlets through which he had recently passed. Daru's mission however was fruitless! Not a Muscovite was to be seen; not the least smoke arose from a single chimney; not the slightest noise issued from this immense and populous city: its three hundred thousand inhabitants seemed to be struck dumb and motionless by enchantment; it was the silence of the desert!

But such was the incredulity of Napoleon, that he was not yet convinced, and waited for farther information. At length an officer, determined to gratify him, or persuaded that whatever the emperor willed must necessarily be accomplished, entered the city, seized five or six vagabonds, drove them before his horse to the emperor, and imagined that he had brought him a deputation.[1] From the first words they uttered, Napoleon discovered that the persons before him were only indigent labourers.

It was not till then that he ceased to doubt the entire evacuation of Moscow, and lost all the hopes that he had built upon it. He shrugged his shoulders, and with that contemptuous look with which he met every thing that crossed his wishes, he exclaimed, "Ah! the Russians know not yet the effect which the taking of their capital will produce upon them!"

1. M. Gourgaud asserts, that the persons thus contemptuously spoken of, were really tradesmen and citizens of Moscow.—*Ed.*

CHAPTER V

MURAT'S ENTRANCE INTO THE CITY

IT was now an hour since Murat, and the long and close column of his cavalry, had entered Moscow; they penetrated into that gigantic body, as yet untouched, but inanimate. Struck with profound astonishment at the sight of this complete solitude, they replied to the taciturnity of this modern Thebes, by a silence equally solemn. These warriors listened, with a secret shuddering, to the steps of their horses resounding alone, amid these deserted palaces. They were astonished to hear nothing but themselves amid such numerous habitations. No one thought of stopping or of plundering, either from prudence, or because great civilised nations respect themselves in enemies' capitals, in the presence of those great centres of civilisation.

Meanwhile they were silently observing this mighty city, which would have been truly remarkable had they met with it in a flourishing and populous country, but which was still more astonishing in these deserts. It was like a rich and brilliant oasis. They had at first been struck by the sudden view of so many magnificent palaces, but they now perceived that they were intermingled with mean cottages; a circumstance which indicated the want of gradation between the classes, and that luxury was not generated there, as in other countries, by industry, but preceded it; whereas, in the natural order, it ought to be its more or less necessary consequence.

Here more especially prevailed inequality—that bane of all human society, which produces pride in some, debasement in others, corruption in all. And yet such a generous abandonment of every thing demonstrated that this excessive luxury, as yet however entirely borrowed, had not rendered these nobles effeminate.

They thus advanced, sometimes agitated by surprise, at others by pity, and more frequently by a noble enthusiasm. Several cited events of the great conquests which history has handed down to us; but it was for the purpose of indulging their pride, not to draw lessons from them; for they thought themselves too lofty and beyond all comparison: they had left behind them all the conquerors of antiquity. They were exalted by that which is second only to virtue, by glory. Then succeeded melancholy; either from the exhaustion consequent on so many sensations, or the effect of the operation produced by such an immeasurable elevation, and of the seclusion in which we were wandering on that height, whence we beheld immensity, infinity, in which our weakness was lost: for the higher we ascend, the more the horizon expands, and the more conscious we become of our own insignificance.

Amid these reflections, which were favoured by a slow pace, the report of fire-arms was all at once heard: the column halted. Its last horses still covered the fields; its centre was in one of the longest streets of the city; its head had reached the Kremlin. The gates of that citadel appeared to be closed. Ferocious cries issued from within it: men and women, of savage and disgusting aspect, appeared fully armed on its walls. In a state of filthy inebriety, they uttered the most horrible imprecations. Murat sent them an amicable message, but to no purpose. It was found necessary to employ cannon to break open the gate.

We penetrated, partly without opposition, partly by force, among these wretches. One of them rushed close to the king, and endeavoured to kill one of his officers. It was thought sufficient to disarm him, but he again fell upon his victim, rolled him on the ground, and attempted to suffocate him; and even after his arms were seized and held, he strove to tear him with his teeth. These were the only Muscovites who had waited our coming, and who seemed to have been left behind as a savage and barbarous token of the national hatred.

It was easy to perceive, however, that there was no unison in this patriotic fury. Five hundred recruits, who had been forgotten in the Kremlin, beheld this scene without stirring. At the first summons they dispersed. Farther on, we overtook a convoy of provisions, the escort of which immediately threw down its arms. Several thousand stragglers and deserters from the enemy voluntarily remained in the power of our advanced guard. The latter left to the corps which followed the task of picking them up; and these to others, and so on: hence they remained at liberty in the midst of us, till the conflagration and pillage of the city having reminded them of their duty, and rallied them all in one general feeling of antipathy, they went and rejoined Kutusoff.

Murat, who had been stopped but a few moments by the Kremlin, dispersed this despicable crew. Ardent and indefatigable as in Italy and Egypt, after a march of 900 leagues, and sixty battles fought to reach Moscow, he traversed that proud city without deigning to halt in it, and pursuing the Russian rear-guard, he boldly, and without hesitation, took the road for Wladimir and Asia.

Several thousand Cossacks, with four pieces of cannon, were retreating in that direction. The armistice was at an end. Murat, tired of this peace of half a day, immediately ordered it to be broken by a discharge of carbines. But our cavalry considered the war as finished; Moscow appeared to them to be the term of it, and the advanced posts of the two empires were unwilling to renew hostilities. A fresh order arrived, and the same hesitation prevailed. At length Murat, irritated at this disobedience, gave his orders in person; and the firing, with which he seemed to threaten Asia, but which was not destined to cease till we reached the banks of the Seine, was renewed.

CHAPTER VI

THE BURNING OF MOSCOW

NAPOLEON did not enter Moscow till after dark.[1] He stopped in one of the first houses of the Dorogomilow suburb. There he appointed marshal Mortier governor of that capital. "Above, all," said he to him, "no pillage! For this you shall be answerable to me with your life. Defend Moscow against all, whether friend or foe."

That night was a gloomy one: sinister reports followed one upon the heels of another. Some Frenchmen, resident in the country, and even a Russian officer of police, came to give intelligence respecting the conflagration. He gave all the particulars of the preparations for it. The emperor, alarmed by these accounts, strove in vain to take some rest. He called every moment, and had the fatal tidings repeated to him. He nevertheless persisted in his incredulity, till about two in the morning, when he was informed that the fire had actually broken out.

It was at the Exchange, in the centre of the city, in its richest quarter. He instantly issued orders upon orders. As soon as it was light, he himself hastened to the spot, and threatened the young guard and Mortier. The marshal pointed out to him some houses covered with iron; they were closely shut up, still untouched and uninjured without, and yet a black smoke was already issuing from them. Napoleon pensively entered the Kremlin.

At the sight of this half Gothic and half modern palace of the Ruriks and the Romanoffs, of their throne still standing, of the cross of the great Ivan, and of the finest part of the city, which is overlooked by the Kremlin, and which the flames, as yet confined to the bazaar, seemed disposed to spare, his former hopes revived. His ambition was flattered by this conquest. "At length, then," he exclaimed, "I am in Moscow, in the ancient palace of the Czars, in the Kremlin!" He examined every part of it with pride, curiosity, and gratification.

He required a statement of the resources afforded by the city; and, in this brief moment given to hope, sent proposals of peace to the emperor Alexander. A superior officer of the enemy's had just been found in the great hospital; he was charged with the delivery of this letter. It was by the baleful light of the flames of the bazaar that Napoleon finished it, and the Russian departed. He was to be the bearer of the news of this disaster to his sovereign, whose only answer was this conflagration.

Day-light favoured the efforts of the Duke of Treviso to subdue the fire. The incendiaries kept themselves concealed. Doubts were entertained of their existence. At length, strict injunctions being issued, order restored, and alarm suspended, each took possession of a commodious house, or sumptuous palace, under the idea of there finding comforts that had been dearly purchased by such long and excessive privations.

Two officers had taken up their quarters in one of the buildings of the Kremlin. The view hence embraced the north and west of the city. About midnight they were awakened by an extraordinary light. They looked and beheld palaces filled with flames, which at first merely illuminated, but presently consumed these elegant and noble structures. They observed that the north wind drove these flames directly towards the Kremlin, and they became alarmed for the safety of that fortress, in which the flower of their army and its commander reposed. They were apprehensive also for the surrounding houses, where our soldiers, attendants, and horses, weary and exhausted, were doubtless buried in profound sleep. Sparks and burning fragments were already flying over the roofs of the Kremlin, when the wind, shifting from north to west, blew them in another direction.

One of these officers, relieved from apprehension respecting his own corps, then composed himself again to sleep, exclaiming, "Let others look to it now; 'tis no affair of ours." For such was the unconcern produced by the multiplicity of events and misfortunes, and such the selfishness arising from excessive suffering and fatigue, that they left to each only just strength and feeling sufficient for his personal service and preservation.

It was not long before fresh and vivid lights again awoke them. They beheld other flames rising precisely in the new direction which the wind had taken towards the Kremlin, and they cursed French imprudence and want of discipline, to which they imputed this disaster. But three times did the wind thus change from north to west, and three times did these hostile fires, as if obstinately bent on the destruction of the imperial quarters, appear eager to follow this new direction.

At this sight a strong suspicion seized their minds. Could the Muscovites, aware of our rash and thoughtless negligence, have conceived the hope of burning, with Moscow, our soldiers, heavy with wine, fatigue, and sleep; or rather, have they dared to imagine that they should involve Napoleon in this catastrophe; that the loss of such a man would be fully equivalent to that of their capital; that it was a result sufficiently important to justify the sacrifice of all Moscow to obtain it; that perhaps Heaven, in order to grant them so signal a victory, had decreed so great a sacrifice; and lastly, that so immense a Colossus required not a less immense funeral pile?

Whether this was their plan we cannot tell, but nothing less than the emperor's good fortune was required to prevent its being realised. In fact, not only did the Kremlin contain, unknown to us, a magazine of gunpowder,[2] but that very night, the guards, asleep and carelessly posted, suffered a whole park of artillery to enter and draw up under the windows of Napoleon.

It was at this moment that the furious flames were driven from all quarters with the greatest violence towards the Kremlin; for the wind, attracted no doubt by this vast combustion, increased every moment in strength. The flower of the army and the emperor would have been destroyed if but one of the brands that flew over our heads had alighted on one of the powder-wagons. Thus upon each of the sparks that were for several hours floating in the air, depended the fate of the whole army.

At length the day, a gloomy day, appeared: it came to add to the horrors of the scene, and to deprive it of its brilliancy. Many of the officers sought refuge in the halls of the palace. The chiefs, and Mortier himself, overcome by the fire with which, for thirty-six hours they had been contending, there dropped down from fatigue and despair.

They said nothing and we accused ourselves. Most of us imagined that want of discipline in our troops and intoxication had begun the disaster, and that the high wind had completed it. We viewed ourselves with a sort of disgust. The cry of horror which all Europe would not fail to set up terrified us. Filled with consternation by so tremendous a catastrophe, we accosted each other with downcast looks: it sullied our glory; it deprived us of the fruits of it; it threatened our present and our future existence; we were now but an army of criminals, whom Heaven and the civilised world would severely judge. From these overwhelming thoughts and paroxysms of rage against the incendiaries, we were roused only by an eagerness to obtain intelligence; and all the accounts now began to accuse the Russians alone of this disaster.

In fact, officers arrived from all quarters, and they all agreed. The very first night, that of the 14th, a fire-balloon had settled on the palace of Prince Trubetskoi, and consumed it: this was a signal. Fire had been immediately set to the Exchange: Russian police soldiers had been seen stirring it up with tarred lances. Here howitzer shells, perfidiously placed, had discharged themselves in the stoves of several houses, and wounded the military who crowded round them. Retiring to other quarters which were still standing, they sought fresh retreats; but when they were on the point of entering houses closely shut up and uninhabited, they had heard faint explosions within; these were succeeded by a light smoke, which immediately became thick and black, then reddish, and lastly the colour of fire, and presently the whole edifice was involved in flames.

All had seen hideous-looking men, covered with rags, and women resembling furies, wandering among these flames, and completing a frightful image of the infernal regions. These wretches, intoxicated with wine and the success of their crimes, no longer took any pains to conceal themselves: they proceeded in triumph through the blazing streets; they were caught, armed with torches, assiduously striving to spread the conflagration; it was necessary to strike down their hands with sabres to oblige them to loose their hold. It was said that these banditti had been released from prison by the Russian generals for the purpose of burning Moscow; and that in fact so grand, so extreme a resolution could only have been conceived by patriotism and executed only by guilt.

Orders were immediately issued to shoot all the incendiaries on the spot. The army was on foot. The old guard, which exclusively occupied one part of the Kremlin, was under arms: the baggage, and the horses ready loaded, filled the courts; we were struck dumb with astonishment, and disappointmeut, on witnessing the destruction of such excellent quarters. Though masters of Moscow, we were forced to go and bivouac without provisions outside its gates.

While our troops were yet struggling with the conflagration, and the army was disputing their prey with the flames, Napoleon, whose sleep none had dared to disturb during the night, was awoke by the twofold light of day and of the fire.[3] His first feeling was that of irritation, and he would have commanded the devouring element: but he soon paused and yielded to impossibility. Surprised, that when he had struck at the heart of an empire, he should find there any other sentiment than submission and terror, he felt himself vanquished, and surpassed in determination.

This conquest, for which he had sacrificed every thing, was like a phantom which he had pursued, and which, at the moment when he imagined he had grasped it, vanished in a mingled mass of smoke and flame. He was then seized with extreme agitation; he seemed to be consumed by the fires which surrounded him. He rose every moment, paced to and fro, and again sat down abruptly. He traversed his apartments with quick steps: his sudden and vehement gestures betrayed painful uneasiness: he quitted, resumed, and again quitted, an urgent occupation, to hasten to the windows and watch the progress of the conflagration. Short and incoherent exclamations burst from his labouring bosom. "What a tremendous spectacle!—It is their own work!—So many palaces!—What extraordinary resolution!—What men!—These are indeed Scythians!"

Between the fire and him there was an extensive vacant space, then the Moskwa and its two quays; and yet the panes of the windows against which he leaned felt already burning to the touch, and the constant exertions of sweepers, placed on the iron roofs of the palace, were not sufficient to keep them clear of the numerous flakes of fire which alighted upon them.

At this moment a rumour was spread that the Kremlin was undermined: this was confirmed, it was said, by Russians, and by written documents. Some of his attendants were beside themselves with fear; while the military awaited unmoved what the orders of the emperor and fate should decree; and to this alarm the emperor replied only with a smile of incredulity.

But he still walked convulsively; he stopped at every window, and beheld the terrible, the victorious element furiously consuming his brilliant conquest; seizing all the bridges, all the avenues to his fortress, inclosing, and as it were besieging him in it; spreading every moment among the neighbouring houses; and, reducing him within narrower and narrower limits, confining him at length to the site of the Kremlin alone.

We already breathed nothing but smoke and ashes. Night approached, and was about to add darkness to our dangers: the equinoctial gales, in alliance with the Russians, increased in violence. The king of Naples and Prince Eugene hastened to the spot; in company with the Prince of Neufchâtel they made their way to the emperor, and urged him by their entreaties, their gestures, and on their knees, and insisted on removing him from this scene of desolation. All was in vain.

Master at length of the palace of the Czars, Napoleon was bent on not yielding that conquest even to the conflagration, when all at once the shout of "the Kremlin is on fire!" passed from mouth to mouth, and roused us from the contemplative stupor with which we had been seized. The emperor went out to ascertain the danger. Twice had the fire communicated to the building in which he was, and twice had it been extinguished; but the tower of the arsenal was still burning. A soldier of the police had been found in it. He was brought in, and Napoleon caused him to be interrogated in his presence. This man was the incendiary; he had executed his commission at the signal given by his chief. It was evident that every thing was devoted to destruction, the ancient and sacred Kremlin itself not excepted.

The gestures of the emperor betokened disdain and vexation: the wretch was hurried into the first court, where the enraged grenadiers despatched him with their bayonets.

1. Napoleon entered the Kremlin at six o'clock next morning.—*Ed.*

2. There was no powder-magazine in the Kremlin. The only magazines of the kind were outside of the city.—*Ed.*

3. "About four o'clock in the morning," says General Gourgaud, "one of the emperor's officers awoke him, to inform him of the conflagration. The monarch had thrown himself on the bed only a few minutes before, after having dictated orders to the various corps of his army, and laboured with his secretaries. It is inconceivable how M. de Segur, who ought to know better what passed in the interior of the palace, can constantly represent Napoleon as being afraid of having his rest broken. He ought to have known that officers of the lowest rank never scrupled to wake him up when they had a report to make. If the aide-de-camp on service had ventured not to have informed him of the arrival of an officer, he would have been severely reprimanded.—*Ed.*

CHAPTER VII

NAPOLEON'S DANGER

THIS incident decided Napoleon.[1] He hastily descended the northern staircase, famous for the massacre of the Strelitzes, and desired to be conducted out of the city, to the distance of a league on the road to Petersburgh, toward the imperial palace of Petrowski.

But we were besieged by an ocean of fire, which blocked up all the gates of the citadel, and frustrated the first attempts that were made to depart. After some search, we discovered a postern gate leading between the rocks to the Moskwa. It was by this narrow passage that Napoleon, his officers and guard, escaped from the Kremlin. But what had they gained by this movement? They had approached nearer to the fire, and could neither retreat nor remain where they were; and how were they to advance? how force a passage through the billows of this sea of flame? Those who had traversed the city, stunned by the tempest, and blinded by the ashes, could not find their way, since the streets themselves were no longer distinguishable amidst smoke and ruins.

There was no time to be lost. The roaring of the flames around us became every moment more violent. A single narrow winding street completely on fire, appeared to be rather the entrance than the outlet to this hell. The Emperor rushed on foot, and without hesitation into this narrow passage. He advanced amid the crackling of the flames, the crash of floors, and the fall of burning timbers, and of the red-hot iron roofs which tumbled around him. These ruins impeded his progress. The flames, which, with impetuous roar, consumed the edifices between which we were proceeding, spreading beyond the walls, were blown out by the wind, and formed an arch over our heads. We walked on a ground of fire, beneath a fiery sky, and between two walls of fire. The intense heat burned our eyes, which we were nevertheless obliged to keep open and fixed on the danger. A consuming atmosphere, glowing ashes, detached flames, parched our throats, and rendered our respiration short and dry; and we were already almost suffocated by the smoke. Our hands were burned, either in endeavouring to protect our faces from the insupportable heat, or in brushing off the sparks which every moment covered and penetrated our garments.

In this inexpressible distress, and when a rapid advance seemed to be our only means of safety, our guide stopped in uncertainty and agitation. Here would probably have terminated our adventurous career, had not some pillagers of the first corps recognised the emperor amidst the whirling flames: they ran up and guided him towards the smoking ruins of a quarter which had been reduced to ashes in the morning.

It was then that we met the prince of Eckmühl. This marshal who had been wounded at the Moskwa, had desired to be carried back among the flames to rescue Napoleon; or to perish with him. He threw himself into his arms with transport; the Emperor received him kindly, but with that composure which in danger he never lost for a moment.

To escape from this vast region of calamities, it was further necessary to pass a long convoy of powder, which was defiling amidst the fire.[2] This was not the least of his dangers, but it was the last, and by nightfall he arrived at Petrowsky.

Next morning, the 17th of September, Napoleon cast his first looks towards Moscow, hoping to see that the conflagration had subsided. He beheld it again raging with the utmost violence:

the whole city appeared like a vast spout of fire rising in whirling eddies to the sky, which it deeply coloured. Absorbed by this melancholy contemplation, he preserved a long and gloomy silence, which he broke only by the exclamation, "This forebodes great misfortunes to us!"

The effort which he had made to reach Moscow had expended all his means of warfare.[3] Moscow had been the term of his projects, the aim of all his hopes, and Moscow was no more! What was now to be done? Here this decisive genius was forced to hesitate. He, who in 1805 had ordered the sudden and total abandonment of an expedition, prepared at an immense cost, and determined at Bologne-sur-mer on the surprise and annihilation of the Austrian army, in short, on all the operations of the campaign between Ulm and Munich exactly as they were executed; the same man, who, in the following year, dictated at Paris with the same infallibility all the movements of his army as far as Berlin, the day fixed for his entrance into that capital, and the appointment of the governor whom he destined for it—he it was, who, astonished in his turn, was now undecided what course to pursue. Never had he communicated his most daring projects to the most confidential of his ministers but in the order for their execution; he was now constrained to consult, and put to the proof, the moral and physical energies of those about him.

In doing this, however, he still preserved the same forms. He declared, therefore, that he should march for Petersburgh. This conquest was already marked out on his maps, hitherto so prophetic: orders were even issued to the different corps to hold themselves in readiness. But his decision was only a feint: it was but a better face that he strove to assume, or an expedient for diverting his grief for the loss of Moscow: so that Berthier, and more especially Bessières, soon convinced him that he had neither time, provisions, roads, nor a single requisite for so extensive an excursion.

At this moment he was apprised that Kutusoff, after having fled eastward, had suddenly turned to the south, and thrown himself between Moscow and Kaluga. This was an additional motive against the expedition to Petersburgh; it was a threefold reason for marching upon this beaten army for the purpose of extinguishing it; to secure his right flank and his line of operation; to possess himself of Kaluga and Tula, the granary and arsenal of Russia; and lastly, to open a safe, short, new, and untouched retreat to Smolensk and Lithuania.

Some one proposed to return upon Wittgenstein and Witepsk. Napoleon remained undecided between all these plans. That for the conquest of Petersburgh alone flattered him: the others appeared but as ways of retreat, as acknowledgments of error: and whether from pride, or policy which will not admit itself to be in the wrong, he rejected them.

Besides, where was he to halt in case of a retreat? He had so fully calculated on concluding a peace at Moscow, that he had no winter quarters provided in Lithuania. Kaluga had no temptations for him. Wherefore lay waste fresh provinces? It would be wiser to threaten them, and leave the Russians something to lose, in order to induce them to conclude a peace by which they might be preserved. Would it be possible to march to another battle, to fresh conquests, without exposing a line of operation, covered with sick, stragglers, wounded and convoys of all sorts? Moscow was the general rallying point; how could it be changed? What other name would have any attraction?

Lastly, and above all, how could he relinquish a hope to which he had made so many sacrifices, when he knew that his letter to Alexander had just passed the Russian advanced posts: when eight days would be sufficient for receiving an answer so ardently desired; when he required that time to rally and reorganise his army, to collect the relics of Moscow, the conflagration of which had but too strongly sanctioned pillage, and to draw his soldiers from that vast infirmary!

Meanwhile, scarcely a third of that army and of that capital now existed. But himself and the Kremlin were still standing: his renown was still entire, and he persuaded himself that those two great names, Napoleon and Moscow, combined, would be sufficient to accomplish every thing. He determined, therefore, to return to the Kremlin, which a battalion of his guard had unfortunately preserved.

1. Napoleon was prevailed on to remove by an observation from Berthier. "Sire," said Berthier, "if the enemy should attack those French corps which are out of Moscow, your majesty has no means of communicating with them."—*Ed.*

2. This assertion respecting the convoy of powder, has no foundation. —*Ed.*

3. This is an exaggeration. The army had been joined by various corps and detachments, and supplies of ammunition had been brought up.—*Ed.*

CHAPTER VII

AFTER THE CONFLAGRATION

THE camps which he traversed on his way thither presented an extraordinary sight. In the fields, amidst thick and cold mud, large fires were kept up with mahogany furniture, windows, and gilded doors. Around these fires, on a litter of damp straw, imperfectly sheltered by a few boards, were seen the soldiers, and their officers, splashed all over with mud, and blackened with smoke, seated in arm-chairs or reclined on silken couches. At their feet were spread or heaped Cashmere shawls, the rarest furs of Siberia, the gold stuffs of Persia, and silver dishes, off which they had nothing to eat but a black dough baked in the ashes, and half broiled and bloody horse-flesh. Singular assemblage of abundance and want, of riches and filth, of luxury and wretchedness!

Between the camp and the city were met troops of soldiers dragging along their booty, or driving before them, like beasts of burden, Muscovites bending under the weight of the pillage of their capital; for the fire brought to view nearly twenty thousand inhabitants, previously unobserved in that immense city. Some of these Muscovites of both sexes were well dressed; they were tradespeople. They came with the wreck of their property to seek refuge at our fires. They lived pell-mell with our soldiers, protected by some, and tolerated, or rather scarcely remarked, by others.

About ten thousand of the enemy's troops were in the same predicament. For several days they wandered about among us free, and some of them even still armed. Our soldiers met these vanquished enemies without animosity, or without thinking of making them prisoners; either because they considered the war at an end, from thoughtlessness, or from pity, and because when not in battle the French delight in having no enemies. They suffered them to share their fires; nay, more, they allowed them to pillage in their company. When some degree of order was restored, or rather when the officers had organised this marauding as a regular system of forage, the great number of these Russian stragglers then attracted notice. Orders were given to secure them; but seven or eight thousand had already escaped. It was not long before we had to fight them.

On entering the city, the Emperor was struck by a sight still more extraordinary: a few houses scattered among the ruins were all that was left of the mighty Moscow. The smell issuing from this colossus, overthrown, burned, and calcined, was horrible. Heaps of ashes, and at intervals, fragments of walls or half demolished pillars, were now the only vestiges that marked the site of streets.

The suburbs were sprinkled with Russians of both sexes, covered with garments nearly burned. They flitted like spectres among the ruins; squatted in the gardens, some of them were scratching up the earth in quest of vegetables, while others were disputing with the crows for the relics of the dead animals which the army had left behind. Farther on, others again were seen plunging into the Moskwa to bring out some of the corn which had been thrown into it by command of Rostopchin, and which they devoured without preparation, soured and spoiled as it already was.

Meanwhile the sight of the booty, in such of the camps where every thing was yet wanting, inflamed the soldiers whom their duty or stricter officers had kept with their colours. They murmured. "Why were they to be kept back? Why were they to perish by famine and want, when every thing was within their reach? Was it right to allow the enemy's fires to destroy what might be saved? Why was such respect to be paid to the conflagration?" They added, that "as the inhabitants of Moscow had not only abandoned, but even endeavoured utterly to destroy it, all that they could save would be fairly gained; that the remains of that city, like the relics of the arms of the conquered, belonged by right to the victors, as the Muscovites had turned their capital into a vast machine of war, for the purpose of annihilating us."

The best principled and the best disciplined were those who argued thus, and it was impossible to reply satisfactorily to them. Exaggerated scruples, however, at first preventing the issuing of orders for pillage, it was permitted, unrestrained by regulations. Then it was, urged by the most imperious wants, all hurried to share the spoil, the soldiers of the *élite*, and even officers. Their chiefs were obliged to shut their eyes; only such guards as were absolutely indispensable remained with the eagles and the piled arms.

The emperor saw his whole army dispersed over the city. His progress was obstructed by a long file of marauders going in quest of booty, or returning with it; by tumultuous assemblages of soldiers grouped around the entrance of cellars, or the doors of palaces shops, and churches, which the fire had nearly reached, and which they were endeavouring to break into.

His steps were impeded by the fragments of furniture of every kind which had been thrown out of the windows to save it from the flames, or by rich pillage which had been abandoned from caprice for some other booty; for such is the way with soldiers; they are incessantly beginning their fortune afresh, taking everything indiscriminately, loading themselves beyond measure, as if they could carry all they find; then, after they have gone a few steps, compelled by fatigue to throw away successively the greatest part of their burden.

The roads were obstructed with it; the open places, like the camps, were turned into markets, whither every one repaired to exchange superfluities for necessaries. There, the rarest articles, the value of which was not known to their possessors, were sold at a low price; others, of deceitful appearance, were purchased at a price far beyond their worth. Gold, from being more portable, was bought at an immense loss with silver, which the knapsacks were incapable of holding. Everywhere soldiers were seen seated on bales of merchandise, on heaps of sugar and coffee, amidst wines and the most exquisite liqueurs, which they were offering in exchange for a morsel of bread. Many, in an intoxication, aggravated by inanition, had fallen near the flames, which reached them, and put an end to their lives.

Most of the houses and palaces which had escaped the fire served nevertheless for quarters for the officers, and all that they contained was respected. All of them beheld with pain this vast destruction, and the pillage which was its necessary consequence. Some of our men belonging to the *élite* were reproached with taking too much pleasure in collecting what they were able to save from the flames; but their number was so few that they were mentioned by name. In these ardent men, war was a passion which presupposed the existence of many others. It was not covetousness, for they did not hoard; they spent lavishly what they picked up, taking in order to give, believing that one hand washed the other, and that they had paid for everything with the danger.

Besides, on such an occasion, there is scarcely any distinction to be made, unless in the motive: some took with regret, others with pleasure, and all from necessity. Amidst wealth which had ceased to belong to any individual, ready to be consumed, or to be buried in ashes, we were placed in a quite novel situation, where right and wrong were confounded, and for which no rule was laid down. The most delicate, either from principle, or because they were richer than others, bought of the soldiers the provision and apparel which they required: some sent agents to plunder for them and the most necessitous were forced to help themselves with their own hands.

As to the soldiers, many of them being embarrassed with the fruits of their pillage, became less active, less thoughtless:

in danger they began to calculate, and in order to save their booty, they did what they would have disdained to do to save themselves.

It was amidst this confusion that Napoleon again entered Moscow. He had allowed this pillage, hoping that his army, scattered over the ruins, would not ransack them in vain. But when he learned that the disorder increased, that the old guard itself was seduced, that the Russian peasants, who were at length allured thither with provisions, for which he caused them to be liberally paid for the purpose of inducing others to come, were robbed of the provisions which they brought us by our famished soldiers—when he was informed that the different corps, destitute of everything, were ready to fight for the relics of Moscow—that, finally, all the existing resources were wasted by this irregular pillage—he then issued strict orders, and forbade his guard to leave their quarters. The churches, in which our cavalry had sheltered themselves, were restored to the Greek worship.[1] The business of plunder was ordered to be taken in turn by the corps, like any other duty, and directions were at length given for securing the Russian stragglers.

But it was too late. These soldiers had fled: the affrighted peasants returned no more; great quantities of provisions were wasted. The French army have sometimes fallen into this fault, but on the present occasion the fire pleads their excuse: no time was to be lost in anticipating the flames. It is, however, a remarkable fact, that at the first command perfect order was restored.

Some writers, and even French ones, have ransacked these ruins in quest of traces of outrages which might have been committed in them. There were very few. Most of our men behaved generously, considering the small number of inhabitants, and the great number of enemies, that they met with. But if in the first moments of pillage some excesses were committed, ought this to appear surprising in an army exasperated by such urgent wants, such severe sufferings, and composed of so many different nations?

Misfortunes having since overwhelmed these warriors, reproaches have, as is always the case, been raised against them. Who can be ignorant that such disorders have always been the bad side of great wars, the inglorious part of glory; that the renown of conquerors casts its shadow like every thing else in this world? Does there exist a creature ever so diminutive, on every side of which the sun, great as is that luminary, can shine at once? It is therefore a law of nature, that great bodies have great shadows.

Moreover, people have been too much astonished at the virtues as well as at the vices of that army. They were the virtues of the moment, the vices of the age; and for that very reason, the former were less praiseworthy, and the latter less reprehensible, inasmuch as they were, if I may so express myself, enjoined by example and circumstances. Thus every thing is relative; this, however, does not exclude fixed principles, the best or absolute good, as the point of departure and aim. But here the question relates to the judgment which has been formed of this army and its chief; and he who would form a correct judgment of them must put himself in their place. As, then, this position was very elevated, very extraordinary, and very complicated, few minds are capable of attaining it, embracing the whole of it, and appreciating all its necessary results.

1. Napoleon also took measures for relieving "the unfortunate of all classes." Among other things, he ordered lists to be made of all the citizens whom the conflagration had deprived of the means of subsistence, opened houses of refuge for them, and supplied them with food.—*Ed.*

CHAPTER IX

RUSSIAN AND FRENCH REACTION

MEANWHILE Kutusoff, on leaving Moscow, had drawn Murat towards Kolomna, to the point where the Moskwa intersects the road. Here, under favour of the night, he suddenly turned to the south, proceeding by way of Podol, to throw himself between Moscow and Kaluga. This nocturnal march of the Russians around Moscow, the ashes and flames of which were wafted to them by the violence of the wind, was gloomy and religious. They were lighted on their march by the baleful conflagration, which was consuming the centre of their commerce, the sanctuary of their religion, the cradle of their empire! Filled with horror and indignation, they all kept a sullen silence, which was unbroken save by the dull and monotonous sound of their footsteps, the roaring of the flames, and the howling of the tempest. The dismal light was frequently interrupted by livid and sudden flashes. The brows of these warriors might then be seen contracted by a savage grief, and the fire of their sombre and threatening looks answered these flames, which they regarded as our work; it already betrayed that ferocious revenge which was rankling in their hearts, which spread throughout the whole empire, and to which so many Frenchmen fell victims.

At that solemn moment, Kutusoff, in a firm and noble tone, informed his sovereign of the loss of his capital. He declared that, "in order to preserve the fertile provinces of the south, and his communication with Tormasoff and Tchitchakoff, he had been obliged to abandon Moscow, but emptied of the inhabitants, who were the life of it; that as the people were the soul of every empire, so wherever the Russian people were, there would be Moscow and the whole empire of Russia."

At this point, however, he seemed to bend under the weight of his grief. He admitted that "this wound was deep and could never be effaced;" but soon recovering himself, he added, that "the loss of Moscow made but one city less in the empire, that it was the sacrifice of a part for the salvation of the whole. That he was throwing himself on the flank of the enemy's long line of operation, keeping him as it were blockaded by his detachments: there he should watch his movements, cover the resources of the empire, and again complete his army;" and already (this was on the 16th of September) he announced, that "Napoleon would be forced to abandon his fatal conquest."

It is said that on the receipt of this intelligence Alexander was thunderstruck. Napoleon built hopes on the weakness of his rival, and the Russians at the same time dreaded the effect of that weakness. The Czar disappointed both these hopes and fears. In his addresses to his subjects he exhibited himself great as his misfortune; "No pusillanimous dejection!" he exclaimed: "Let us vow redoubled courage and perseverance! The enemy is in deserted Moscow as in a tomb, without means of domination or even of existence. He entered Russia with three hundred thousand men of all countries, without union or any national or religious bond;—he has lost half of them by the sword, famine, and desertion: he has but the wreck of this army in Moscow; he is in the heart of Russia, and not a single Russian is at his feet.

"Meanwhile, our forces are increasing and inclosing him. He is in the midst of a mighty population, encompassed by armies which are waiting for, and keeping him in check. To escape famine, he will soon be obliged to direct his flight through the close ranks of our brave soldiers. Shall we then recede, when all Europe is looking on and encouraging us? Let us, on the contrary, set it an example, and kiss the hand which has chosen us to be the first of the nations in the cause of virtue and independence." He concluded with an invocation to the Almighty.

The Russians entertain different opinions respecting their general and their emperor. We, for our part, as enemies, can only judge of our enemies by their actions. Now such were their words, and their actions corresponded with them! Comrades! let us do them justice! their sacrifice was complete, without reserve, without tardy regrets. They have since claimed nothing, even when in the heart of the enemy's capital which they preserved. Their renown has therefore remained great and unsullied. They have known what is real glory; and when a more advanced civilisation shall have spread among all classes, that great nation will also have its brilliant era, and will sway in its turn the sceptre of glory, which it seems to be decreed that the nations of the earth shall successively relinquish to each other.

This circuitous march of Kutusoff, whether made from indecision or stratagem, turned out fortunate for him. Murat lost all traces of him for three days. The Russian employed this interval in studying the ground and entrenching himself. His advanced-guard had nearly reached Woronowo, one of the finest domains belonging to count Rostopchin, when that nobleman proceeded forward before it. The Russians supposed that he was going to take a last look at this mansion, when all at once the edifice was wrapt from their sight by clouds of smoke.

They hurried on to extinguish the fire, but Rostopchin himself rejected their aid. They beheld him amid the flames which he was encouraging, smiling at the demolition of this splendid mansion, and then with a firm hand penning these words, which the French, shuddering with surprise, read on the iron gate of a church which was left standing:—"For eight years I have been embellishing this country-seat, where I have lived happily in the bosom of my family. The inhabitants of this estate, to the number of 1720, leave it on your approach, while

I have set fire to my house, that it may not be polluted by your presence. Frenchmen, I have relinquished to you my two houses at Moscow, with their furniture, worth half a million of rubles. Here you will find nothing but ashes!"

It was near this place that Murat came up with Kutusoff. On the 29th of September there was a smart engagement of cavalry towards Czerikowo, and another on the 4th of October, near Winkowo. But there, Miloradowitch, too closely pressed, turned round furiously, with 12,000 horse, upon Sebastiani. He brought him into such danger, that Murat, in the heat of the action, dictated a proposal for a suspension of arms, announcing to Kutusoff the approach of a flag of truce. It was Lauriston that he expected. But as the arrival of Poniatowski at that moment gave us some superiority, the king made no use of the letter which he had written; he fought till nightfall, and repulsed Miloradowitch.

Meanwhile the conflagration at Moscow, which commenced in the night of the 14th of September, suspended through our exertions during the day of the 15th, revived in the following night, and raging in its utmost violence on the 16th, 17th, and 18th, abated on the 19th. It ceased on the 20th. That very day, Napoleon, whom the flames had driven from the Kremlin, returned to the palace of the Czars. He attracted thither the looks of all Europe. There he awaited his convoys, his reinforcements, and the stragglers of his army; certain that all his men would be rallied by his victory, by the allurements of the rich booty, by the astonishing sight of captive Moscow, and, above all, by his own glory, which, from the top of this immense pile of ruins, still shone attractive like a beacon upon a rock.

Twice, however, on the 22nd and 28th of September, letters from Murat had well nigh drawn Napoleon from this fatal abode. They announced a battle; but twice the orders for departure, written in consequence, were burned. It seemed as though the war was finished for our emperor, and that he was only waiting for an answer from Petersburgh. He nourished his hopes with the recollections of Tilsit and Erfurt. Was it possible that at Moscow he should have less ascendency over Alexander? Then, like men who have long been favourites of fortune, what he ardently wished he confidently expected.

His genius possessed, besides, that extraordinary faculty which consisted in throwing aside the most important occupation whenever he pleased, either for the sake of variety or of rest: for in him the power of volition surpassed that of imagination. In this respect he reigned over himself as much as he did over others.

Thus, Paris diverted his attention from Petersburgh. His accumulating affairs, and the couriers, which, in the first days, succeeded each other without intermission, served to engage him. But the rapidity with which he transacted business soon left him nothing to do. His expresses, which at first came from France in a fortnight, ceased to arrive. A few military posts, placed in four towns reduced to ashes, and in wooden houses rudely palisaded, were not sufficient to guard a road of ninety-three leagues: for we had not been able to fix more than a few steps, and those too far apart, on so long a ladder. This too lengthened line of operation was broken at every point where it was touched by the enemy: a few peasants and a handful of Cossacks were quite sufficient for the purpose.

Still no answer was received from Alexander. The uneasiness of Napoleon increased, and his means of diverting his attention from it diminished. The activity of his genius, accustomed to the government of all Europe, had nothing wherewith to occupy itself but the management of one hundred thousand men; and then, the organisation of his army was so perfect that this was scarcely any occupation. Here every thing was fixed; he held all the wires in his hand: he was surrounded by ministers who could tell him immediately, at any hour of the day, the position of each man in the morning or at night, whether alone or not, whether with his colours, in the hospital, on leave of absence, or wherever else he might be, and that from Moscow to Paris—to such a degree of perfection had the science of a concentrated administration been then brought, so experienced and well chosen were the officers, and so much was required by their commander.

But eleven days had now elapsed; still Alexander was silent, and still did Napoleon hope to overcome his rival in obstinacy: thus losing the time which he ought to have gained, and which is always serviceable to defence against attack.

From this period all his actions indicated to the Russians still more strongly than at Witepsk, that their mighty foe was resolved to fix himself in the heart of their empire. Moscow, though in ashes, received an intendant and municipalities. Orders were issued to provision it for the winter. A theatre was formed amidst the ruins. The first-rate actors of Paris were, it is said, sent for. An Italian singer strove to reproduce, in the Kremlin, the evening entertainments of the Tuileries. By such means Napoleon expected to dupe a government which the habit of reigning over error and ignorance had rendered an adept in all these deceptions.

He was himself sensible of the inadequacy of these means, and yet September was past, October had begun. Alexander had not deigned to reply! it was an affront! he was exasperated. On the 3rd of October, after a night of restlessness and anger, he summoned his marshals. "Come in," said he, as soon as he perceived them, "hear the new plan which I have conceived; Prince Eugene, read it." They listened. "We must burn the remains of Moscow, march by Twer to Petersburgh, where we shall be joined by Macdonald. Murat and Davoust will form the rear-guard."—The emperor, all animation, fixed his sparkling eyes on his generals, whose frigid and silent countenances expressed nothing but astonishment.

Then exalting himself in order to rouse them—"What!" said he, "and are *you* not inflamed by this idea? Was there ever so great a military achievement? Henceforth this conquest is the only one that is worthy of us! With what glory we shall be covered, and what will the whole world say, when it learns that, in three months we have conquered the two great capitals of the North!"

But Davoust, as well as Daru, objected to him, "the season, the want of supplies, a sterile, desert, and artificial road, that from Twer to Petersburgh runs for a hundred leagues through morasses, and which three hundred peasants might in one day render impassable. Why keep proceeding northward? why go to meet, to provoke and to defy the winter?—it was already too near; and what was to become of the six thousand wounded still in Moscow? were they then to be left to the mercy of Kutusoff? That general would not fail to follow close at our heels. We should have at once to attack and to defend ourselves, and to march to a conquest as though we were in flight."

These officers have declared that they then proposed various plans; a useless trouble with a prince whose genius outstripped all other imaginations, and whom their objections would not have stopped, had he been really determined to march to Petersburgh. But that idea was in him only a sally of anger, an inspiration of despair, on finding himself obliged in the face of Europe to give way, to relinquish a conquest, and to fall back.

It was more especially a threat to frighten his officers as well as the enemy, and to bring about and promote a negociation which Caulaincourt was to open. That officer had made himself agreeable to Alexander; he was the only one of the grandees of Napoleon's court who had acquired any influence over his rival; but for some months past Napoleon had kept him at a distance, because he had not been able to persuade him to approve his expedition.

It was nevertheless to this very man that he was that day obliged to have recourse, and to disclose his anxiety. He sent for him; but when alone with him, he hesitated. Taking him by the arm, he walked to and fro a long time in great agitation, while his pride prevented him from breaking so painful a silence: at length it yielded, but in a threatening manner. Caulaincourt was to beg the enemy to solicit peace of him, as if he deigned to grant it.

After a few words, which were scarcely articulate, he said, that "he was about to march to Petersburgh. He knew that the destruction of that city would no doubt give pain to his grand equerry. Russia would then rise against the emperor Alexander: there would be a conspiracy against that monarch; he would be assassinated, which would be a most unfortunate circumstance. He esteemed that prince, and should regret him, both for his own sake and that of France. His disposition," he added, "was suitable to our interests; no prince could replace him with such advantage to us. He thought, therefore, of sending Caulaincourt to him, to prevent such a catastrophe."

The duke of Vicenza, however, more obstinate than disposed to flattery, did not alter his tone. He maintained that "these overtures would be useless; that so long as the Russian territory was not entirely evacuated, Alexander would not listen to any proposals; that Russia was sensible of all her advantage at this season of the year; nay, more, that this step would be detrimental to himself, inasmuch as it would demonstrate the need which Napoleon had of peace, and betray all the embarrassment of our situation."

He added, "that the more particular the selection of the negociator, the more clearly he would show his anxiety; that therefore he would be more likely to fail than any other, especially as he should go with the certainty of failing." The emperor abruptly terminated the conversation by these words: "Well, then, I will send Lauriston."

The latter asserts, that he added fresh objections to the preceding, and that, being urged by the emperor, he recommended to him to begin his retreat that very day by way of Kaluga. Napoleon, irritated at this, acrimoniously replied, "that he liked simple plans, less circuitous routes, high roads, the roads by which he had come, yet he would not retread it but with peace." Then showing to him, as he had done to the duke of Vicenza, the letter which he had written to Alexander, he ordered him to go and obtain of Kutusoff a safe-conduct to Petersburgh. The last words of the emperor to Lauriston were: "I want peace, I must have peace, I absolutely will have peace; only save my honour!"

CHAPTER X

ARMISTICE

THE general set out, and reached the advanced posts on the 5th of October. Hostilities were instantly suspended, and an interview granted, at which Wolkonsky, aide-de-camp to Alexander, and Beningsen were present without Kutusoff. Wilson asserts, that the Russian generals and officers, suspicious of their commander, and accusing him of weakness, had raised a cry of treason, and that the latter had not dared to leave his camp.

As Lauriston's instructions purported that he was to address himself to no one but Kutusoff, he peremptorily rejected any intermediate communication, and seizing, as he said, this occasion for breaking off a negociation which he disapproved, he retired in spite of all the solicitations of Wolkonsky, with the intention of returning to Moscow. In that case, no doubt, Napoleon, exasperated, would have fallen upon Kutusoff, overthrown him and destroyed his army, as yet very incomplete, and have forced him into a peace. In case of less decisive success, he would at least have been able to retire without loss upon his reinforcements.

Unfortunately, Beningsen desired an interview with Murat. Lauriston waited. The chief of the Russian staff, an abler negociator than soldier, strove to charm this monarch of yesterday, by demonstrations of respect; to seduce him by praises; to deceive him with smooth words, breathing nothing but a weariness of war and the hope of peace: and Murat, tired of battles, anxious respecting their result, and, as it is said, regretting his throne, now that he had no hope of a better, suffered himself to be charmed, seduced, and deceived.

Beningsen was equally successful in persuading his own commander, and the leader of our vanguard; he sent in great haste for Lauriston, and had him conducted to the Russian camp, where Kutusoff was waiting for him at midnight. The interview began inauspiciously. Konownitzin and Wolkonsky wished to be present. This shocked the French general: he insisted that they should retire, and they complied.

As soon as Lauriston was alone with Kutusoff, he explained his motives and his object, and applied for a safe conduct to Petersburgh. The Russian general replied, that a compliance with this demand exceeded his powers; but he immediately proposed to send Wolkonsky with the letter from Napoleon to Alexander, and offered an armistice till the return of that officer. He accompanied these proposals with pacific protestations, which were subsequently repeated by all his generals.

According to their account, "they all deplored the continuance of the war. And what was its object? Their nations, like their emperors, ought to esteem, to love, and to be allies of one another. It was their ardent wish that a speedy peace might arrive from Petersburgh. Wolkonsky could not make haste enough." They pressed round Lauriston, drawing him aside, taking him by the hand, and lavishing upon him those caressing manners which they have inherited from Asia.

It was soon demonstrated that the chief point in which they were all agreed was to deceive Murat and his emperor; and in this they succeeded. These details transported Napoleon with joy. Credulous from hope, perhaps from despair, he was for some moments dazzled by these appearances; eager to escape from the inward feeling which oppressed him, he seemed desirous to deaden it by resigning himself to an expansive joy.

He summoned all his generals; he triumphantly announced to them a very speedy peace. "They had but to wait another fortnight. None but himself was acquainted with the Russian character. On the receipt of his letter, Petersburgh would be illuminated."

But the armistice proposed by Kutusoff was so unsatisfactory to him, that he ordered Murat to break it instantly; it nevertheless continued to be observed, the cause of which is unknown.

This armistice was a singular one. If either party wished to break it, three hours notice was to be sufficient. It was confined to the fronts of the two camps, but did not extend to their flanks. Such at least was the interpretation put upon it by the Russians. We could not bring up a convoy, or send out a foraging party, without fighting; so that the war continued everywhere, excepting where it could be favourable to us.

In the first of the succeeding days, Murat took it into his head to show himself at the enemy's advanced posts. There he was gratified by the notice which his fine person, his reputation for bravery, and his rank, procured him. The Russian officers took good care not to displease him; they were profuse of all the marks of respect calculated to strengthen his illusion. He could give his orders to their videttes just as he did to the French. If he took a fancy to any part of the ground which they occupied, they cheerfully gave it up to him.

Some Cossack chiefs even went so far as to affect enthusiasm, and to tell him that they had ceased to acknowledge any other as emperor but him who reigned at Moscow. Murat believed for a moment that they would no longer fight against him. He went even farther. Napoleon was heard to exclaim, while reading his letters, "Murat, king of the Cossacks! What madness!" The most extravagant ideas were conceived by men on whom fortune had lavished all sorts of favours.

As for the emperor, who was not so easily deceived, he had but a few moments of a factitious joy. He soon complained "that an annoying warfare of partisans hovered around him;

that notwithstanding all these pacific demonstrations, he was sensible that bodies of Cossacks were prowling on his flanks and in his rear. Had not one hundred and fifty dragoons of his old guard been surprised and routed by a number of these barbarians? And this two days after the armistice, on the road to Mojaisk, on his line of operation, that by which the army communicated with its magazines, its reinforcements, its depôts, and himself with Europe?"

In fact two convoys had just fallen into the enemy's hands on that road: one through the negligence of its commander, who put an end to his life in despair; and the other through the cowardice of an officer, who was about to be punished when the retreat commenced. The destruction of the army was his salvation.[1]

Our soldiers, and especially our cavalry, were obliged every morning to go to a great distance in quest of provisions for the evening and the next day; and as the environs of Moscow and Winkowo became gradually more and more drained, they were daily necessitated to extend their excursions. Both men and horses returned worn out with fatigue, that is to say, such of them as returned at all; for we had to fight for every bushel of rye, and for every truss of forage. It was a series of incessant surprises and skirmishes, and of continual losses. The peasantry took a part in it. They punished with death such of their number as the prospect of gain had allured to our camp with provisions. Others set fire to their own villages, to drive our foragers out of them, and to give them up to the Cossacks whom they had previously summoned, and who kept us there in a state of siege.

It was the peasantry also who took Veria, a town in the neighbourhood of Moscow. One of their priests is said to have planned and executed this *coup-de-main*. He armed the inhabitants, obtained some troops from Kutusoff, then on the 10th. of October, before day-break, he caused the signal of a false attack to be given in one quarter while in another he himself made an attack upon our palisades, destroyed them, penetrated into the town, and put the whole garrison to the sword.

Thus the war was every where: in our front, on our flanks, and in our rear: our army was weakening, and the enemy becoming daily more enterprising. This conquest was destined to fare like many others, which are won in the mass, and lost piecemeal.

Murat himself at length grew uneasy. In these daily skirmishes he had seen half the remnant of his cavalry melted away. At the advanced posts, the Russian officers on meeting with ours, either from weariness, vanity, or military frankness carried to indiscretion, exaggerated the disasters which threatened us. Showing us those wild-looking horses, scarcely at all broken in, whose long manes swept the dust of the plain, they said, "Did not this tell us that a numerous cavalry was joining them from all quarters while ours was gradually perishing? Did not the continual discharges of fire within their line apprize us that a multitude of recruits were there training under favour of the armistice?"

And in fact, notwithstanding the long journeys which they had to make, all these recruits joined the army. There was no occasion to defer calling them together as in other years, till deep snows, obstructing all the roads excepting the high road rendered their desertion impossible. Not one failed to obey the national appeal; all Russia rose: mothers, it was said, wept for joy on learning that their sons had been selected for soldiers: they hastened to acquaint them with this glorious intelligence, and even accompanied them to see them marked with the sign of the Crusaders, to hear them cry, *'Tis the will of God!*

The Russian officers added, "That they were particularly astonished at our security on the approach of their mighty winter, which was their natural and most formidable ally, and which they expected every moment: they pitied us and urged us to fly. In a fortnight," said they, "your nails will drop off, and your arms will fall from your benumbed and half-dead fingers."

The language of some of the Cossack chiefs was also remarkable. They asked our officers, "if they had not, in their own country, corn enough, air enough, graves enough—in short, room enough to live and die? Why then did they come so far from home to throw away their lives and to fatten a foreign soil with their blood?" They added, that "this was a robbery of their native land, which, while living it is our duty to cultivate, to defend and to embellish; and to which after our death we owe our bodies, which we received from it, which it has fed, and which in their turn ought to feed it."

The emperor was not ignorant of these warnings, but he would not suffer his resolution to be shaken by them. The uneasiness which had again seized him betrayed itself in angry orders. It was then that he caused the churches of the Kremlin to be stripped of every thing that could serve for a trophy to the grand army. These objects, devoted to destruction by the Russians themselves, belonged, he said, to the conquerors by the double right conferred by victory, and by the conflagration.

It required long efforts to remove the gigantic cross from the steeple of Ivan the Great, to the possession of which the Russians attached the salvation of their empire. The emperor determined that it should adorn the dome of the Invalids at Paris. During the work it was remarked that a great number of ravens kept flying round this cross, and that Napoleon, weary of their hoarse croaking, exclaimed, that "it seemed as if these flocks of ill-omened birds meant to defend it." We cannot pretend to tell all that he thought in this critical situation, but it is well known that he was accessible to every kind of presentiment.

His daily excursions, always illumined by a brilliant sun, in which he strove himself to perceive and to make others recognise his star, did not amuse him. To the sullen silence of inanimate Moscow was superadded that of the surrounding deserts, and the still more menacing silence of Alexander. It was not the faint sound of the footsteps of our soldiers, wandering in this vast sepulchre, that could rouse our emperor from his reverie, and snatch him from his painful recollections and still more painful anticipations.

His nights in particular became irksome to him. He passed part of them with count Daru. It was then only that he admitted the danger of his situation. "From Wilna to Moscow what submission, what point of support, of rest, or of retreat, marked his power? It was a vast, bare and desert field of battle, in which his diminished army was imperceptible, insulated, and as it were lost in the horrors of an immense void. In this country of foreign manners and religion, he had not conquered a single individual; he was in fact master only of the ground on which he stood. That which he had just quitted and left behind him was no more his than that which he had not reached. Insufficient for these vast deserts, he was lost as it were in their immense space."

He then reviewed the different resolutions of which he still had the choice. "People imagined," he said, "that he had nothing to do but march, without considering that it would take a month to refit his army and to evacuate his hospitals; that if he relinquished his wounded, the Cossacks would daily be seen triumphing over his sick and his stragglers. He would appear to fly. All Europe would resound with the report! Europe, which envied him, which was seeking a rival under whom to rally, and would imagine that it had found such a rival in Alexander."

Then, appreciating all the power which he derived from the notion of his infallibility, he trembled at the idea of giving it the first blow. "What a frightful succession of dangerous wars would date from his first retrograde step! Let not then his inactivity be censured! As if I did not know," added he, "that in a military point of view Moscow is of no value! But Moscow is not a military position, it is a political position. People look upon me as a general there, when in fact I am only emperor!" He then exclaimed that "in political measures we ought never to recede, never to retrograde, never to admit ourselves to be wrong, as it lessened our consideration; that even when in error, we ought to persist in it, in order to have the appearance of being in the right."

On this account he adhered to his own opinion with that tenacity which, on other occasions, was his best quality, but in this case his worst defect.

His distress meanwhile increased. He knew that he must not depend upon the Prussian army: an intimation from too authentic a source, addressed to Berthier, extinguished his confidence in the support of the Austrians. He was sensible that Kutusoff was only trifling with him, but he had so far committed himself, that he could neither advance nor stay where he was; nor retreat, nor fight, with honour and success. Thus alternately impelled and held back by all that can decide and dissuade, he remained upon those ashes, almost ceasing to hope, but continuing to desire.

The letter of which Lauriston was the bearer had been despatched on the 6th of October; the answer to it could scarcely arrive before the 20th; and yet, in spite of so many threatening demonstrations, the pride, the policy, and perhaps the health of Napoleon induced him to pursue the worst of all courses, that of waiting for this answer, and of trusting to time, which was destroying him. Daru, as well as his other officers, was astonished to find in him no longer that prompt decision, variable and rapid as the circumstances that called it forth; they asserted, that his genius could no longer accommodate itself to them; they placed it to the account of his natural persistence, which led to his elevation, and was likely to cause his downfall.

But in this extremely critical military position, which, by its complication with a political position, became the most delicate which ever existed, it was hardly to be expected that a character which had hitherto been so great, from its unshaken constancy, would make a speedy renunciation of the object which he had proposed to himself ever since he left Witepsk.

1. This is not the fact. An inquiry was instituted into the conduct of the officer, and he was acquitted.—*Ed.*

CHAPTER XI

THE ILLUSION OF HOPE

NAPOLEON, however, was completely aware of his situation. To him everything seemed lost if he receded in the face of astonished Europe, and every thing saved if he could yet overcome Alexander in determination. He appreciated but too well the means that were left him to shake the constancy of his rival; he knew that the number of effective troops, that his situation, the season, in short every thing, would become daily more and more unfavourable to him; but he reckoned upon that force of illusion which his renown gave him. Hitherto, that had lent to him a real and never-failing strength; he endeavoured therefore to keep up by specious arguments the confidence of his people, and perhaps also the faint hope that was yet left to himself.

Moscow, empty of inhabitants, no longer furnished him with anything to lay hold of. "It is no doubt a misfortune," said he, "but this misfortune is not without its advantage. Had it been otherwise, he would not have been able to keep order in so large a city, to overawe a population of three hundred thousand souls, and to sleep in the Kremlin without having his throat cut. They have left us nothing but ruins, but at least we are quiet among them. Millions have no doubt slipped through our hands, but how many thousand millions is Russia losing! Her commerce is ruined for. a century to come. The nation is thrown back fifty years; this of itself is an important result. When the first moment of enthusiasm is past, this reflection will fill them with consternation." The conclusion which he drew was, that so violent a shock would convulse the throne of Alexander, and force that prince to sue for peace.

If he reviewed his different *corps d'armée*, as their reduced battalions now presented but a narrow front, which he had traversed in a moment, this diminution vexed him; and whether he wished to dissemble for the sake of his enemies or his own people, he declared that the practice hitherto pursued, of ranging the men three deep, was wrong, and that two were sufficient; he therefore ordered that in future his infantry should be drawn up in two ranks only.

Nay, more, he insisted that the inflexibility of the regimental returns should give way to this illusion. He disputed their results. The obstinacy of count Lobau could not overcome his: he was desirous, no doubt, of making his aide-de-camp understand what he wished others to believe, and that nothing could shake his resolution.

Murat, nevertheless, transmitted to him tidings of the distressed state of his advanced-guard. They terrified Berthier; but Napoleon sent for the officer who brought them, pressed him with his interrogatories, daunted him with his looks, and dumbfounded him with his incredulity. The statements of Murat's envoy lost much of their assurance. Napoleon took advantage of his hesitation to keep up the hopes of Berthier, and to persuade him that matters were not yet so very urgent; and he sent back the officer to Murat's camp with the opinion, which he would no doubt propagate, that the emperor was immoveable, that he doubtless had his reasons for thus persisting, and that they must all redouble their exertions. And really, for several more days, the pride of an unshaken countenance was the only means by which he could keep up the prospect of negociation.

Meanwhile the attitude of his army seconded his wishes. Most of the officers persevered in their confidence. The common soldiers, who, seeing their whole lives in the present moment, and expecting but little from the future, concerned themselves but little about it, retained their thoughtlessness, the most valuable of their qualities. The rewards, however, which the emperor bestowed profusely upon them in the daily reviews, were received only with a sedate joy, mingled with some degree of dejection. The vacant places that were about to be filled up were yet dyed with blood. These favours were threatening.

On the other hand, ever since they had left Wilna, many of them had thrown away their winter garments, that they might load themselves with provisions. Their shoes were worn out by the length of the march, and the rest of their apparel by the actions in which they had been engaged; but, in spite of all, their attitude was still lofty. They carefully concealed their wretched plight from the notice of the emperor, and appeared before him with their arms bright and in the best order. In this first court of the palace of the Czars, eight hundred leagues from their resources, and after so many battles and bivouacs, they were anxious to appear still clean, ready, and smart; for herein consists the pride of the soldier; here they piqued themselves upon it the more on account of the difficulty, in order to astonish, and because man prides himself on everything that requires extraordinary effort.

The emperor complaisantly affected to know no better, catching at every thing to keep up his hopes, when all at once the first snows fell. With them fell all the illusions with which he had endeavoured to surround himself. From that moment he thought of nothing but retreat without, however, pronouncing the word, and yet no positive order for it could be obtained from him. He merely said, that in twenty days the army must be in winter-quarters, and he urged the departure of his wounded. On this, as on other occasions, he would not consent to the voluntary relinquishment of any thing, however trifling; there was a deficiency of horses for his artillery, now too numerous for an army so reduced; it did not signify, and he flew into a passion at the proposal to leave part of it in Moscow.

"No; the enemy would make a trophy of it,"—and he insisted that every thing should go along with him.

In this desert country, he gave orders for the purchase of 20,000 horses[1] and he expected forage for two months to be provided on a tract where the most distant and dangerous excursions were not sufficient for the supply of the passing day. Some of his officers were astonished to hear orders which it was so impossible to execute; but we have already seen that he sometimes issued such orders to deceive his enemies, and most frequently to indicate to his own troops the extent of his necessities, and the exertions which they ought to make for the purpose of supplying them.

His distress manifested itself only in some paroxysms of ill-humour. It was in the morning at his levee. There, amid the assembled chiefs, in whose anxious looks he imagined he could read disapprobation, he seemed desirous to awe them by the severity of his manner, by his sharp tone, and his abrupt language. From the paleness of his face, it was evident that Truth, whose best time for obtaining a hearing is in the darkness of night, had oppressed him grievously by her presence, and tired him with her unwelcome light. Sometimes, on these occasions, his bursting heart would overflow, and pour forth his sorrows around him by movements of impatience; but so far from lightening his griefs, he aggravated them by those acts of injustice for which he reproached himself, and which he was afterwards anxious to repair.

It was only to count Daru that he unbosomed himself frankly, but without weakness. He said, "he should march upon Kutusoff, crush or drive him back, and then turn suddenly towards Smolensk." Daru, who had before approved this course, replied, that "it was now too late; that the Russian army was reinforced, his own weakened; his victory forgotten; that the moment his troops should turn their faces towards France, they would slip away from him by degrees; that each soldier, laden with booty, would try to get the start of the army, for the purpose of selling it in France."—"What, then, is to be done?" exclaimed the emperor.

"Remain here," replied Daru, "make one vast entrenched camp of Moscow and pass the winter in it. He would answer for it that there would be no want of bread and salt: the rest foraging on a large scale would supply. Such of the horses as they could not procure food for might be salted down. As to lodgings, if there were not houses enough, the cellars might make up the deficiency. Here we might stay till the return of spring, when our reinforcements and all Lithuania in arms should come to relieve, to join us, and to complete the conquest."

After listening to this proposal the emperor was for some time silent and thoughtful; he then replied, "This is a lion's counsel! But what would Paris say? what would they do there? what have they been doing there for the last three weeks that they have not heard from me? who knows what would be the effect of a suspension of communications for six months? No; France would not accustom itself to my absence, and Prussia and Austria would take advantage of it."[2]

Still Napoleon could not make up his mind either to stay or to depart. Overcome in this struggle of obstinacy, he deferred from day to day the avowal of his defeat. Amid the dreadful storm of men and elements which was gathering around him, his ministers and his aides-de-camp saw him pass whole days in discussing the merits of some new verses which he had received, or the regulations for the *Comédie Française* at Paris, which he took three evenings to finish. As they were acquainted with his deep anxiety, they admired the strength of his genius, and the facility with which he could take off or fix the whole force of his attention on whatever he pleased.

It was merely remarked that he prolonged his meals, which had hitherto been so simple and so short. He seemed desirous of stifling thought by repletion. He would then pass whole hours half reclined, as if torpid, and awaiting with a novel in his hand the catastrophe of his terrible history. On beholding this obstinate and inflexible character, struggling with impossibility, his officers would then observe to one another, that, having arrived at the summit of his glory, he no doubt foresaw that from his first retrograde step would date its decline; that for this reason he continued immoveable, clinging to and lingering a few moments longer on this elevation.

Kutusoff, meanwhile, was gaining the time which we were losing. His letters to Alexander described "his army as being in the midst of plenty; his recruits arriving from all quarters and being trained; his wounded recovering in the bosom of their families; the whole of the peasantry on foot, some in arms, some on the look-out from the tops of steeples, or in our camp, while others were stealing into our habitations, and even into the Kremlin. Rostopchin received a daily report of what was passing at Moscow, as regularly as before its capture. If they undertook to be our guides, it was for the purpose of delivering us into his hands. His partisans were every day bringing in some hundreds of prisoners. Every thing concurred to destroy the enemy's army and to strengthen his own; to serve him and to betray us; in a word, the campaign, which was over for us, was but just about to begin for them."

Kutusoff neglected no advantage. He made his camp ring with the news of the victory of Salamanca. "The French," said he, "are expelled from Madrid. The hand of the Most High presses heavily upon Napoleon. Moscow will be his prison, his grave, and that of all his grand army. We shall soon take France in Russia!" It was in such language that the Russian general addressed his troops and his emperor; and nevertheless he still kept up appearances with Murat. At once bold and crafty, he contrived slowly to prepare a sudden and impetuous warfare, and to cover his plans for our destruction with demonstrations of kindness and honeyed words.

At length, after several days of illusion, the charm was dispelled. A Cossack completely dissolved it. This barbarian fired at Murat, at the moment when that prince came as usual to show himself at the advanced posts. Highly exasperated, Murat immediately declared to Miloradowitch that an armistice which was incessantly violated was at an end; and that thenceforward each must only look to himself.[3]

At the same time he apprised the emperor, that the woody country on his left might favour the enemy's attempts against his flank and rear; that his first line, being backed against a ravine, might be precipitated into it; that, in short, the position which he occupied, in advance of a defile, was dangerous, and rendered a retrograde movement absolutely necessary. But Napoleon would not consent to this step, though he had at first pointed out Woronowo as a more secure position. In this war, still in his view rather political than military, he dreaded above all the appearance of receding. He preferred risking every thing.

However, on the 13th of October, he sent back Lauriston to Murat, to examine the position of the vanguard. As to the emperor, either from a tenacious adherence to his first hope, or that any disposition which might be construed into a preparation for retreat, equally shocked his pride and his policy, a singular negligence was remarked in his preparations for departure. He nevertheless thought of it, for that very day he traced his plan of retreat by Woloklamsk, Zubtzow, and Bieloi, on Witepsk. A moment afterwards he dictated another on Smolensk. Junot received orders to burn on the 21st, at Kolotskoi, all the muskets of the wounded, and to blow up the ammunition wagons. D'Hilliers was to occupy Elnia, and to form magazines at that place. It was not till the 17th, at Moscow, that Berthier thought of causing leather to be distributed for the first time among the troops.

This major-general was a wretched substitute for his principal on this critical occasion. In a strange country and climate, he recommended no new precaution, and he expected the minutest details to be dictated by his emperor. They were forgotten. This negligence or want of foresight was attended with fatal consequences. In an army, each division of which was commanded by a marshal, a prince, or even a king, one relied perhaps too much on the other. Besides, Berthier gave no orders of himself; he thought it enough to repeat exactly the very letter of Napoleon's commands; for, as to their spirit, either from fatigue or habit, he was incessantly confounding the positive with the conjectural parts of those instructions.

Napoleon meanwhile rallied his *corps d'armée*. The reviews which he held in the Kremlin were more frequent; he formed all the dismounted cavalry into battalions, and lavishly distributed rewards. The division of Claparède, the trophies and all the wounded that could be removed, set out for Mojaisk; the rest were collected in the great Foundling Hospital; French surgeons were placed there; and the Russian wounded, intermixed with ours, were intended to serve them for a safeguard.

But it was too late. Amid these preparations, and at the moment when Napoleon was reviewing Ney's divisions in the first court of the Kremlin, a report was all at once circulated around him, that the report of cannon was heard towards Winkowo. It was some time before any one durst apprise him of the circumstance; some from incredulity or uncertainty, and dreading the first movement of his impatience; others from weakness, hesitating to provoke a terrible signal, or apprehensive of being sent to verify this assertion, and of exposing themselves to a fatiguing excursion.

Duroc, at length, took courage to inform him. The emperor was at first agitated, but, quickly recovering himself, he continued the review. An aide-de-camp, young Beranger, arrived shortly after with the intelligence that Murat's first line had been surprised and overthrown, his left turned by favour of the woods, his flank attacked, his retreat cut off: that twelve pieces of cannon, twenty ammunition wagons, and thirty wagons belonging to the train, were taken, two generals killed, three or four thousand men lost as well as the baggage; and, lastly, that the king was wounded. He had not been able to rescue the relics of his advanced-guard from the enemy but by repeatedly charging their numerous troops, which already occupied the high road in his rear, his only retreat.

Our honour however was saved. The attack in front, directed by Kutusoff, was feeble; Poniatowski, at some leagues' distance on the right, made a glorious resistance; Murat and his carabineers, by supernatural exertions, checked Bagawout, who was ready to penetrate our left flank, and restored the fortune of the day. Claparède and Latour-Maubourg cleared the defile of Spaskapli, two leagues in the rear of our line, which was already occupied by Platoff. Two Russian generals were killed, and others wounded: the loss of the enemy was considerable, but the advantage of the attack, our cannon, our position, the victory in short, were theirs.

As for Murat, he had no longer an advanced-guard. The armistice had destroyed half the remnant of his cavalry. This engagement finished it; the survivors, emaciated with hunger, were so few as scarcely to furnish a charge. Thus had the war recommenced. It was now the 18th of October.

At these tidings Napoleon recovered the fire of his early years. A thousand orders, general and particular, all differing, yet all in unison and all necessary, burst at once from his impetuous genius. Night had not yet arrived, and the whole army was already in motion for Woronowo: Broussier was sent in the direction of Fominskoë, and Poniatowski toward Medyn. The emperor himself quitted Moscow before day-light on the 19th of October. "Let us march upon Kaluga," said he, "and woe be to those whom I meet with by the way!"

1. M. de Segur is in error here. The simple fact is, that a great number of individuals in the army having more horses than the regulations allowed, Napoleon purchased the surplus for the use of the artillery &c.—*Ed*.

2. General Gourgaud maintains that it is impossible for any such conversation to have taken place. It is certain that the plan attributed to Daru is absurd in the extreme.—*Ed*.

3. No such declaration was made by Murat. The Russians are said to have violated the armistice without giving any notice, in the hope of destroying the French advanced-guard.—*Ed*.

BOOK IX

———•———

CHAPTER I

DEPARTURE FROM MOSCOW

IN the southern part of Moscow, near one of its gates, one of its most extensive suburbs is divided by two high roads; both run to Kaluga: the one, that on the right, is the more ancient; the other is new. It was on the first that Kutusoff had just beaten Murat. By the same road Napoleon left Moscow on the 19th of October, announcing to his officers his intention to return to the frontiers of Poland by Kaluga, Medyn, Yuknow, Elnia, and Smolensk. One of them, Rapp, observed that "it was late, and that winter might overtake them by the way." The emperor replied, "that he had been obliged to allow time to the soldiers to recruit themselves, and to the wounded collected in Moscow, Mojaisk, and Kolotskoi, to move off towards Smolensk." Then, pointing to a still serene sky, he asked, "if in that brilliant sun they did not recognise his star?" But this appeal to his fortune, and the sinister expression of his looks, belied the security which he affected.

Napoleon entered Moscow with ninety thousand fighting men, and twenty thousand sick and wounded, and quitted it with more than a hundred thousand combatants. He left there only twelve hundred sick. His stay, notwithstanding daily losses, had therefore served to rest his infantry, to complete his stores, to augment his force by ten thousand men, and to protect the recovery or the retreat of a great part of his wounded. But on this very first day he could perceive that his cavalry and artillery might be said rather to crawl than to march.

A melancholy spectacle added to the gloomy presentiments of our chief. The army had ever since the preceding day been pouring out of Moscow without intermission. In this column of one hundred and forty thousand men and about fifty thousand horses of all kinds, a hundred thousand combatants marching at the head with their knapsacks, their arms, upwards of five hundred and fifty pieces of cannon, and two thousand artillery wagons still exhibited a formidable appearance worthy of soldiers who had conquered the world. But the rest, in an alarming proportion, resembled a horde of Tartars after a successful invasion. It consisted of three or four files of infinite length, in which there was a mixture, a confusion of chaises, ammunition wagons, handsome carriages, and vehicles of every kind. Here trophies of Russian, Turkish, and Persian colours, and the gigantic cross of Ivan the Great[1]—there, long-bearded Russian peasants carrying or driving along our booty, of which they constituted a part: others dragging even wheelbarrows filled with whatever they could remove. The fools were not likely to proceed in this manner till the conclusion of the first day: yet their senseless avidity made them think nothing of battles and a march of eight hundred leagues.

In these followers of the army were particularly remarked a multitude of men of all nations, without uniform and without arms, and servants swearing in every language, and urging by dint of shouts and blows the progress of elegant carriages, drawn by pigmy horses harnessed with ropes. They were filled with provisions, or with the booty saved from the flames. They carried also French women with their children. Formerly these females were happy inhabitants of Moscow; they now fled from the hatred of the Muscovites, which the invasion had drawn upon their heads; the army was their only asylum.

A few Russian girls, voluntary captives, also followed. It looked like a caravan, a wandering nation, or rather one of those armies of antiquity returning loaded with slaves and spoil after a great devastation. It was inconceivable how the head of this column could draw and support such a heavy mass of equipages in so long a route.

Notwithstanding the width of the road and the shouts of his escort, Napoleon had great difficulty to obtain a passage through this immense throng. No doubt the obstruction of a defile, a few forced marches and a handful of Cossacks, would have been sufficient to rid us of all this incumbrance: but fortune or the enemy had alone a right to lighten us in this manner. As for the emperor, he was fully sensible that he could neither deprive his soldiers of this fruit of so many toils, nor reproach them for securing it. Besides, the provisions concealed the booty, and could he, who could not give his troops the subsistence which he ought to have done, forbid their carrying it along with them? Lastly, in case of the failure of military conveyances, these vehicles would be the only means of preservation for the sick and wounded.

Napoleon, therefore, extricated himself in silence from the immense train which he drew after him, and advanced on the old road leading to Kaluga. He pushed on in this direction for some hours, declaring that he should go and beat Kutusoff on the very field of his victory. But all at once, about midday, opposite to the castle of Krasnopachra, where he halted, he suddenly turned to the right with his army, and in three marches across the country gained the new road to Kaluga.

The rain, which overtook him in the midst of this manœuvre, spoiled the cross-roads, and obliged him to halt in them. This was a most unfortunate circumstance. It was with great difficulty that our cannon were drawn out of the sloughs.

At any rate the emperor had masked his movement by Ney's corps and the relics of Murat's cavalry, which had remained behind the Motscha and at Woronowo. Kutusoff, deceived by this feint, was still waiting for the grand army on the old road, whilst on the 3rd of October, the whole of it had been transferred to the new one, and had but one march to make in order to pass quietly by him, and to get between him and Kaluga.

A letter from Berthier to Kutusoff, dated on the first day of this flanking march, was at once a last attempt at peace, and perhaps a *ruse de guerre*. No satisfactory answer was returned to it.

1. The cross which was carried away by the French was *not* gigantic. The large cross, on the summit of the tower of Ivan Veliki, was of wood, thirty feet high, and covered with thin plates of gilded silver. In the midst of it was a cross, about ten inches long, of pure gold. In taking the great cross down, the French sappers let it fall, and it was broken to pieces. It was the golden cross which was taken away by the French when they retreated—*Ed.*

CHAPTER II

BATTLE OF MALO-YAROSLAWETZ

ON the 23rd the imperial quarters were at Borowsk. That night was an agreeable one for the emperor: he was informed that at six in the evening Delzons and his division, who was four leagues in advance of him, had found Malo-Yaroslawetz and the woods which command it unoccupied; this was a strong position within reach of Kutusoff, and the only point where he could cut us off from the new road to Kaluga.

The emperor wished first to secure that advantage by his presence; the order to march was even given, but withdrawn, we know not why. He passed the whole of that evening on horseback far from Borowsk, on the left of the road, the side on which he supposed Kutusoff to be. He reconnoitred the ground in the midst of a heavy rain, as if he anticipated that it might become a field of battle. Next day, the 24th, he learned that the Russians had disputed the possession of Malo-Yaroslawetz with Delzons. Either from confidence or uncertainty in his plans, this intelligence appeared to give him very little concern.

He quitted Borowsk, therefore, late and leisurely, when the noise of a very smart engagement reached where he was; he then became uneasy, hastened to an eminence and listened. "Had the Russians anticipated him? Was his manœuvre thwarted? Had he not used sufficient expedition in that march, the object of which was to pass the left flank of Kutusoff?"

In reality there was in this whole movement a little of that torpor which succeeds a long repose. Moscow is but one hundred and ten wersts from Malo-Yaroslawetz; four days would have been sufficient to march that distance; we took six. The army was heavy laden with provision and pillage, and the roads were deep. A whole day had been sacrificed in the passage of the Nara and its morass, as well as in the rallying of the different corps. It is true that in defiling so near the enemy, it was necessary to march close, that we might not present him too long a flank. Be this as it may, we may date all our calamities from that delay.

The emperor was still listening; the noise increased. "Is it then a battle?" he exclaimed. Every discharge agitated him, for the chief point with him was no longer to conquer, but to preserve, and he urged on Davoust, who accompanied him; but he and that marshal did not reach the field of battle till dark, when the firing was subsiding and the whole was over.

The emperor saw the end of the battle, but without being able to assist the viceroy. A band of Cossacks from Twer had nearly captured one of his officers, who was only a very short distance from him.

It was not till then that an officer, sent by Prince Eugene, came to him to explain the whole affair. "The troops had," he said, "in the first place, been obliged to cross the Louja at the foot of Malo-Yaroslawetz, at the bottom of an elbow which the river makes in its course; and then to climb a steep hill: it is on this rapid declivity, broken by pointed crags, that the town is built. Beyond is an elevated plain, surrounded with woods, from which run three roads, one in front, coming from Kaluga, and two on the left, from Lectazowo, the seat of the entrenched camp of Kutusoff.

On the preceding day Delzons found no enemy there; but he did not think it prudent to place his whole division in the upper town, beyond a river and a defile, and on the margin of a precipice, down which it might have been thrown by a nocturnal surprise. He remained, therefore, on the low bank of the Louja, sending only two battalions to occupy the town and to watch the elevated plain.

"The night was drawing to a close; it was four o'clock, and all were already asleep in Delzons's bivouacs, excepting a few sentinels, when Doctoroff's Russians suddenly rushed in the dark out of the woods with tremendous shouts. Our sentinels were driven back on their posts, the posts on their battalions, the battalions on the division; and yet it was not a *coup-de-main*, for the Russians had brought up cannon. At the very commencement of the attack, its discharges conveyed the tidings of a serious affair to the viceroy, who was three leagues distant."

The report added, that "the Prince had immediately hastened up with some officers, and that his divisions and his guard had precipitately followed him. As he approached, a vast amphitheatre, where all was bustle, opened before him; the Louja marked the foot of it, and a multitude of Russian light troops already disputed its banks."

Behind them, from the summit of the declivities on which the town was situated, their advanced-guard poured their fire on Delzons; beyond that, on the elevated plain, the whole army of Kutusoff was rapidly advancing in two long black columns, by the two roads from Lectazowo. They were seen stretching out and entrenching themselves on this bare slope, upon a line of about half a league, where they commanded and embraced every thing by their number and position: they were already placing themselves across the old road to Kaluga, which was open the preceding day, which we might have occupied and travelled if we had pleased, but of which Kutusoff would now have it in his power to defend every inch.

The enemy's artillery had at the same time taken advantage of the heights which bordered the river on their side; their fire traversed the low ground in the bend of the river, in which were Delzons and his troops. The position was untenable, and hesitation would have been fatal. It was necessary to get out of it either by a prompt retreat, or by an impetuous attack; but it was before us that our retreat lay, and the viceroy gave orders for the attack.

After crossing the Louja by a narrow bridge, the high road from Kaluga runs along the bottom of a ravine, which ascends to the town, and then enters Malo-Yaroslawetz. The Russians in mass occupied this hollow way; Delzons and his Frenchmen rushed upon them pell-mell; the Russians were broken and overthrown; they gave way, and presently our bayonets glistened on the heights.

Delzons, conceiving himself sure of the victory, announced it as won. He had nothing but a pile of buildings to storm, but his soldiers hesitated. He himself advanced, and was encouraging them by his words, actions, and example, when a ball struck him on the forehead, and extended him on the ground. His brother threw himself upon him, covered him with his body, clasped him in his arms, and strove to bear him off out of the fire and the fray, but a second ball hit him also, and both expired together.

This loss left a great void, which required to be filled up. Guilleminot succeeded Delzons, and the first thing he did was to throw a hundred grenadiers into a church and church-yard, in the walls of which they made loop-holes. This church stood on the left of the high road, which it commanded, and to the possession of this edifice we owed the victory. Five times during the day was this post passed by the Russian columns, which were pursuing ours, and five times did its fire, seasonably poured upon their flank and rear, harass them and retard their progress: afterwards, when we resumed the offensive, this position placed them between two fires, and ensured the success of our attacks.

Scarcely had that general made this disposition when he was assailed by hosts of Russians; he was driven back towards the bridge, where the viceroy had stationed himself, in order to judge how to act and prepare his reserves. At first the reinforcements which he sent came up but slowly, one after another: and, as is almost always the case, each of them being inadequate to any great effort, was successively destroyed without result.

At length the whole of the 14th division was engaged: the combat was then carried, for the third time, to the heights. But when the French had passed the houses, when they had removed from the central point from which they set out; when they had reached the plain, where they were exposed, and where the circle expanded, they could advance no farther: overwhelmed by the fire of a whole army they were daunted and shaken: fresh Russians incessantly came up: our thinned ranks gave way and were broken; the obstacles of the ground increased their confusion: they again descended precipitately and abandoned every thing.

Meanwhile the shells having set fire to the wooden town behind them, in their retreat they were stopped by the conflagration; one fire drove them back upon another; the Russian recruits, wrought up to a pitch of fanatic fury, closely pursued them; our soldiers became enraged; they fought man to man; some were seen seizing each other by one hand and striking with the other, until both victors and vanquished rolled down precipices into the flames, without quitting their hold. There the wounded expired, either suffocated by the smoke or consumed by the fire. Their blackened and calcined skeletons soon presented a hideous sight, when the eye could still discover in them the traces of a human form.

All, however, were not equally intent on doing their duty. There was one officer, a man who was known to talk very big, and who, at the bottom of a ravine, wasted the time for action in making speeches. In this place of security he kept a sufficient number of troops about him to authorise his remaining himself, leaving the rest to expose themselves in detail, without unison and at random.

The 15th division was still left. The viceroy summoned it: as it advanced, it threw a brigade into the suburb on the left, and another into the town on the right. It consisted of Italians, recruits, who had never before been in action. They ascended, shouting enthusiastically, ignorant of the danger or despising it, from that singular disposition which renders life less dear in its flower than in its decline, either because while young we fear death less from the feeling of its distance, or because at that age, rich in years and prodigal of every thing, we are prodigal of life as the wealthy are of their fortune.

The shock was terrible; every thing was reconquered for the fourth time; and lost in like manner. More eager to begin than their seniors, these young troops were sooner disheartened, and returned flying to the old battalions, which supported and were obliged to lead them back to the danger.

The Russians, emboldened by their incessantly increasing numbers and success, then descended by their right to gain possession of the bridge and to cut off our retreat. Prince Eugene had nothing left but his last reserve: he and his guard now took part in the combat. At this sight, and in obedience to his call, the remains of the 13th, 14th, and 15th divisions mustered their courage; they made a last and powerful effort, and for the fifth time the combat was transferred to the heights.

At the same time colonel Peraldi and the Italian chasseurs overthrew with their bayonets the Russians, who were already approaching the left of the bridge; intoxicated by the smoke and the fire through which they had passed, by the havoc which they made, and by their victory, they pushed forward without stopping on the elevated plain, and endeavoured to make themselves masters of the enemy's cannon: but one of those deep clefts, with which the soil of Russia is intersected, stopped them in the midst of a destructive fire; their ranks opened, the enemy's cavalry attacked them, and they were driven back to the very gardens of the suburb. There they paused and rallied: all, both French and Italians, obstinately defended the upper avenues of the town, and the Russians, being at length repulsed, drew back and concentrated themselves on the road to Kaluga, between the woods and Malo-Yaroslawetz.

In this manner did 18,000 Italians and French, crowded together at the bottom of a ravine, defeat 50,000 Russians[1] posted over their heads, and seconded by all the obstacles that a town built on a steep declivity is capable of presenting.

The army, however, surveyed with sorrow this field of battle, where seven generals and 4000 Italians had been killed or wounded. The sight of the enemy's loss afforded no consolation; it was not twice the amount of ours, and their wounded would be saved. It was moreover recollected that in a similar situation Peter I., in sacrificing ten Russians for one Swede, thought that he was not sustaining merely an equal loss, but even gaining by so terrible a bargain. But what caused the greatest pain, was the reflection that so sanguinary a conflict might have been spared.

In fact, the fires which were discovered on our left, in the night between the 23rd and 24th, had apprised us of the movement of the Russians towards Malo-Yaroslawetz; and yet the French army had marched thither languidly; a single division had been thrown to the distance of three leagues from all succour, and carelessly risked; the different corps had remained out of reach of each other. Where were now the rapid movements of Marengo, Ulm, and Eckmühl? Why so slow and drawling a march on such a critical occasion? Was it our artillery and baggage that had caused this tardiness? Such was at least the most plausible presumption.

1. The French army consisted of three divisions containing 16,000 men; the Russian army formed sixteen divisions, 90,000 strong. The former lost 3000 men, the latter lost 8000.—*Ed.*

CHAPTER III

DISTRESS OF THE EMPEROR

WHEN the emperor received the report of this combat, he was a few paces to the right of the high road, at the bottom of a ravine, close to the rivulet and village of Ghorodinia, in the habitation of a weaver, an old crazy, filthy, wooden hut.[1] Here he was half a league from Malo-Yaroslawetz, at the commencement of the bend of the Louja. It was in this worm-eaten dwelling, and in a dirty dark room, parted off in two by a cloth, that the fate of the army and of Europe was about to be decided.

The first hours of the night were spent in receiving reports. All agreed that the enemy was making preparations for a battle on the following day, which all were disposed to decline. About eleven o'clock Bessières entered. This marshal owed his elevation to honourable services, and above all to the affection of the emperor, who had become attached to him as to a creation of his own. It is true that a man could not be a favourite with Napoleon as with any other monarch; it was necessary at least to have followed and been of some service to him, for he sacrificed little to the graces; in short, it was requisite that he should have been more than a witness of so many victories: and the emperor, when fatigued, accustomed himself to see with eyes which he believed to be of his own formation.

He had sent this marshal to examine the attitude of the enemy, and in obedience to his orders Bessières had carefully explored the front of the Russian position. "It is," said he, "unassailable!"[2] "Oh heavens!" exclaimed the emperor, clasping his hands, "have you examined it well? Are you not mistaken? Will you answer for that?" Bessières repeated his assertion; he affirmed that "three hundred grenadiers would there be sufficient to keep in check a whole army." Napoleon then crossed his arms with a look of consternation, hung his head and remained as if overwhelmed with the deepest dejection. "His army was victorious and himself conquered. His route was intercepted, his manœuvre thwarted: Kutusoff, an old grey-headed Scythian, had been beforehand with him! And he could not accuse his star. Did not the sun of France seem to have followed him to Russia? Was not the road to Malo-Yaroslawetz open but the preceding day? It was not his fortune then that had failed him, but he who had been wanting to his fortune!"

Absorbed in this abyss of painful reflections, he fell into so profound a stupor that none of those about him could draw from him a single word. Scarcely could a nod of the head be obtained from him by dint of importunity. At length he tried to take some rest: but a feverish anxiety prevented him from closing his eyes. During all the rest of that cruel night he kept rising, lying down again,[3] and calling incessantly, but yet not a word escaped him to betray his distress: it was only from the agitation of his body that the anguish of his mind was to be inferred.

About four in the morning, one of his orderly officers, the prince D'Armberg, came to inform him that under favour of the night, of the woods, and some inequalities of ground, the Cossacks were slipping in between him and his advanced posts. The emperor had just sent off Poniatowski on his right to Kremenskoe. So little did he expect the enemy on that side, that he had neglected to order out any scouts on his right flank. He therefore slighted the report of his orderly officer.

No sooner did the sun appear above the horizon on the 25th, than he mounted his horse, and advanced on the Kaluga road, which to him was now nothing more than the road to Malo-Yaroslawetz. To reach the bridge of that town, he had to cross the plain, about a league in length and breadth, embraced by the bend of the Louja: a few officers only attended him. The four squadrons of his usual escort, not having been previously apprized, hastened to rejoin, but had not yet overtaken him. The road was covered with hospital artillery, and vehicles of luxury: it was the interior of the army, and every one was marching on without mistrust.

In the distance, towards the right, a few small bodies of men were first seen running, and then large black lines advancing. Outcries were presently heard: some women and attendants on the army were met running back, too much frightened and out of breath, either to listen to any thing, or to answer any question. At the same time the file of vehicles stopped in uncertainty; disorder arose in it: some endeavoured to proceed, others to turn back; they crossed, jostled, and upset one another: and the whole was soon a scene of complete uproar and confusion.

The emperor looked on and smiled, still advancing, and believing it to be a groundless panic. His aides-de-camp suspected that it was the Cossacks they saw, but they marched in such regular platoons that they still had doubts on the subject; and if those wretches had not howled at the moment of attack, as they all do to stifle the sense of danger, it is probable that Napoleon would not have escaped them. A circumstance which increased the peril was, that their cries were at first mistaken for acclamations, and their hurrahs for shouts of *Vive l'Empereur!*

It was Platoff and six thousand Cossacks, who in the rear of our victorious advanced-guard had ventured to cross the river, the low plain, and the high road, driving all before them: and it was at the very moment when the emperor, perfectly tranquil in the midst of his army, and the windings of a deep river, was advancing, refusing belief to so audacious a plan, that they put it in execution.

When they had once started, they approached with such speed, that Rapp had but just time to say to the emperor, "It is the Cossacks!—turn back!" The emperor, whose eyes deceived him, or who disliked running away, stood firm, and was on the point of being surrounded, when Rapp seized the bridle of his horse, and turned him round, crying "Indeed you must!" And really it was high time to fly, although Napoleon's pride would not allow him to do so. He drew his sword, the prince of Neufchatel and the grand equerry did the same; then placing themselves on the left side of the road, they waited the approach of the horde, from which they were scarcely forty paces distant. Rapp had barely time to turn himself round to face these barbarians, when the foremost of them thrust his lance into the chest of his horse with such violence as to throw him down.[4] The other aides-de-camp, and a few horse belonging to the guard, extricated the general. This action, the bravery of Lecoulteux, the efforts of a score of officers and chasseurs, and above all, the thirst of these barbarians for plunder, saved the emperor. And yet they needed only to have stretched out their hands and seized him; for, at the same moment, the horde, in crossing the high-road, overthrew every thing before them, horses, men, and carriages, wounding and killing some, and dragging them into the woods for the purpose of plundering them; then, loosing the horses' harness to the guns, they took them along with them across the country. But they had only a momentary victory, a triumph of surprise. The cavalry of the guard galloped up; at this sight they let go their prey and fled: and this torrent subsided, leaving indeed melancholy traces, but abandoning all that it was hurrying away in its course.

Some of these barbarians, however, carried their audacity even to insolence. They were seen retiring at a foot pace across the interval between our squadrons, and coolly reloading their arms. They reckoned upon the heaviness of our cavalry of the *élite*, and the swiftness of their own horses, which they urge with a whip. Their flight was effected without disorder; they faced round several times, but without waiting till within reach of fire, so that they left scarcely any wounded, and not one prisoner. At length they enticed us on to ravines covered with bushes, where we were stopped by their artillery, which was waiting for them. All this furnished subject for reflection. Our army was worn down; and the war had begun again with new and undiminished spirit.

The emperor, struck with astonishment that the enemy had dared to attack him, halted until the plain was cleared; after which he returned to Malo-Yaroslawetz, where the viceroy pointed out to him the obstacles which had been conquered the preceding day.

The ground itself spoke sufficiently. Never was field of battle more terribly eloquent. Its marked features; its ruins covered with blood; the streets, the lines of which could no longer be recognised but by the long train of the dead, and of heads crushed by the wheels of the cannon; the wounded, who were still seen issuing from the rubbish, and crawling along, with their garments, their hair, and their limbs half consumed by the fire, and uttering lamentable cries; finally, the doleful sound of the last melancholy honours which the grenadiers were paying to the remains of their colonels and generals who had been slain—all attested the extreme obstinacy of the conflict. In this scene the emperor, it was said, beheld nothing but glory: he exclaimed, that "the honour of so proud a day belonged exclusively to Prince Eugene." This sight, nevertheless, aggravated the painful impression which had already seized him. He then advanced to the elevated plain.

1. During the whole of this combat, Napoleon was on the road leading to the bridge of Malo-Yaroslawetz, from whence he witnessed the action, and issued his orders.—*Ed.*

2. To this it is replied, that the really formidable points of the Russian position were the bridge and the town, and that the French made themselves masters.—*Ed.*

3. When his army was in the field, it was the custom of Napoleon to rise between midnight and two o'clock, to receive the reports which usually arrived about that time.—*Ed.*

4. It is not the fact, that Rapp seized Napoleon's bridle, or that his own horse was killed by a Cossack.—*Ed.*

CHAPTER IV

COUNCIL OF THE OFFICERS

DO you recollect, comrades, the fatal field which put a stop to the conquest of the world, where the victories of twenty years were blasted, where the great edifice of our fortune began to totter to it foundation? Do you not still figure to yourselves the blood ruins of that town, those deep ravines, and the woods which surround that elevated plain, and convert it as it were into a field of combat? On one side were the French, quitting the north, which they shunned; on the other, at the entrance of the wood, were the Russians, guarding the south, and striving to drive us back upon their mighty winter. In the midst of this plain, between the two armies, was Napoleon, his steps and his eyes wandering from south to west, along the roads to Kaluga and Medyn, both which were closed against him. On that to Kaluga, were Kutusoff and one hundred and twenty thousand men, ready to dispute with him twenty leagues of defiles; towards Medyn he beheld a numerous cavalry: it was Platoff and those same hordes which had just penetrated into the flank of the army, had traversed it through and through, and burst forth, laden with booty, to form again on his right flank, where reinforcements and artillery were waiting for them. It was on that side that the eyes of the emperor were fixed longest; it was there that he received the reports of his officers and consulted his maps: then, oppressed with regret and gloomy forebodings, he slowly returned to his head-quarters.

Murat, Prince Eugene, Berthier, Davoust, and Bessières followed him. This mean habitation of an obscure artisan contained within it an emperor, two kings, and three generals. Here they were about to decide the fate of Europe, and of the army which had conquered it. Smolensk was the goal.

Should they march thither by Kaluga, Medyn, or Mojaisk? Napoleon was seated at a table, his head supported by his hands, which concealed his features, as well as the anguish which they no doubt expressed.[1]

A silence fraught with such imminent destinies continued to be respected, until Murat, whose actions were always the result of impetuous feeling, became weary of this hesitation. Yielding to the dictates of his genius, which was wholly directed by his ardent temperament, he was eager to burst from that uncertainty, by one of those first movements which elevate to glory, or hurry to destruction.

Rising, he exclaimed, that "he might possibly be again accused of imprudence, but that in war circumstances decided and gave to everything its name; that where there is no other course than to attack, prudence becomes temerity and temerity prudence; that to stop was impossible, to fly dangerous, consequently they ought to pursue. What signified the menacing attitude of the Russians and their impenetrable woods? For his part he cared not for them. Give him but the remnant of his cavalry, and that of the guard, and he would force his way into their forests and their battalions, overthrow all before him, and open anew to the army the road to Kaluga."

Here Napoleon, raising his head, extinguished all this fire, by saying, that "we had exhibited temerity enough already; that we had done but too much for glory, and it was high time to give up thinking of any thing but how to save the rest of the army."

Bessières, either because his pride revolted at the idea of being put under the command of the king of Naples, or from a desire to preserve uninjured the cavalry of the guard, which he had formed, for which he was answerable to Napoleon, and which he exclusively commanded; Bessières, finding himself supported, then ventured to add, that "neither the army nor even the guard had sufficient spirit left for such efforts. It was already said in both, that as the means of conveyance were inadequate, henceforth the victor, if overtaken, would fall a prey to the vanquished; that of course every wound would be mortal. Murat would therefore be but feebly seconded. And in what a position! its strength had just been but too well demonstrated. Against what enemies! had they not remarked the field of the preceding day's battle, and with what fury the Russian recruits, only just armed and clothed, had there fought and fell?" The marshal concluded by voting in favour of retreat, which the emperor approved by his silence.

The prince of Eckmühl immediately observed, that, "as a retreat was decided upon, he proposed that it should be by Medyn and Smolensk." But Murat interrupted Davoust, and whether from enmity, or from that discouragement which usually succeeds the rejection of a rash measure, he declared his astonishment "that any one should dare to propose so imprudent a step to the emperor. Had Davoust sworn the destruction of the army? Would he have so long and so heavy a column trail along, without guides and in uncertainty, on an unknown track, within reach of Kutusoff, presenting its flank to all the attacks of the enemy? Would he, Davoust, defend it? Why—when in our rear, Borowsk and Vereria would lead us without danger to Mojaisk—why reject that safe route? There, provisions must have been collected, there every thing was known to us, and we could not be misled by any traitor."

At these words Davoust, burning with a rage which he had great difficulty to repress, replied, that "he proposed a retreat through a fertile country, by an untouched, plentiful, and well-supplied route, villages still standing, and by the shortest road, that the enemy might not avail himself of it, to cut us off from the route from Mojaisk to Smolensk, recommended by Murat.

And what a route! a desert of sand and ashes, where convoys of wounded would increase our embarrassment, where we should meet with nothing but ruins, traces of blood, skeletons and famine!

"Moreover, though he deemed it his duty to give his opinion when it was asked, he was ready to obey orders contrary to it with the same zeal as if they were consonant with his suggestions; but that the emperor alone had a right to impose silence on him and not Murat, who was not his sovereign, and never should be!"

The quarrel growing warm, Bessières and Berthier interposed. As for the emperor, still absorbed in the same attitude, he appeared insensible to what was passing. At length he broke up this council with the words, "Well, gentlemen, I will decide."

He decided on retreat, and by that road which would carry him most speedily to a distance from the enemy; but it required another desperate effort before he could bring himself to give an order of march so new to him. So painful was this effort, that in the inward struggle which it occasioned, he lost the use of his senses. Those who attended him have asserted, that the report of another warm affair with the Cossacks, towards Borowsk, a few leagues in the rear of the army, was the last shock which induced him finally to adopt this fatal resolution.

It is a remarkable fact, that he issued orders for this retreat northward, at the very moment that Kutusoff, and his Russians, dismayed by the defeat of Malo-Yaroslawetz, were retiring southward.

1. This council was never assembled. The retreat to Smolensk was decided upon by Napoleon before he quitted the battle field of Malo-Yaroslawetz.—*Ed.*.

CHAPTER V

MUTUAL RETREAT

THE very same night a similar anxiety had agitated the Russian camp. During the combat of Malo-Yaroslawetz, Kutusoff had approached the field of battle, merely groping his way, as it were, pausing at every step, and examining the ground, as if he was afraid of its sinking beneath him; he did not send off the different corps which were despatched to the assistance of Doctoroff, till the orders for that purpose were absolutely extorted from him. He durst not place himself in person across Napoleon's way, till an hour when general battles are not to be apprehended.

Wilson, warm from the action, then hastened to him—Wilson, that active bustling Englishman, whom we had seen in Egypt, in Spain, and every where else, the enemy of the French and of Napoleon. He was the representative of the allies in the Russian army; he was in the midst of Kutusoff's army an independent man, an observer, nay, even a judge—infallible motives of aversion; his presence was odious to the old Russian general; and, as hatred never fails to beget hatred, both cordially detested each other.

Wilson reproached him with his excessive dilatoriness: he reminded him that five times in one day it had caused him to lose the victory, in the battle of Winkowo, on the 18th of

October. In fact, on that day Murat would have been destroyed, had Kutusoff fully occupied the front of the French by a brisk attack, while Beningsen was turning their left wing. But either from negligence, from the tardiness which is the fault of age, or, as several Russians assert, because Kutusoff was more envious of Beningsen than inimical to Napoleon, the veteran had attacked too faintly, and too late, and had stopped too soon.

Wilson continued to insist on his agreeing to a decisive engagement on the following day, and on his refusal, he asked, "Was he then determined to open a free passage for Napoleon? to allow him to escape with his victory? What a cry of indignation would be raised in Petersburgh, in London, throughout all Europe! Did he not already hear the murmurs of his own troops?"

Kutusoff, irritated at this, replied, that "he would certainly rather make a bridge of gold for the enemy than compromise his army, and with it the fate of the whole empire. Was not Napoleon fleeing? why then stop him and force him to conquer? The season was sufficient to destroy him: of all the allies of Russia, they could rely with most confidence on winter; and he should wait for its assistance. As for the Russian army, it was under his command, and it would obey him in spite of the clamours of Wilson; Alexander, when informed of his proceedings, would approve them. What did he care for England? was it for her that he was fighting? He was a true-born Russian, his fondest wish was to see Russia delivered, and delivered she would be without risking the chance of another battle; and as for the rest of Europe, it was nothing to him whether it was under the dominion of France or England."

Thus was Wilson repulsed; and yet Kutusoff, shut up with the French army in the elevated plain of Malo-Yaroslawetz was compelled to put himself into the most threatening attitude. He there drew up, on the 25th, all his divisions, and seven hundred pieces of artillery. No doubts were any longer entertained in the two armies that a decisive day had arrived; Wilson was of that opinion himself. He remarked that the

Russian lines had at their back a muddy ravine, across which there was an unsafe bridge. This only way of retreat, in the sight of an enemy, appeared to him to be impracticable. Kutusoff was now in such a situation that he must either conquer or perish; and the Englishman was hugging himself at the prospect of a decisive engagement: whether its issue proved fatal to Napoleon or dangerous to Russia, it must be bloody, and England could not but be a gainer by it.

Still uneasy, however, he went at night through the ranks: he was delighted to hear Kutusoff swear that he was at length going to fight; he triumphed on seeing all the Russian generals preparing for a terrible conflict; Beningsen alone had still his doubts on the subject. The Englishman, nevertheless, considering that the position no longer admitted of falling back, at length lay down to wait for daylight, when about three in the morning a general order for retreat awoke him. All his efforts to prevent it were ineffectual. Kutusoff had resolved to direct his flight southward, first to Gonczarewo, and then beyond Kaluga; and at the Oka every thing was by this time ready for his passage.

It was at that very instant that Napoleon ordered his troops to retire northward on Mojaisk. The two armies therefore turned their backs on each other, mutually deceiving each other by means of their rear-guards.

On the part of Kutusoff, Wilson asserts, that his retreat was like a rout. Cavalry, cannon, carriages, and battalions thronged from all sides to the entrance of the bridge, against which the Russian army was backed. There all these columns, hurrying from the right, the left, and the centre, met, clashed, and became blended into so enormous and so dense a mass, that it lost all power of motion. It took several hours to disentangle it, and to clear the passage. A few balls discharged by Davoust, which he regarded as thrown away, fell among this confused crowd.

Napoleon needed but to have advanced upon this disorderly rabble. It was after the greatest effort, that of Malo-Yaroslawetz, had been made, and when he had nothing to do but to march, that he retreated. But such is war! in which it is impossible to attempt too much, or to be too daring. One army knows not what the other is doing. The advanced posts are the exterior of these two great hostile bodies, by means of which they overawe one another. What an abyss there is between two armies in the presence of each other!

Besides, it was perhaps because the emperor had been wanting in prudence at Moscow that he was now deficient in audacity: he was worn out; the two affairs with the Cossacks had disgusted him: he felt for his wounded; so many horrors disheartened him, and like men of extreme resolutions, having ceased to hope for a complete victory, he determined upon a precipitate retreat.

From that moment he had nothing in his view but Paris, just as on leaving Paris he saw nothing but Moscow. It was on the 26th of October that the fatal movement of our retreat commenced. Davoust with twenty-five thousand men remained as a rear-guard. While he advanced a few paces, and, without being aware of it, spread consternation among the Russians, the grand army in astonishment turned its back on them. It marched with downcast eyes; as if ashamed and humbled. In the midst of it, its commander, gloomy and silent, seemed to be anxiously measuring his line of communication with the fortresses on the Vistula.

For the space of more than two hundred and fifty leagues it offered but two points where he could halt and rest, the first Smolensk, and the second Minsk. He had made those towns his two great depôts, where immense magazines were established. But Wittgenstein, who was still before Polotsk, threatened the left flank of the former, and Tchitchakoff, already at Bresk-litowsky, the right flank of the latter. Wittgenstein's force was gaining strength by recruits and fresh corps which he was daily receiving, and by a gradual diminution of that of Saint Cyr.

Napoleon, however, reckoned upon the duke of Belluno, and his thirty-six thousand fresh troops. That corps had been at

Smolensk ever since the beginning of September. He reckoned also upon detachments being sent from his depôts, on the sick and wounded who had recovered, and on the stragglers, who would be rallied and formed at Wilna into marching battalions. All these would successively come into line, and fill up the chasms made in his ranks by the sword, famine, and disease. He should therefore have time to regain that position on the Dwina and the Borysthenes, where he wished it to be believed that his presence, added to that of Victor, Saint Cyr, and Macdonald, would overawe Wittgenstein, check Kutusoff, and threaten Alexander even in his second capital.

He therefore announced that he was going to take post on the Dwina. But it was not upon that river and the Borysthenes that his thoughts rested: he was sensible that it was not with a harassed and reduced army that he could guard the interval between those two rivers and their courses, which the ice would speedily efface. He placed no reliance on a sea of snow six feet deep, with which winter would speedily cover those parts, but to which it would also give solidity; the whole then would be one wide road for the enemy to reach him, to penetrate into the intervals between his wooden cantonments, scattered over a frontier of two hundred leagues, and to burn them.

Had he at first stopped there, as he declared he should on his arrival at Witepsk—had he there taken proper measures for preserving and recruiting his army—had Tormasoff, Tchitchakoff, and Hoertel been driven out of Volhynia—had he raised a hundred thousand Cossacks in those rich provinces— his winter quarters would then have been habitable. But now, nothing was ready for him there; and not only was his force inadequate to the purpose, but Tchitchakoff, a hundred leagues in his rear, would still threaten his communications with Germany and France and his retreat. It was therefore at a hundred leagues beyond Smolensk, in a more compact position, behind the morasses of the Berezina, it was to Minsk, that it was necessary to repair in search of winter-quarters, from which he was forty marches distant.[1]

But should he arrive there in time? He had reason to think so. Dombrowski and his Poles, placed around Bobruisk, would be sufficient to keep Hoertel in check. As for Schwartzenberg, that general was at the head of forty-two thousand Austrians, Saxons, and Poles, whom Durutte, and his French division, from Warsaw, would augment to more than fifty thousand men. He had been victorious over Tormasoff, and pursued him as far as the Styr.

It was true that the Russian army of Moldavia had just formed a junction with the remains of the army of Volhynia—that Tchitchakoff, an active and resolute general, had assumed the command of fifty-five thousand Russians—that the Austrian general had paused and even thought it prudent, on the 23rd of September, to retire behind the Bug; but he was to have recrossed that river at Bresk-litowsky, and Napoleon knew no more.

At any rate, without a defection, which it was too late to foresee, and which a precipitate return could alone prevent, he flattered himself that Schwartzenberg, Regnier, Durutte, Dombrowski, and twenty thousand men, divided between Minsk, Slonim, Grodno, and Wilna—in short, that seventy thousand men would not allow sixty thousand Russians to gain possession of his magazines, and to cut off his retreat.

1. It was not till after his arrival at Smolensk that Napoleon resolved to fall back behind the Berezina.—*Ed.*

CHAPTER VI

DEVASTATION
OF THE COUNTRY

NAPOLEON, reduced to such hazardous conjectures, arrived quite pensive at Vereïa, when Mortier presented himself before him. But I perceive that, hurried along, just as we then were, by the rapid succession of violent scenes and memorable events, my attention has been diverted from a fact worthy of notice. On the 23rd of October, at half-past one in the morning, the air was shaken by a tremendous explosion, which for a moment astonished both armies, though amid such mighty expectations scarcely anything now excited astonishment.

Mortier had obeyed his orders—the Kremlin was no more—barrels of powder had been placed in all the halls of the palace of the Czars, and one hundred and eighty-three thousand pounds under the vaults which supported them. The marshal, with eight thousand men, had remained on this volcano, which a Russian howitzer shell might have exploded. Here he covered the march of the army upon Kaluga, and the retreat of our different convoys towards Mojaisk.

Among these eight thousand men there were scarcely two thousand on whom Mortier could rely; the others were dismounted cavalry, men of different countries and regiments, under new officers, without similar habits, without common recollections, in short, without any bond of union, who formed rather a rabble than an organised body; they could scarcely fail in a short time to disperse.

This marshal was looked upon as a devoted victim. The other chiefs, his old companions in glory, had left him with tears in their eyes, as well as the emperor, who said to him, "that he relied on his good fortune; but still in war we must sometimes make part of a fire." Mortier resigned himself without hesitation. His orders were to defend the Kremlin, and on retreating to blow it up, and to burn what yet remained of the city. It was from the castle of Krasno-pachra, on the 21st of October, that Napoleon sent him his last orders. After executing them, Mortier was to march upon Vereïa, and to form the rear-guard of the army.

In this letter Napoleon particularly recommended to him "to put the men still remaining in the hospitals into the carriages belonging to the young guard, those of the dismounted cavalry, and any others that he might find. The Romans," added he, "awarded civic crowns to those who saved citizens: so many soldiers as he should save, so many crowns would the duke of Treviso deserve. He must put them on his horses and those of any of his troops. It was thus that he, Napoleon, acted at St. Jean d'Acre. He ought so much the more to take this measure, since, as soon as the convoy should have rejoined the army, there would be plenty of horses and carriages, which the consumption would have rendered useless for its supply. The emperor hoped that he should have to testify his satisfaction to the duke of Treviso for having saved him five hundred men. He must begin with the officers and then with the subalterns, and give the preference to Frenchmen. He would for that purpose assemble all the generals and officers under his command, and make them sensible of the importance of this measure, and how well they would deserve of the emperor if they saved him five hundred men."

Meanwhile, as the grand army was leaving Moscow, the Cossacks were penetrating into the suburbs, and Mortier had retired towards the Kremlin, as the last spark of life retires towards the heart, when death has begun to seize the extremities. These Cossacks were the scouts to ten thousand Russians under the command of Winzingerode.

This foreigner, inflamed with hatred of Napoleon, and animated by the desire of retaking Moscow and naturalising himself in Russia by this single exploit, pushed on to a considerable distance from his men; he traversed, at a running pace, the Georgian colony, hastened towards the Chinese town and the Kremlin, met with advanced posts, mistook them, fell into an ambuscade, and finding himself a prisoner in a city which he had come to take, he suddenly changed his part, waving his handkerchief in the air, and declaring that he had brought a flag of truce.

He was conducted to the duke of Treviso. There he claimed, in a high tone, the protection of the law of nations, which, he said, was violated in his person. Mortier replied, that "a general-in-chief, coming in this manner, might be taken for a rash soldier, but never for a flag of truce, and that he must immediately deliver his sword." The Russian general, having no longer any hope of imposing upon him, complied and admitted his imprudence.

At length, after four days' resistance, the French bade an eternal adieu to that fatal city. They carried with them four hundred wounded, and, on retiring, deposited, in a safe and secret place, a fire-work skilfully prepared, which a slow fire was already consuming; its progress was minutely calculated; so that it was known at what hour the fire would reach the immense heap of powder buried among the foundations of these condemned palaces.

Mortier hastened his flight; but while he was rapidly retiring, some greedy Cossacks and squalid Muscovites, allured probably by the prospect of pillage, approached; they listened, and emboldened by the apparent quiet which pervaded the fortress, they ventured to penetrate into it; they ascended, and their greedy hands were already stretched forth to plunder, when in a moment they were all destroyed, crushed, hurled into the air, with the buildings which they had come to pillage, and thirty thousand stand of arms that had been left behind there: and then their mangled limbs, mixed with fragments of walls and shattered weapons, blown to a great distance, descended in a horrible shower.

The earth shook under the feet of Mortier; at Fominskoé, ten leagues off, the emperor heard the explosion. He himself, in that tone of anger in which he sometimes addressed Europe, published the following day a bulletin, dated from Borowsk, announcing, that "the Kremlin, the arsenal the magazines were all destroyed; that that ancient citadel, which dated from the origin of the monarchy, and the first palace of the Czars, no longer existed; that Moscow was now but a heap of ruins, a filthy and unwholesome sink, without importance, either political or military. He had abandoned it to Russian beggars and plunderers, in order to march against Kutusoff, to throw himself on the left wing of that general, to drive him back, and then to proceed quietly to the banks of the Dwina, where he should take up his winter-quarters." Then, apprehensive lest he should appear to be retreating, he added, that "there he should be within eighty leagues of Wilna and of Petersburgh, a double advantage; that is to say, twenty marches nearer to his resources and his object." By this remark he hoped to give to his retreat the air of an offensive march.

It was on this occasion that he declared, that "he had refused to give orders for the destruction of the whole country which he was quitting; he felt a repugnance to aggravate the miseries of its inhabitants. To punish the Russian incendiary and a hundred wretches who make war like Tartars, he would not ruin nine thousand proprietors, and leave two hundred thousand serfs, innocent of all these barbarities, absolutely destitute of resources."

He had not then been soured by misfortune; but in three days every thing had changed. After coming in collision with Kutusoff, he retreated through this same town of Borowsk, and no sooner had he passed through it than it ceased to exist. It was thus that in future all was destined to be burned behind him. While conquering, he had preserved: when retiring, he resolved to destroy: either from necessity, to ruin the enemy and to retard his march, every thing being imperative in war; or by way of reprisal, the dreadful consequence of wars of invasion, which in the first place authorise every means of defence, while these afterwards operate as motives to those of attack.

It must be admitted, however, that the aggression in this terrible species of warfare was not on the side of Napoleon. On the 19th of October, Berthier wrote to Kutusoff, proposing "to regulate hostilities in such a manner that they might not inflict on the Muscovite empire more evils than were inseparable from a state of war; the devastation of Russia being as detrimental to that empire as it was painful to Napoleon." But Kutusoff replied, that "it was not in his power to restrain the Russian patriotism," which amounted to an approval of the Tartar warfare made upon us by his militia, and authorised us in some measure to repay them in their own coin.

Similar flames consumed Vereïa, where Mortier rejoined the emperor, bringing Winzingerode along with him. At sight of that German general, all the secret resentments of Napoleon took fire; his dejection gave place to anger, and he discharged on this enemy all the spleen that oppressed him "Who are you?" he exclaimed, crossing his arms with violence, as if to grasp and restrain himself, "a man without country! You have always been my personal enemy. When I was at war with the Austrians, I found you in their ranks. When Austria became my ally, you entered into the Russian service. You have been one of the warmest instigators of the present war. Nevertheless you are a native of the states of the Confederation of the Rhine; you are my subject. You are not an ordinary enemy, you are a rebel; I have a right to bring you to trial! *Gendarmes d'élite*, seize this man!" The *gendarmes* remained motionless, like men accustomed to see these violent scenes terminate without effect, and sure of obeying best by disobeying.

The emperor resumed: "Do you see, sir, this devastated country, these villages in flames? To whom are these disasters to be charged? to fifty adventurers like yourself, paid by England, which has thrown them upon the continent; but the weight of this war will ultimately fall on those who have excited it. In six months I shall be at Petersburgh, and I will call them to account for all this swaggering."

Then addressing the aide-de-camp of Winzingerode, who was a prisoner like himself, "As for you, count Narischkin," said he, "I have nothing to upbraid you with; you are a Russian, you are doing your duty; but how could a man of one of the first families in Russia condescend to become the aide de-camp of a foreign mercenary? Be the aide-de camp of a Russian general; that will be far more honourable."

Till then general Winzingerode had had no opportunity to answer this violent language except by his attitude: it was calm as his reply. " The emperor Alexander," he said, "was the benefactor of himself and of his family: all that he possessed he owed to him; gratitude had made him his subject; he was at the post which his benefactor had allotted to him, and consequently he was only doing his duty."

Napoleon added some threats, but in a less violent strain, and he confined himself to words, either because he had vented all his wrath in the first explosion, or because he merely designed to frighten the Germans who might be tempted to abandon him. Such at least was the interpretation which those about him put upon his violence. It was disapproved; no account was taken of it, and each was eager to accost the captive general to tranquillise and to console him. These attentions were continued till the army reached Lithuania, where the Cossacks retook Winzingerode and his aide-de-camp. The emperor affected to treat this young Russian nobleman with kindness, at the same that he stormed so loudly against his general—a proof that there was calculation even in his wrath.

CHAPTER VII

MOJAISK AND BEYOND

ON the 28th of October we again beheld Mojaisk. That town was still full of wounded; some were carried away, and the rest collected together and abandoned, as at Moscow, to the generosity of the Russians. Napoleon had proceeded but a few wersts from that place when the winter began.[1] Thus, after an obstinate combat, and ten days' marching and counter-marching, the army, which had brought from Moscow only fifteen rations of flour per man, had advanced but three days' march on its retreat. It was in want of provisions, and overtaken by the winter.

Some men had already sunk under these hardships. In the first days of the retreat, on the 26th of October, carriages, laden with provisions, which the horses could no longer draw, were burned. The order for setting fire to all behind the army then followed; in obedience to it, powder-wagons, the horses of which were already worn out, were blown up together with the horses. But at length, as the enemy had not again shown himself, we seemed to be but once more setting out on a toilsome journey; and Napoleon, on again seeing the well-known road, was recovering his confidence, when, towards evening, a Russian chasseur, who had been made prisoner, was sent to him by Davoust.

At first he questioned him carelessly; but as chance would have it, this Russian had some knowledge of roads, names, and distances. He answered, that "the whole Russian army was marching by Medyn upon Viasma." The emperor then became attentive. Did Kutusoff mean to forestall him there, as at Malo-Yaroslawetz, to cut off his retreat upon Smolensk, as he had done that upon Kaluga, and to coop him up in this desert without provisions, without shelter, and in the midst of a general insurrection? His first impulse, however, inclined him to reject this notion; for, whether owing to pride or experience, he was accustomed not to give his adversaries credit for that ability which he would have displayed in their place.

In this instance, however, he had another motive. His security was but affected: for it was evident that the Russian army was taking the Medyn road, the very one which Davoust had recommended for the French army: and Davoust, either from vanity or inadvertence, had not confided this alarming intelligence to his despatch alone. Napoleon feared its effects on his troops, and therefore affected to disbelieve and to despise it; but at the same time he gave orders that his guard should march next day in all haste, and so long as it should be light, as far as Gjatz. Here he proposed to afford rest and provisions to this flower of his army, to ascertain, so much nearer, the direction of Kutusoff's march, and to be beforehand with him at that point.

But he had not consulted the season, which seemed to avenge the slight. Winter was so near at hand, that a blast of a few minutes was sufficient to bring it on, sharp, biting, intense. We were immediately sensible that it was indigenous to the country, and that we were strangers in it. Every thing was altered: roads, faces, courage: the army became sullen, the march toilsome, and consternation began.

Some leagues from Mojaisk, we had to cross the Kologa. It was but a large rivulet: two trees, the same number of props, and a few planks were sufficient to ensure the passage: but such was the confusion and inattention, that the emperor was detained there.[2] Several pieces of cannon, which it was attempted to get across by fording, were lost. It seemed as if each corps was marching separately, as if there was no staff, no general order, no common tie, nothing that bound these corps together. In reality, the elevation of each of their chiefs rendered them too independent of one another. The emperor himself had become so exceedingly great, that he was at an immeasurable distance from the details of his army; and Berthier, holding an intermediate place between him and officers, who were all kings, princes, or marshals, was obliged to act with a great deal of caution. He was besides incompetent to his situation.

The emperor, stopped by the trifling obstacle of a broken bridge, confined himself to a gesture expressive of dissatisfaction and contempt, to which Berthier replied only by a look of resignation. On this particular point he had received no orders from the emperor: he therefore conceived that he was not to blame; for Berthier was a faithful echo, a mirror, and nothing more. Always ready, clear and distinct, he reflected, he repeated the emperor, but added nothing, and what Napoleon forgot was irretrievably forgotten.

After passing the Kologa, we marched on, absorbed in thought, when some of us, raising our eyes, uttered an exclamation of horror. Each instantly looked around him, and beheld a plain trampled, bare, and devastated, all the trees cut down within a few feet from the surface, and farther off craggy hills, the highest of which appeared to be the most misshapen. It had all the appearance of an extinguished and destroyed volcano. The ground was covered all round with fragments of helmets and cuirasses, broken drums, gun-stocks, tatters of uniforms, and standards dyed with blood.

On this desolate spot lay thirty thousand half-devoured corpses. A number of skeletons, left on the summit of one of the hills, overlooked the whole. It seemed as if death had here fixed his empire: it was that terrible redoubt, the conquest and the grave of Caulaincourt. Presently the cry, "It is the field of the great battle!" formed a long and doleful murmur.

The emperor passed quickly. Nobody stopped. Cold, hunger, and the enemy urged us on: we merely turned our faces as we proceeded to take a last melancholy look at the vast grave of so many companions in arms, uselessly sacrificed, and whom we were obliged to leave behind.

It was here that we had inscribed with the sword and blood one of the most memorable pages of our history. A few relics yet recorded it, and they would soon be swept away. Some day the traveller will pass with indifference over this plain, undistinguished from any other; but when he shall learn that it was the theatre of the great battle, he will turn back, long survey it with inquisitive looks, impress its minutest features on his greedy memory, and doubtless exclaim, "What men! what a commander! what a destiny! These were the soldiers, who thirteen years before in the south attempted a passage to the east, through Egypt, and were dashed against its gates. They afterwards conquered Europe, and hither they came by the north to present themselves again before that same Asia, to be again foiled. What then urged them into this roving and adventurous life? They were not barbarians, seeking a more genial climate, more commodious habitations, more enchanting spectacles, greater wealth; on the contrary, they possessed all these advantages, and all possible pleasures; and yet they forsook them, to live without shelter, and without food, to fall daily and in succession, either slain or mutilated. What necessity drove them to this?—Why, what but confidence in a leader hitherto infallible! the ambition to complete a great work gloriously begun! the intoxication of victory, and, above all, that insatiable thirst of fame, that powerful instinct, which impels man to seek death, in order to obtain immortality."

1. The winter did not begin till the 6th of November. "Previous to that day," says Gen. Gourgaud, "the weather was fine, and the cold much less than it was for some months during the Prussian and Polish campaigns,

and than it was, even in Spain, in the mountains of Castile, when in 1808 the emperor in person made a winter campaign there."—*Ed.*

2. The bridge was not broken. The artillery was not under the necessity of fording; it passed by a bridge, which was constructed for the purpose to the right of Borodino.—*Ed.*

CHAPTER VIII

ABANDONING THE WOUNDED

WHILE the army was passing this fatal field in grave and silent meditation, one of the victims of that sanguinary day was perceived, it is said, still living, and piercing the air with his groans. It was found by those who ran up to him that he was a French soldier. Both his legs had been broken in the engagement; he had fallen among the dead, where he remained unnoticed. The body of a horse, gutted by a shell, was at first his asylum; afterwards, for fifty days, the muddy water of a ravine, into which he had rolled, and the putrefied flesh of the dead, had served for dressing for his wounds, and food for the support of his languishing existence. Those who say that they discovered this man affirm that they saved him.

Farther on, we again beheld the great abbey or hospital of Kolotskoi, a sight still more hideous than that of the field of battle. At Borodino all was Death, but not without its quiet; there at least the battle was over; at Kolotskoi it was still raging. The victims who had escaped from the engagement, death here seemed to be pursuing with the utmost malignity; he penetrated into them by all their senses at once. They were destitute of every means for repelling his attacks, excepting orders, which it was impossible to execute in these deserts, and which, moreover, issuing from too high and too distant a quarter, passed through too many hands to be executed.

Still, in spite of famine, cold, and the most complete destitution, the devotedness of a few surgeons, and a remnant of hope, still supported a great number of wounded in this pestiferous abode. But when they saw the army repass, and that they were about to be left behind, the least infirm crawled to the threshold of the door, lined the way, and extended towards us their supplicating hands.

The emperor had just given orders that each carriage, of whatever kind it might be, should take up one of these unfortunate creatures, that the weakest should be left, as at Moscow, under the protection of such of the wounded and captive Russian officers as had been recovered by our attentions. He halted to see this order carried into execution, and it was at a fire kindled with his forsaken wagons that he and most of his attendants warmed themselves. Ever since the morning a multitude of explosions proclaimed the numerous sacrifices of this kind which it already had been found necessary to make.

During this halt, an atrocious action was witnessed. Several of the wounded had just been placed in the suttlers' carts. These wretches, whose vehicles were overloaded with plunder of Moscow, murmured at the new burden imposed upon them; but being compelled to admit it, they held their peace. No sooner, however, had the army recommenced it march, than they slackened their pace, dropped behind their columns, and, taking advantage of a lonely situation, they threw all the unfortunate men committed to their care into the ditches. One only lived long enough to be picked up by the next carriages that passed: he was a general, and through him this atrocious procedure became known. A shudder of horror spread throughout the column; it reached the emperor; for the sufferings of the army were not yet so severe and so universal as to stifle pity, and to concentrate all his affections within the bosom of each individual.

In the evening of this long day, as the imperial column was approaching Gjatz, it was surprised to find Russians quite recently killed on the way. It was remarked, that each of them had his head shattered in the same manner, and that his bloody brains were scattered near him. It was known that two thousand Russian prisoners were marching on before, and that their guard consisted of Spaniards Portuguese and Poles. On this discovery, each, according to his dispositions was indignant, approved, or remained indifferent. Around the emperor these various feelings were mute. Caulaincourt broke out into the exclamation, that "it was an atrocious cruelty. Here was a pretty specimen of the civilisation which we were introducing into Russia! What would be the effect of this barbarity on the enemy? Were we not leaving our wounded and a multitude of prisoners at his mercy? Did he want the means of wreaking the most horrible retaliation?"[1]

Napoleon preserved a gloomy silence, but on the ensuing day these murders ceased. These unfortunate people were then merely left to die of hunger in the enclosures where, at night, they were confined like cattle. This was no doubt a barbarity too; but what could we do? Exchange them? the enemy rejected the proposal. Release them? they would have gone and published the general distress, and, soon joined by others, they would have returned to pursue us. In this mortal warfare, to give them their lives would have been sacrificing our own. We were cruel from necessity. The mischief arose from our having involved ourselves in so dreadful an alternative.

Besides, in their march to the interior of Russia, our soldiers, who had been made prisoners, were not more humanely treated, and there, certainly, imperious necessity was not an excuse.

At length the troops arrived with the night at Gjatz; but this first day of winter had been cruelly occupied. The sight of the field of battle and of the two forsaken hospitals, the multitude of wagons consigned to the flames, the Russians with their brains blown out, the excessive length of the march, the first severities of winter, all concurred to render it horrible: the retreat became a flight; and Napoleon, compelled to yield and run away, was a spectacle perfectly novel.

Several of our allies enjoyed it with that inward satisfaction which is felt by inferiors, when they see their chiefs at length thwarted, and obliged in their turn, to give way. They indulged the miserable envy that is excited by extraordinary success, which rarely occurs without being abused, and which shocks that equality which is the first feeling of man. But this malicious joy was soon extinguished and lost in the universal distress.

The wounded pride of Napoleon justified the supposition of such reflections. This was perceived in one of the halts of that day; there on the rough furrows of a frozen field, strewed with wrecks both Russian and French, he attempted, by the energy of his words, to relieve himself from the weight of the insupportable responsibility of so many disasters. "He had in fact dreaded this war, and he devoted its author to the execration of the whole world. It was —— whom he accused of this; it was that Russian minister, sold to the English, who had fomented it, and the traitor had drawn into it both Alexander and himself."

These words, uttered before two of his generals, were heard with that silence enjoined by old respect, added to that which is due to misfortune. But the duke of Vicenza, perhaps too impatient, betrayed his indignation by a gesture of anger and incredulity, and, abruptly retiring, put an end to this painful conversation.

1. On an inquiry being instituted, the escort pleaded, that, having found brandy in a deserted wagon, the Russian prisoners got intoxicated, and some of them tried to disarm the escort, which was compelled to fire in self-defence.—*Ed.*

CHAPTER IX

DAVOUST'S PROBLEMS

FROM Gjatz the emperor proceeded in two marches to Viazma. He there halted to wait for Prince Eugene and Davoust, and to reconnoitre the road of Medyn and Yucknow, which runs at that place into the high road to Smolensk. It was this cross-road which might bring the Russian army from Malo-Yaroslawetz on his passage. But on the first of November, after waiting thirty-six hours, Napoleon had not seen any avant-courier of that army; he set out, therefore, wavering between the hope that Kutusoff had fallen asleep, and the fear lest the Russian had left Viazma on his right, and proceeded two marches farther towards Dorogobouje to cut off his retreat. At any rate, he left Ney at Viazma, to collect the first and fourth corps, and to relieve, as the rear-guard, Davoust, whom he judged to be fatigued.

He complained of the tardiness of the latter: he wrote to reproach him with being still five marches behind him, when he ought to have been no more than three days later; he considered the genius of that marshal to be too methodical to direct, in a suitable manner, so irregular a march.

The whole army, and the corps of Prince Eugene in particular, repeated these complaints. They said, "that owing to his spirit of order and obstinacy Davoust had suffered the enemy to overtake him at the abbey of Kolotskoi; that he had there done the rascally Cossacks the honour of retiring before them, step by step, and in square battalions, as if they had been Mamelukes; that Platoff, with his cannon, had played at a distance on the deep masses which he had presented to him; that then only the marshal had opposed to them merely a few slender lines, which had speedily formed again, and some light pieces, the first fire of which had produced the desired effect; but that these manœuvres and regular foraging excursions had occasioned a great loss of time, which is always valuable in retreat, and especially amidst famine, through which the most skilful manœuvre was to pass with all possible expedition."

In reply to this, Davoust pleaded his natural horror of every kind of disorder, which had at first led him to attempt to introduce regularity into this flight; he had endeavoured to cover the wrecks of it, fearing the shame and the danger of leaving for the enemy these evidences of our disastrous state.

He added, that "people were not aware of all that he had had to surmount; he had found the country completely devastated, houses demolished, and the trees burned to their very roots; for it was not to him who came last that the work of general destruction had been left; the conflagration preceded him. It appeared as if the rear-guard had been totally forgotten! No doubt, too, people forgot the frozen road rough with the tracks of all who had gone before him; as well as the deep fords and broken bridges, which no one thought of repairing, as each corps, when not engaged, cared but for itself alone.

"Did they not know, besides, that the whole tremendous train of stragglers, belonging to the other corps, on horseback, on foot, and in vehicles, aggravated these embarrassments, just as in a diseased body all the complaints fly to and unite in the part most affected? Every day he had to march between these wretches and the Cossacks, driving forward the one, and pressed by the other.

"Thus, after passing Gjatz, he had found the slough of Czarewo-Zaimcze without a bridge, and completely encumbered with carriages. He had dragged them out of the marsh in sight of the enemy, and so near to them that their fires lighted his labours, and the sound of their drums mingled with that of his voice." For the marshal and his generals could not yet resolve to relinquish to the enemy so many trophies; nor did they make up their minds to it till after superfluous exertions, and in the last extremity, which happened several times a-day.

The road was in fact crossed every moment by marshy hollows. A slope, slippery as glass with the frost, hurried the carriages into them, and there they stuck; to draw them out it was necessary to climb the opposite ascent by an icy road, where the horses, whose shoes were worn quite smooth, could not obtain a footing, and where every moment they and their drivers dropped exhausted one upon the other. The famished soldiers immediately fell upon these luckless animals and tore them to pieces; then at fires, kindled with the remains of their carriages, they broiled the yet bleeding flesh, and devoured it.

Meanwhile the artillery-men, a chosen corps, and their officers, all brought up in the first school in the world, kept off these unfortunate wretches whenever they could, and took the horses from their own chaises and wagons, which they abandoned to save the guns. To these they harnessed their horses, nay, even themselves: the Cossacks, observing this disaster from a distance, durst not approach; but with their light pieces mounted on sledges, they threw their balls into all this disorder, and served to increase it.

The first corps had already lost ten thousand men; nevertheless, by dint of efforts and sacrifices, the viceroy and the prince of Eckmühl were, on the 2nd of November, within two leagues of Viazma. It is certain that the same day they might have passed that town, joined Ney, and avoided a disastrous engagement. It is affirmed that such was the opinion of Prince Eugene, but that Davoust believed his troops to be too much fatigued; on which the viceroy, sacrificing himself to his duty, stayed to share a danger which he had foreseen. Davoust's generals say, on the contrary, that Prince Eugene, who was already encamped, could not find it in his heart to make his soldiers leave their fires and their meal, which they had already begun, and the cooking of which always cost them a great deal of trouble.

Be that as it may, during the deceptive tranquillity of that night, the advanced guard of the Russians arrived from Malo-Yaroslawetz, our retreat from which place had put an end to theirs; it skirted along the two French corps and that of Poniatowski, passed their bivouacs, and disposed its columns of attack against the left flank of the road, in the intermediate two leagues which Davoust and Eugene had left between themselves and Viazma.

Miloradowitch, whom we denominated the Russian Murat, commanded this advanced-guard. He was, according to his countrymen, an indefatigable and successful warrior, impetuous as that soldier-king, of a stature equally remarkable, and, like him, a favourite of fortune. He was never known to be wounded, though numbers of officers and soldiers had fallen around him, and several horses had been killed under him. He despised the principles of war; he even made an art of not following the rules of that art, pretending to surprise the enemy by unexpected blows, for he was prompt in decision; he disdained to make any preparations, leaving places and circumstances to suggest what was proper to be done, and guiding himself only by sudden inspirations. In other respects, a general in the field of battle alone, he was destitute of foresight in the management of any affairs; either public or private, a notorious spendthrift, and, what is rare, not less upright than prodigal.

It was this general, with Platoff and twenty thousand men, whom we had now to fight.

CHAPTER X

BATTLE NEAR VIAZMA

ON the 3rd of November, Prince Eugene was proceeding towards Viazma, preceded by his equipages and his artillery, when the first light of day shewed him at once his retreat threatened by an army on his left; behind him his rear-guard cut off;[1] and on his left the plain covered with stragglers and scattered vehicles, fleeing before the lances of the enemy. At the same time, towards Viazma, he heard marshal Ney, who should have assisted him, fighting for his own preservation.

That prince was not one of those generals, the offspring of favour, to whom every thing is unexpected and cause of astonishment, for want of experience. He immediately looked the evil in the face, and set about remedying it. He halted, turned about, deployed his divisions on the right of the high road, and checked in the plain the Russian columns, who were striving to cut him off from that road. Their foremost troops, overpowering the right of the Italians, had already seized one point, of which they kept possession, when Ney despatched from Viazma one of his regiments, which attacked them in the rear and dislodged them.

At the same time, Compans, a general of Davoust's, joined the Italian rear-guard with his division. These cleared a way for themselves, and while they, united with the viceroy, were engaged, Davoust with his column passed rapidly behind them, along the left side of the high road, then crossing it as soon as he had got beyond them, he claimed his place in the order of battle, took the right wing, and found himself between Viazma and the Russians. Prince Eugene gave up to him the ground which he had defended, and crossed to the other side of the road. The enemy then began to extend himself before them, and endeavoured to outflank their wings.

By the success of this first manœuvre, the two French and Italian corps had not conquered the right to continue their retreat, but only the possibility of defending it. They were still 80,000 strong; but in the first corps, that of Davoust, there was some disorder. The hastiness of the manœuvre, the surprise, so much wretchedness, and, above all, the fatal example of a multitude of dismounted cavalry, without arms, and running to and fro bewildered with fear, threw it into confusion.

This sight encouraged the enemy; he took it for a rout. His artillery, superior in number, manœuvred at a gallop: it took obliquely and in flank our lines, which it cut down, while the French cannon, already at Viazma, and which had been ordered to return in haste, could with difficulty be brought along. However, Davoust and his generals had still their firmest troops about them. Several of these officers, still suffering from the wounds received at the Moskwa, one with his arm in a sling, another with his head wrapped in cloths, were seen supporting the best, encouraging the most irresolute, dashing at the enemy's batteries, forcing them to retire, and even seizing three of their pieces; in short, astonishing both the enemy and their own fugitives, and combating a mischievous example by their noble behaviour.

Miloradowitch, perceiving that his prey was escaping, now applied for reinforcements, and it was again Wilson, who was sure to be present wherever he could be most injurious to France, who hastened to summon Kutusoff. He found the old marshal unconcernedly resting himself with his army within hearing of the action. The ardent Wilson, urgent as the occasion, excited him in vain; he could not induce him to stir. Transported with indignation, he called him traitor, and declared that he would instantly despatch one of his Englishmen full speed to Petersburgh, to denounce his treason to his emperor and his allies.

This threat had no effect on Kutusoff: he persisted in remaining inactive; either because to the frost of age was superadded that of winter, and that in his shattered frame his mind was depressed by the sight of so many ruins; or that, from another effect of old age, a person becomes prudent when he has scarcely any thing to risk, and a temporiser when he has no more time to lose. He seemed still to be of the opinion, as at Malo-Yaroslawetz, that the Russian winter alone could overthrow Napoleon; that this genius, the conqueror of men, was not yet sufficiently conquered by Nature; that it was best to leave to the climate the honour of that victory, and to the Russian atmosphere the work of vengeance.

Miloradowitch, left to himself, then tried to break the French line of battle, but he could not penetrate it except by his fire, which made dreadful havoc in it. Eugene and Davoust were growing weak; and as they heard another action in the rear of their right, they imagined that the rest of the Russian army was approaching Viazma by the Yuknof road, the outlet of which Ney was defending.

It was only an advanced guard: but they were alarmed at the noise of this fight in the rear of their own, threatening their retreat. The action had lasted ever since seven in the morning; night was approaching; the baggage must by this time have got away; the French generals therefore began to retire.

This retrograde movement increased the ardour of the enemy, and but for a memorable effort of the 25th, 57th, and 85th regiments, and the protection of a ravine, Davoust's corps would have been broken, turned by its right and destroyed. Prince Eugene, who was not so briskly attacked, was able to effect his retreat more rapidly through Viazma; but the Russians followed him thither, and had penetrated into the town, when

Davoust, pursued by 20,000 men, and overwhelmed by eighty pieces of cannon, attempted to pass in his turn.

Morand's division first entered the town: it was marching on with confidence, under the idea that the action was over, when the Russians, who were concealed by the windings of the streets, suddenly fell upon it. The surprise was complete, and the confusion great: Morand, nevertheless, rallied and encouraged his men, retrieved matters, and fought his way through.

It was Compans who put an end to the whole. He closed the march with his division. Finding himself too closely pressed by the bravest troops of Miloradowitch, he turned about, dashed in person at the most eager, overthrew them, and having thus made them fear him, he finished his retreat without further molestation. This conflict was glorious to each, and its result disastrous to all: it was without order and unity. There would have been troops enough to conquer, had there not been too many commanders. It was not till near two o'clock that the latter met to concert their manœuvres, and these were even then executed without harmony.

When at length the river, the town of Viazma, night, mutual fatigue, and marshal Ney, had separated them from the enemy, the danger being adjourned and the bivouacs established, the numbers were counted. Several pieces of cannon which had been broken, the baggage, and four thousand killed or wounded, were missing. Many of the soldiers had dispersed. Their honour was saved, but there were immense gaps in the ranks. It was necessary to close them up, to bring every thing within a narrower compass, to form what remained into a more compact whole. Each regiment scarcely composed a battalion, each battalion a platoon. The soldiers had no longer their accustomed places, comrades or officers.

This sad re-organisation took place by the light of the conflagration of Viazma, and during the successive discharges of the cannon of Ney and Miloradowitch, the thunders of which were prolonged amid the double darkness of the night and the forests. Several times the relics of these brave troops, conceiving that they were attacked, crawled to their arms. Next morning, when they again fell into their ranks, they were astonished at the smallness of their numbers.

1. The assertion that the rear-guard was cut off is incorrect.—*Ed.*

CHAPTER XI

A FATAL SNOWSTORM

THE spirits of the troops were, nevertheless, still supported by the example of their leaders, by the hopes of finding all their wants supplied at Smolensk, and still more by the aspect of a yet brilliant sun, of that universal source of hope and life, which seemed to contradict and deny the spectacles of despair and death that already encompassed us.

But on the 6th of November, the heavens declared against us. Their azure disappeared. The army marched enveloped in cold fogs. These fogs became thicker, and presently an immense cloud descended upon it in large flakes of snow. It seemed as if the very sky was falling, and joining the earth and our enemies to complete our destruction. All objects changed their appearance, and became confounded, and not to be recognised again; we proceeded, without knowing where we were, without perceiving the point to which we were bound; every thing was transformed into an obstacle. While the soldier was struggling with the tempest of wind and snow, the flakes, driven by the storm, lodged and accumulated in every hollow: their surfaces concealed unknown abysses, which perfidiously opened beneath our feet. There the men were engulfed, and the weakest, resigning themselves to their fate, found a grave in these snow-pits.

Those who followed turned aside, but the storm drove into their faces both the snow that was descending from the sky, and that which it raised from the ground: it seemed bent on opposing their progress. The Russian winter, under this new form, attacked them on all sides: it penetrated through their light garments and their torn shoes and boots. Their wet clothes froze upon their bodies: an icy envelope encased them and stiffened all their limbs. A keen and violent wind interrupted respiration: it seized their breath at the moment when they exhaled it, and converted it into icicles, which hung from their beards all round their mouths.

The unfortunate creatures still crawled on, shivering, till the snow, gathering like balls under their feet, or the fragment of some broken article, a branch of a tree, or the body of one of their comrades, caused them to stumble and to fall. There they groaned in vain; the snow soon covered them: slight hillocks marked the spot where they lay: such was their only grave! The road was studded with these undulations like a cemetery: the most intrepid and the most indifferent were affected; they passed on quickly with averted looks. But before them, around them, there was nothing but snow: this immense and dreary uniformity extended farther than the eye could reach; the imagination was astounded; it was like a vast winding-sheet which Nature had thrown over the army. The only objects not enveloped by it were some gloomy pines, trees of the tombs, with their funereal verdure, the motionless aspect of their gigantic black trunks and their dismal look, which completed the doleful appearance of a general mourning, and of an army dying amidst a nature already dead.

Every thing, even to their very arms, still offensive at Malo-Yaroslawetz, but since defensive only, now turned against them. These seemed to their frozen limbs insupportably heavy. In the frequent falls which they experienced, they dropped from their hands and were broken or buried in the snow. If they rose again it was without them; for they did not throw them away; hunger and cold wrested them from their grasp. The fingers of many others were frozen to the muskets which they still held, which deprived them of the motion necessary for keeping up some degree of warmth and life.

We soon met with numbers of men belonging to all the corps, sometimes singly, at others in troops. They had not basely deserted their colours; it was cold and inanition which had separated them from their columns. In this general and individual struggle, they had parted from one another, and there they were, disarmed, vanquished, defenceless, without leaders, obeying nothing but the urgent instinct of self-preservation.

Most of them, attracted by the sight of by-paths, dispersed themselves over the country, in hopes of finding bread and shelter for the coming night: but, on their first passage, all had been laid waste to the extent of seven or eight leagues; they met with nothing but Cossacks, and an armed population, which encompassed, wounded, and stripped them naked, and then left them, with ferocious bursts of laughter, to expire on the snow. These people, who had risen at the call of Alexander and Kutusoff, and who had not then learned, as they since have, to avenge nobly a country which they had been unable to defend, hovered on both flanks of the army under favour of the woods. Those whom they did not despatch with their pikes and hatchets, they brought back to the fatal and all-devouring high road.

Night then came on—a night of sixteen hours! But on that snow, which covered every thing, they knew not where to halt, where to sit, where to lie down, where to find some root or other to eat, and dry wood to kindle a fire! Fatigue, darkness, and repeated orders nevertheless stopped those whom their moral and physical strength and the efforts of their officers had kept together. They strove to establish themselves; but the tempest, still active, dispersed the first preparations for bivouacs. The pines, laden with frost, obstinately resisted the flames; their snow, that from the sky which still continued to fall fast, and that on the ground, which melted with the efforts of the soldiers and the effect of the first fires, extinguished those fires, as well as the strength and spirits of the men.

When at length the flames gained the ascendency, the officers and soldiers around them prepared their wretched repast; it consisted of lean and bloody pieces of flesh torn from the horses that were knocked up, and at most a few spoonfuls of rye-flour mixed with snow-water. Next morning circular ranges of soldiers extended lifeless marked the bivouacs; and the ground about them was strewed with the bodies of several thousand horses.

From that day we began to place less reliance on one another. In that lively army, susceptible of all impressions, and taught to reason by an advanced civilisation, despondency and neglect of discipline spread rapidly, the imagination knowing no more bounds in evil than in good. Henceforward, at every bivouac, at every difficult passage, at every moment, some portion separated from the yet organised troops, and fell into disorder. There were some, however, who were proof against this wide-spread contagion of indiscipline and despondency. These were officers, non-commissioned officers, and steady soldiers. These were extraordinary men: they encouraged one another by repeating the name of Smolensk, which they knew they were approaching, and where they had been promised that all their wants should be supplied.

It was in this manner that, after this deluge of snow, and the increase of cold which it foreboded, each, whether officer or soldier, preserved or lost his fortitude, according to his disposition, his age, and his constitution; that one of our leaders who had hitherto been the strictest in enforcing discipline, now paid little attention to it. Thrown out of all his fixed ideas of regularity, order and method, he was seized with despair at the sight of such universal disorder, and conceiving, before the others, that all was lost, he felt himself ready to abandon all.

From Gjatz to Mikalewska, a village between Dorogobouje and Smolensk, nothing remarkable occurred in the imperial column, unless that it was found necessary to throw the spoils of Moscow into the lake of Semlewo: cannon, gothic armour, the ornaments of the Kremlin, and the cross of Ivan the Great, were buried in its waters; trophies, glory, all those acquisitions to which we had sacrificed every thing, became a burden to us; our object was no longer to embellish, to adorn life, but to preserve it. In this vast wreck, the army, like a great ship tossed by the most tremendous of tempests, threw without hesitation into that sea of ice and snow, every thing that could slacken or impede its progress.

CHAPTER XII

NEY'S PERILOUS SITUATION

DURING the 3rd and 4th of November Napoleon halted at Slawkowo. This repose, and the shame of appearing to flee, inflamed his imagination. He dictated orders, according to which his rear-guard, by appearing to retreat in disorder, was to draw the Russians into an ambuscade, where he should be waiting for them in person; but this vain project passed off with the pre-occupation which gave it birth. On the 5th he slept at Dorogobouje. Here he found the handmills which were ordered for the expedition, at the time the cantonments of Smolensk were projected; of these a late and totally useless distribution was made.

Next day, the 6th of November, opposite to Mikalewska, at the moment when the clouds, laden with sleet and snow, were bursting over our heads, count Daru was seen hastening up, and a circle of vedettes forming around him and the emperor.

An express, the first that had been able to reach us for ten days, had just brought intelligence of that strange conspiracy which had been hatched in Paris itself, and in the depth of a prison, by an obscure general. He had no other accomplices than the false news of our destruction, and forged orders to some troops to apprehend the minister, the prefect of police, and the commandant of Paris. His plan had completely succeeded, from the impulse of a first movement, from ignorance, and the general astonishment; but no sooner was a rumour of the affair spread abroad, than an order was sufficient again to consign the leader, with his accomplices or dupes, to a prison.

The emperor was apprised at the same moment of their crime and their punishment. Those who at a distance strove to read his thoughts in his countenance could discover nothing. He repressed his feelings; his first and only words to Daru were, "How now, if we had remained at Moscow!" He then hastened into a house surrounded with a palisade, which had served for a post of correspondence.

The moment he was alone with the most devoted of his officers, all his emotions burst forth at once in exclamations of astonishment, humiliation, and anger. Presently afterwards he sent for several other officers to observe the effect which so extraordinary a piece of intelligence would produce upon them. He perceived in them a painful uneasiness and consternation, and their confidence in the stability of his government completely shaken. He had occasion to know that they accosted each other with a sigh, and the remark, that it thus appeared that the great revolution of 1789, which was thought to be finished, was not yet over. Grown old in struggles to get out of it, were they to be again plunged into it, and to be thrown once more into the dreadful career of political convulsions? Thus war was coming upon us in every quarter, and we were liable to lose every thing at once.

Some rejoiced in this intelligence, in the hope that it would hasten the return of the emperor into France; that it would fix him there, and that he would no longer risk himself abroad, since he was not safe at home. On the following day, the sufferings of the moment put an end to these conjectures. As for Napoleon, all his thoughts again flew before him to Paris, and he was advancing mechanically towards Smolensk, when his whole attention was recalled to the present place and time, by the arrival of an aide-de-camp of Ney.

From Viazma that marshal had begun to protect this retreat, which proved mortal to so many others, but immortal for himself. As far as Dorogobouje, it had been molested only by some bands of Cossacks, troublesome insects, attracted by our dying and by our forsaken carriages, flying away the moment a hand was lifted, but harassing by their continual return.

They were not the subject of Ney's message. On approaching Dorogobouje he had met with the traces of the disorder which prevailed in the corps that preceded him, and which it was not in his power to efface. So far he had made up his mind to leave the baggage to the enemy: but he blushed with shame at the sight of the first pieces of cannon abandoned before Dorogobouje.

The marshal had halted there. After a dreadful night, in which snow, wind, and famine had driven most of his men from the fires, the dawn, which is always awaited with such impatience in a bivouac, had brought him a tempest, the enemy, and the spectacle of an almost general defection. In vain he had just fought in person at the head of what men and officers he had left: he had been obliged to retreat precipitately behind the Dnieper; and of this he sent to apprise the emperor.

He wished him to know the worst. His aide de-camp, colonel Dalbignac, was instructed to say, that "the first movement of retreat from Malo-Yaroslawetz, for soldiers who had never yet fallen back, had dispirited the army; that the affair at Viazma had shaken its firmness; and that lastly, the deluge of snow and the increased cold which it betokened, had completed its disorganisation: that a multitude of officers, having lost every thing, their platoons, battalions, regiments, and even divisions, had joined the roving masses: generals, colonels, and officers of all ranks, were seen mingled with the privates, and marching at random, sometimes with one column, sometimes with another; that as order could not exist in the presence of disorder, this example was seducing even the veteran regiments, which had served during the whole of the wars of the revolution: that in the ranks, the best soldiers were heard asking one another, why they alone were required to fight in order to secure the flight of the rest; and how any one could expect to keep up their courage, when they heard the cries of despair issuing from the neighbouring woods, in which the large convoys of their wounded, who had been dragged to no purpose all the way from Moscow, had just been abandoned? Such then was the fate which awaited themselves! what had they to gain by remaining by their colours? Incessant toils and combats by day, and famine at night; shelterless bivouacs still more destructive than battle: famine and cold drove sleep far away from them, or if fatigue got the better of these for the moment, that repose which ought to refresh them put a period to their lives. In short, the eagles had ceased to protect—they destroyed. Why then remain around them to perish by battalions, by masses? It would be better to disperse, and since there was no other course than flight, to try who could run fastest. It would not then be the best that would fall: the cowards behind them would no longer eat up the relics of the high road." Lastly, the aide-de-camp was commissioned to explain to the emperor all the horrors of his situation, the responsibility of which Ney absolutely declined.

But Napoleon saw enough around himself to judge of the rest. The fugitives were passing him; he was sensible that nothing could now be done but to sacrifice the army successively, part by part, beginning at the extremities, in order to save the head. When, therefore, the aide-de camp was beginning, he sharply interrupted him with these words, "Colonel, I do not ask you for these details." The colonel was silent, aware that in this disaster, now irremediable, and in which every one had occasion for all his energies, the emperor was afraid of complaints, which could have no other effect but to discourage those who indulged in and those who listened to them.

He remarked the attitude of Napoleon, the same which he retained throughout the whole of this retreat. It was grave, silent, and resigned; suffering much less in body than others, but much more in mind, and brooding over his misfortunes. At that moment general Charpentier sent him from Smolensk a convoy of provisions. Bessières wished to take possession of them, but the emperor instantly had them forwarded to the prince of the Moskwa, saying, "that those who were fighting must eat before the others." At the same time he sent word to Ney "to defend himself long enough to allow him some stay at Smolensk, where the army should eat, rest, and be re-organised."

But if this hope kept some to their duty, many others abandoned every thing, to hasten towards that promised term of their sufferings. As for Ney, he saw that a sacrifice was required, and that he was marked out as the victim: he resigned himself, ready to meet the whole of a danger great as his courage: thenceforward he neither attached his honour to baggage, nor to cannon, which the winter alone wrested from him. An elbow of the Borysthenes stopped and kept back part of his guns at the foot of its icy slopes; he sacrificed them without hesitation, passed that obstacle, faced about, and made the hostile river, which crossed his route, serve him as the means of defence.

The Russians, however, advanced under favour of a wood and our forsaken carriages, whence they kept up a fire of musketry on Ney's troops. Half of the latter, whose icy arms froze their stiffened fingers, got discouraged; they gave way, justifying themselves by their faint-heartedness on the preceding day, fleeing because they had fled; which before they would have considered as impossible. But Ney rushed in amongst them, snatched one of their muskets, and led them back to action, which he was the first to renew; exposing his life like a private soldier, with a musket in his hand, the same as when he was neither husband nor father, neither possessed of wealth, nor power, nor consideration: in short, as if he had still every thing to gain, when in fact he had every thing to lose. At the same time that he again turned soldier, he ceased not to be the general; he took advantage of the ground, supported himself against a height, and covered himself with a palisaded house. His generals and his colonels, among whom he himself remarked Fezenzac, strenuously seconded him; and the enemy, who expected to pursue, was obliged to retreat.

By this action, Ney gave the army a respite of twenty-four hours: it profited by it to proceed towards Smolensk. The next day, and all the succeeding days, he manifested the same heroism. Between Viazma and Smolensk he fought ten whole days.

CHAPTER XIII

THE PASSAGE OF THE WOP

ON the 13th of November he was approaching that city, which he was not to enter till the ensuing day, and had faced about to keep off the enemy, when all at once the hills upon which he intended to support his left were seen covered with a multitude of fugitives. In their fright, these unfortunate wretches fell and rolled down to where he was upon the frozen snow, which they stained with their blood. A band of Cossacks, which was soon perceived in the midst of them, sufficiently accounted for this disorder. The astonished marshal, having caused this flock of enemies to be dispersed, discovered behind it the army of Italy, returning completely stripped, without baggage, and without cannon.

Platoff had kept it besieged, as it were, all the way from Dorogobouje. Near that town Prince Eugene had quitted the high road, and in order to proceed towards Witepsk, had taken that which, two months before, had brought him from Smolensk; but the Wop, which, when he crossed it before, was a mere brook, and had scarcely been noticed, he now found swelled into a river. It ran over a bed of mud, and was bounded by two steep banks. It was found necessary to cut a way in these rough and frozen banks, and to give orders for the demolition, during the night, of the neighbouring houses, in order to build a bridge with the materials. But those who had taken shelter in them opposed their destruction. The viceroy, who was more beloved than feared, was not obeyed. The pontonniers were disheartened, and when daylight appeared with the Cossacks, the bridge, after being twice broken down, was abandoned.

Five or six thousand soldiers, still in order, twice the number of disbanded men, sick and wounded, upwards of a hundred pieces of cannon, ammunition-wagons, and a multitude of other vehicles, lined the bank and covered a league of ground. An attempt was made to ford through the ice which was carried along by the torrent. The first guns that tried to cross reached the opposite bank; but the water kept rising every moment, while at the same time the bed of the river at the ford was deepened by the wheels and the efforts of the horses. One carriage stuck fast, others did the same, and the stoppage became general.

Meanwhile the day was advancing; the men were exhausting themselves in vain efforts: hunger, cold, and the Cossacks became pressing, and the viceroy at length found himself necessitated to order his artillery and all his baggage to be left behind. A distressing spectacle ensued. The owners had scarcely time to part from their effects; while they were selecting from them the articles which they most needed, and loading horses with them, a multitude of soldiers hastened up; they fell in preference upon the vehicles of luxury; they broke in pieces and rummaged every thing, revenging their poverty on this wealth, their privations on these superfluities, and snatching them from the Cossacks, who looked on at a distance.

It was provisions of which most of them were in quest. They threw aside embroidered clothes, pictures, ornaments of every kind, and gilt bronzes, for a few handfuls of flour. In the evening it was a singular sight to behold the riches of Paris and of Moscow, the luxuries of two of the largest cities in the world, lying scattered and despised on the snow of the desert.

At the same time most of the artillery-men spiked their guns in despair, and scattered their powder about. Others laid a train with it as far as some ammunition-wagons, which had been left at a considerable distance behind our baggage. They waited till the most eager of the Cossacks had come up to them, and when a great number of them, greedy of plunder, had collected about them, they threw a brand from a bivouac upon the train. The fire ran, and in a moment reached its destination: the wagons were blown up, the shells exploded, and such of the Cossacks as were not killed on the spot dispersed in dismay.

A few hundred men, who were still called the 14th division, were opposed to these hordes, and sufficed to keep them at a respectful distance till the next day. All the rest, soldiers, administrators, women and children, sick and wounded, driven by the enemy's balls, crowded the bank of the torrent. But at the sight of its swollen current, of the sharp and massive sheets of ice flowing down the stream, and the necessity of aggravating their already intolerable sufferings from cold by plunging into its chilling waves, they all hesitated.

An Italian, Colonel Delfanti, was obliged to set the example and cross first. The soldiers then moved and the crowd followed. The weakest, the least resolute, or the most avaricious, stayed behind. Such as could not make up their minds to part from their booty, and to forsake fortune which was forsaking them, were surprised in the midst of their hesitation. Next day the savage Cossacks were seen amid all this wealth, still covetous of the squalid and tattered garments of the unfortunate creatures who had become their prisoners: they stripped them, and then collecting them in troops, drove them along naked on the snow, by hard blows with the shaft of their lances.

The army of Italy, thus dismantled, thoroughly soaked in the waters of the Wop, without food, without shelter, passed the night on the snow near a village, where its officers expected to have found lodging for themselves. Their soldiers, however, beset its wooden houses. They rushed, like mad men, and in swarms, on each habitation, profiting by the darkness, which prevented them from recognising their officers or being known by them. They tore down every thing, doors, windows, and even the wood-work of the roofs, feeling little compunction to compel others, be they who they might, to bivouac like themselves.

Their generals attempted in vain to drive them off; they took their blows without murmur or opposition, but without desisting—even the men of the royal and imperial guards: for, throughout the whole army, such were the scenes that occurred every night. The unfortunate fellows remained silently but actively engaged on the wooden walls, which they pulled in pieces on every side at once, and which, after vain efforts, their officers were obliged to relinquish to them, for fear they should fall upon their own heads. It was an extraordinary mixture of perseverance in their design, and respect for the anger of their generals.

Having kindled good fires, they spent the night in drying themselves, amid the shouts, imprecations, and groans of those who were still crossing the torrent, or who, slipping from its banks, were precipitated into it and drowned.

It is a fact which reflects disgrace on the enemy, that during this disaster, and in sight of so rich a booty, a few hundred men, left at the distance of half a league from the viceroy, on the other side of the Wop, were sufficient to curb, for twenty hours, not only the courage, but also the cupidity of Platoff's Cossacks.

It is possible, indeed, that the hetman made sure of destroying the viceroy on the following day. In fact, all his measures were so well planned, that at the moment when the army of Italy, after an unquiet and disorderly march, came in sight of Dukhowtchina, a town yet uninjured, and was joyfully hastening forward to shelter itself there, several thousand Cossacks sallied forth from it with cannon, and suddenly stopped its progress; at the same time Platoff, with all his hordes, came up and attacked its rear-guard and both flanks.

Several eye-witnesses assert that a complete tumult and disorder then ensued; that the disbanded men, the women, and the attendants, ran over one another, and broke quite through the ranks; that, in short, there was a moment when this unfortunate army was but a shapeless mass, a mere rabble rout whirling round and round. All seemed to be lost; but the coolness of the prince, and the efforts of the officers, saved all. The best men disengaged themselves; the ranks were again formed. They advanced, firing a few volleys, and the enemy, who had everything on his side excepting courage, the only advantage yet left us, opened and retired, confining himself to a useless demonstration.

The army took his place still warm in that town, beyond which he went to bivouac, and to prepare similar surprises to the very gates of Smolensk. For this disaster at the Wop had made the viceroy give up the idea of separating from the emperor: there these hordes grew bolder; they surrounded the 14th division. When Prince Eugene would have gone to its relief, the men and their officers, stiffened with a cold of twenty degrees, which the wind rendered most piercing, continued stretched on the warm ashes of their fires. To no purpose did he point out to them their comrades surrounded, the enemy approaching, the bullets and balls which were already reaching them; they refused to rise, protesting that they would rather perish than any longer have to endure such cruel hardships. The videttes themselves had abandoned their posts. Prince Eugene, nevertheless, contrived to save his rear-guard.

It was in returning with it towards Smolensk that his stragglers had been driven back on Ney's troops, to whom they communicated their panic; all hurried together towards the Dnieper; here they crowded together at the entrance of the bridge, without thinking of defending themselves, when a charge made by the 4th regiment stopped the advance of the enemy.

Its colonel, young Fezenzac, contrived to infuse fresh life into these men, who were half perished with cold. There, as in everything that can be called action, was manifested the superiority of the sentiments of the soul over the sensations of the body; for every physical sensation tended to encourage despondency and flight; nature advised it with her hundred most urgent voices; and yet a few words of honour were sufficient to produce the most heroic devotedness. The soldiers of the 4th regiment rushed like furies upon the enemy, against the mountain of snow and ice of which he had taken possession, and in the teeth of the northern hurricane, for they had everything against them. Ney himself was obliged to moderate their impetuosity.

A reproach from their colonel had effected this change. These private soldiers devoted themselves, that they might not be wanting to their own characters, from that instinct which requires courage in a man, as well as from habit and the love of glory. A splendid word for so obscure a situation! For what is the glory of a common soldier, he perishes unseen, who is neither praised, censured, nor regretted, but by his own squad! The circle of each, however, is sufficient for him; a small society embraces the same passions as a large one. The proportions of the bodies differ; but they are composed of the same elements; it is the same life that animates them, and the looks of a platoon stimulate a soldier, just as those of an army inflame a general.

CHAPTER XIV

ARRIVAL AT SMOLENSK

AT length the army again came in sight of Smolensk: it approached the term so often held forth to its sufferings. The soldiers pointed it out to each other. *There* was that land of promise where their famine was to find abundance, their fatigue rest; where bivouacs in a cold of nineteen degrees would be forgotten in houses warmed by good fires. *There* they should enjoy refreshing sleep; there they might repair their apparel; there they should be furnished with new shoes, and clothing adapted to the climate.

At this sight, the *corps d'élite*, some soldiers, and the veteran regiments, alone kept their ranks; the rest ran forward with all possible speed. Thousands of men, chiefly unarmed, covered the two steep banks of the Borysthenes: they crowded in masses round the lofty walls and gates of the city; but their disorderly multitude, their haggard faces, begrimed with dirt and smoke, their tattered uniforms and the grotesque habiliments which they had substituted for them, in short, their strange, hideous look, and their extreme ardour, excited alarm. It was conceived that if the irruption of this crowd, maddened with hunger, were not repelled, a general pillage would be the consequence, and the gates were closed against it.

It was also hoped that by this rigour these men would be forced to rally. A horrid struggle between order and disorder then commenced in the remnant of that unfortunate army. In vain did some entreat, weep, conjure, threaten, strive to burst the gates, and drop down dead at the feet of their comrades, who had orders to repel them; they found them inexorable: they were forced to wait the arrival of the first troops, who were still officered and in order.

These were the old and young guard. It was not till afterwards that the disbanded men were allowed to enter; they and the other corps which arrived in succession, from the 8th to the 14th, believed that their entry had been delayed merely to give more rest and more provisions to this guard. Their sufferings rendered them unjust; they execrated it. "Were they then to be for ever sacrificed to this privileged class, fellows kept for mere parade, who were never foremost but at reviews, festivities, and distributions? Was the army always to put up with their leavings; and in order to obtain them, was it always to wait till they had glutted themselves?" It was impossible to tell them in reply, that to attempt to save all was the way to lose all; that it was necessary to keep at least one corps entire, and to give the preference to that which in the last extremity would be capable of making the most powerful effort.

Meanwhile, these poor creatures were admitted into that Smolensk for which they had so ardently wished; they left the banks of the Borysthenes strewed with the dying bodies of the weakest of their number, whom impatience and several hours' waiting had brought to that state. They left others on the icy steep which they had to climb to reach the upper town. The rest ran to the magazines, and there more of them expired while they beset the doors; for there they were again repulsed. "Who were they? To what corps did they belong? What had they to prove it? The persons who had to distribute the provisions were responsible for them; they had orders to deliver them only to authorised officers, bringing receipts, for which they would exchange the rations committed to their care." Those who applied had no officers, nor could they tell where their regiments were. Two thirds of the army were in this predicament.

These unfortunate men then dispersed through the streets, having no longer any other hope than pillage. But horses dissected to the very bones every where denoted a famine; the doors and windows of the houses had been all broken and torn away to feed the bivouac-fires: they found no shelter in them, no winter quarters prepared, no wood. The sick and wounded were left in the streets, in the carts which had brought them. It was again, it was always the fatal high-road, passing through an empty name; it was a new bivouac among deceitful ruins; colder even than the forests which they had just quitted.

Then only did these disorganised troops seek their colours; they rejoined them for a moment in order to obtain food; but all the bread that could be baked had been distributed: there was no more biscuit, no butcher's meat. Rye-flour, dry vegetables, and spirits, were delivered out to them. It required the most strenuous efforts to prevent the detachments of the different corps from murdering one another at the doors of the magazines: and when, after long formalities, their wretched fare was delivered to them, the soldiers refused to carry it to their regiments; they fell upon their sacks, snatched out of them a few pounds of flour, and ran to hide themselves till they had devoured it. The same was the case with the spirits. Next day the houses were found full of the bodies of these unfortunate wretches.

In short, that fatal Smolensk, which the army had looked forward to as the term of its sufferings, marked only their commencement. Inexpressible hardships awaited us: we had yet to march forty days under that yoke of iron. Some, already overloaded with present miseries, sunk under the alarming prospect of those which awaited them. Others revolted against their destiny; finding they had nothing to rely on but themselves, they resolved to live at any rate.

Thenceforward, according as they found themselves the stronger or the weaker, they plundered their dying companions, by violence or stealth, of their subsistence, of their garments, and even of the gold with which they had filled their knapsacks instead of provisions. These wretches, whom despair had made robbers, then threw away their arms to save their infamous booty, profiting by the general confusion, an obscure name, a uniform no longer distinguishable, and night—in short, by all kinds of obscurities favourable to cowardice and guilt. If works already published had not exaggerated these horrors, I should have passed over in silence details so disgusting; for these atrocities were rare, and justice was dealt to the most criminal.

The emperor arrived, on the 9th of November, amid this scene of desolation. He shut himself up in one of the houses in the new square, and never quitted it till the 14th, to continue his retreat. He had calculated upon fifteen days' provisions and forage for an army of one hundred thousand men; there was not more than half the quantity of flour, rice, and spirits, and no meat at all. Cries of rage were set up against one of the persons appointed to provide these supplies.[1] The commissary saved his life only by crawling for a long time on his knees at the feet of Napoleon. Probably the reasons which he assigned did more for him than his supplications.

"When he arrived," he said, "bands of stragglers, whom, when advancing, the army left behind it, had, as it were, involved Smolensk in terror and destruction. The men died there of hunger as they had done upon the road. When some degree of order had been restored, the Jews alone had at first offered to furnish the necessary provisions. More generous motives subsequently engaged the aid of some Lithuanian noblemen. At length the foremost of the long convoys of provisions collected in Germany appeared. These were the carriages called *comtoises,* and were the only ones which had traversed the sands of Lithuania; they brought no more than two hundred quintals of flour and rice; several hundred German and Italian bullocks had also arrived with them.

"Meanwhile the accumulation of dead bodies in the houses, courts, and gardens, and their unwholesome effluvia, infected the air. The dead were killing the living. The civil officers, as well as many of the military, were attacked: some had become to all appearance idiots, weeping, or fixing their hollow eyes steadfastly on the ground. There were others whose hair had become stiff, erect, and ropy, and who, amidst a torrent of blasphemies, a horrid convulsion, or a still more frightful laugh, had dropped down dead.

"At the same time it had been found necessary to kill without delay the greatest part of the cattle brought from Germany and Italy. These animals would neither walk any farther nor eat. Their eyes, sunk in their sockets, were dull and motionless. They were killed without seeking to avoid the fatal blow. Other misfortunes followed: several convoys had been intercepted, magazines taken, and a drove of 800 oxen had just been carried off from Krasnoë."

This man added, that "regard ought also to be had to the great quantity of detachments which had passed through Smolensk; to the stay which marshal Victor, 28,000 men, and about 15,000 sick, had made there; to the multitude of posts and marauders whom the insurrection and the approach of the enemy had driven back into the city. All had subsisted upon the magazines; it had been necessary to deliver out nearly 60,000 rations per day; and lastly, provisions and cattle had been sent forward towards Moscow as far as Mojaisk, and towards Kaluga as far as Elnia."

Many of these allegations were well founded. A chain of other magazines had been formed from Smolensk to Minsk and Wilna. These two towns were, in a still greater degree than Smolensk, centres of provisioning, of which the fortresses of the Vistula formed the first line. The total quantity of provisions distributed over this space was incalculable, the efforts for transporting them thither gigantic, and the result little better than nothing. They were insufficient in that immensity.

Thus great expeditions are crushed by their own weight. Human limits had been surpassed; the genius of Napoleon, in attempting to soar above time, climate, and distances, had, as it were, lost itself in space: great as was its measure, it had gone beyond it.

Moreover, he was passionate from necessity. He had not deceived himself in regard to the inadequacy of his supplies. Alexander alone had deceived him. Accustomed to triumph over every thing by the terror of his name, and the astonishment produced by his daring, he had ventured his army, himself, his fortune, his all, on a first movement of Alexander's. He was still the same man as in Egypt, at Marengo, Ulm, and Esslingen; it was Ferdinand Cortes; it was the Macedonian burning his ships,[2] and above all solicitous, in spite of his troops, to penetrate still farther into unknown Asia; finally, it was Cæsar risking his whole fortune in a fragile bark.

1. This man was charged with having made false entries in his account stating that he had sent on a thousand oxen to meet the retreating army, whereas he had, in fact, sold them to the Jews, who forwarded then to the Russian army. Napoleon ordered him to be tried by a military commission.—*Ed.*

2. This is an oversight of M. de Segur's. Alexander did not burn his ships.—*Ed.*

BOOK X

— • —

CHAPTER I

ATTACK UPON SAINT CYR

THE surprise of Winkowo, however, that unexpected attack of Kutusoff in front of Moscow, was only the spark of a great conflagration. On the same day, at the same hour, the whole of Russia had resumed the offensive. The general plan of the Russians was at once developed. The inspection of the map became truly alarming.

On the 18th of October, at the very moment that the cannon of Kutusoff were destroying Napoleon's illusions of glory and of peace, Wittgenstein, at 100 leagues in the rear of his left wing, had thrown himself upon Polotsk; Tchitchakoff, behind his right, and 200 leagues farther off, had taken advantage of his superiority over Schwartzenberg; and both of them, one descending from the north, and the other ascending from the south, were endeavouring to unite their forces at Borizoff.

This was the most difficult passage in our retreat, and both these hostile armies were already close to it, at the time when Napoleon was at the distance of twelve days' journey, with the winter, famine, and the grand Russian army between them.

At Smolensk it was only suspected that Minsk was in danger; the officers who were present at the loss of Polotsk gave the following details respecting it:—

Ever since the battle of the 18th of August, which raised him to the dignity of marshal, Saint Cyr had remained on the Russian bank of the Dwina, in possession of Polotsk, and of an entrenched camp in front of its walls. This camp showed how easy it would have been for the whole army to have taken up its winter-quarters on the frontiers of Lithuania. Its barracks, constructed by our soldiers, were more spacious than the houses of the Russian peasantry, and equally warm: they were beautiful military villages, properly entrenched, and equally protected from the winter and from the enemy.

For two months the two armies carried on merely a war of partisans. With the French the object was to extend themselves through the country in search of provisions; on the part of the Russians, to strip them of what they found. A war of this sort was entirely in favour of the Russians, as our people, being ignorant of the country as well as of the language, even of the names of the places where they attempted to enter, were incessantly betrayed by the inhabitants, and even by their guides.

In consequence of these checks, and of hunger and disease, the strength of Saint Cyr's army was diminished one half, while that of Wittgenstein had been more than doubled by the arrival of recruits. By the middle of October, the Russian army at that point amounted to fifty-two thousand men, while ours was only seventeen thousand. In this number must be included the 6th corps, or the Bavarians, reduced from twenty-two thousand to eighteen hundred men, and two thousand cavalry. The latter were then absent; Saint Cyr being without forage, and uneasy respecting the attempts of the enemy upon his flanks, had sent them to a considerable distance up the river, with orders to return by the left bank, in order to procure subsistence, and to gain intelligence.

For this marshal was afraid of having his right turned by Wittgenstein and his left by Steingell, who was advancing at the head of two divisions of the army of Finland, which had recently arrived at Riga. Saint Cyr had sent a very pressing letter to Macdonald, requesting him to use his efforts to stop the march of these Russians, who would have to pass his army, and to send him a reinforcement of fifteen thousand men; or if he would not do that, to come himself with succours to that amount, and take the command. In the same letter he also submitted to Macdonald all his plans of attack and defence. But Macdonald did not feel himself authorised to operate so important a movement without orders. He distrusted Yorck, whom he perhaps suspected of an intention of allowing the Russians to get possession of his park of besieging artillery. His reply was, that he must first of all think of defending that, and he remained stationary.

In this state of affairs, the Russians became daily more and more emboldened; and finally, on the 17th of October, the outposts of Saint Cyr were driven back upon his camp, and Wittgenstein possessed himself of all the outlets of the woods which surround Polotsk. He threatened us with a battle, which he did not believe we would venture to accept.

The French marshal, without orders from his emperor, had been too late in his determination to entrench himself. His works were only marked out as much as was necessary, not to cover their defenders, but to point out the place where their efforts would be principally required. Their left, resting on the Dwina, and defended by batteries placed on the left bank of the river, was the strongest. Their right was weak. The Polota, a stream which flows into the Dwina, separated them.

Wittgenstein sent Yacthwil to threaten the least accessible side, and on the 18th he himself advanced against the other; at first with some rashness, for two French squadrons, the only ones which Saint Cyr had retained, overthrew his advance column, took his artillery, and made himself prisoner, it is said, without being aware of it; so that they abandoned this general-in-chief, as an insignificant prize, when they were forced by numbers to retreat.

Rushing from their woods, the Russians then exhibited their whole force, and attacked Saint Cyr in the most furious manner.

In one of the first discharges of their musketry, the marshal was wounded by a ball. He remained, however, in the midst of the troops, but being unable to support himself, was obliged to be carried about. Wittgenstein's determination to carry this point lasted as long as it was day-light. The redoubts, which were defended by Maison, were taken and retaken seven times. Seven times did Wittgenstein believe himself the conqueror; Saint Cyr finally wore him out. Legrand and Maison remained in possession of their entrenchments, which were bathed with the blood of the Russians.

But while on the right the victory appeared completely gained, on the left every thing seemed to be lost: the eagerness of the Swiss and the Croats was the cause of this reverse. Their rivalry had up to that period wanted an opportunity of showing itself. From a too great anxiety to show themselves worthy of belonging to the grand army, they acted rashly. Having been placed carelessly in front of their position, in order to draw on Yacthwil, they had, instead of abandoning the ground which had been prepared for his destruction, rushed forward to meet his masses, and were overwhelmed by numbers. The French artillery, being prevented from firing on this medley, became useless, and our allies were driven back into Polotsk.

It was then that the batteries on the left bank of the Dwina discovered and were able to commence firing on the enemy, but instead of arresting, they only quickened his march. The Russians under Yacthwil, in order to avoid that fire, threw themselves with great rapidity into the ravine of the Polota, by which they were about to penetrate into the town, when at last three cannon, which were hastily directed against the head of their column, and a last effort of the Swiss, succeeded in driving them back. At five o'clock the battle terminated; the Russians retreated on all sides into their woods; fourteen thousand men had beat fifty thousand.

The night which followed was perfectly tranquil, even to Saint Cyr. His cavalry were deceived, and brought him wrong intelligence; they assured him that no enemy had passed the

Dwina either above or below his position: this was incorrect, as Steingell and thirteen thousand Russians had crossed the river at Drissa, and gone up the left bank, with the object of taking the marshal in the rear, and shutting him up in Polotsk, between them, the Dwina, and Wittgenstein.

The morning of the 19th exhibited the latter under arms, and making every disposition for an attack, the signal for which he appeared to be afraid of giving. Saint Cyr, however, was not to be deceived by these appearances; he was satisfied that it was not his feeble entrenchments which kept back an enterprising and numerous enemy, but that he was doubtless waiting the effect of some manœuvre, the signal of an important co-operation, which could only be effected in his rear.

In fact, about ten o'clock in the morning, an aide-de-camp came in full gallop from the other side of the river, with the intelligence that another hostile army, that of Steingell, was marching rapidly along the Lithuanian side of the river, and that it had defeated the French cavalry. He required immediate assistance, without which this fresh army would speedily get in the rear of the camp and surround it. The news of this engagement soon reached the army of Wittgenstein, where it excited the greatest joy, while it carried dismay into the French camp. Their position became dreadfully critical. Let any one figure to himself these brave fellows, hemmed in, against a wooden town, by a force treble their number, with a great river behind them, and no other means of retreat but by a bridge, the passage from which was threatened by another army.

It was in vain that, to meet Steingell, Saint Cyr then weakened his force by detaching three regiments to the other side, whose march he contrived to conceal from Wittgenstein's observation. Every moment the noise of Steingell's artillery was approaching nearer and nearer to Polotsk. The batteries, which from the left side protected the French camp, were now turned round, ready to fire upon this new enemy. At sight of this, loud shouts of joy burst out from the whole of Wittgenstein's line; but that officer still remained immoveable. To make him begin it was not merely necessary that he should *hear* Steingell; he seemed absolutely determined to *see* him make his appearance.

Meanwhile, all Saint Cyr's generals, in consternation, were surrounding him, and urging him to order a retreat, which would soon become impossible. Saint Cyr refused; convinced that the 50,000 Russians before him under arms, and on the tiptoe of expectation, only waited for his first retrograde movement to dart upon him, he remained immoveable, availing himself of their unaccountable inaction, and still flattering himself that night would cover Polotsk with its shades before Steingell made his appearance.

He has since been heard to confess, that never in his life was his mind in such a state of agitation. A thousand times, in the course of these three hours of suspense, he was seen looking at his watch and at the sun, as if he could hasten his setting.

At last, when Steingell was within half an hour's march of Polotsk, when he had only to make a few efforts to appear in the plain, to reach the bridge of the town, and shut Saint Cyr from the only outlet by which he could escape from Wittgenstein, he halted. Soon after, a thick fog, which the French looked upon as an interposition from heaven, preceded the approach of night, and shut out the three armies from the sight of each other.

Saint Cyr had only waited for that moment. His numerous artillery were already silently crossing the river, his divisions were about to follow it and conceal their retreat, when the soldiers of Legrand, either from habit, or regret at abandoning their camp entire to the enemy, set fire to it; the other two divisions, fancying that this was a signal agreed upon, followed their example, and in an instant the whole line was illuminated.

This blaze disclosed their movement; the whole of Wittgenstein's batteries immediately began firing; his columns rushed forward, his shells set fire to the town; the French troops were obliged to contend every inch of ground with the flames, the fire throwing light on the engagement the same as broad daylight. The retreat, however, was effected in good order; on both sides the loss was great; but it was not until three o'clock in the morning of the 20th of October that the Russian eagle resumed possession of Polotsk.

As good luck would have it, Steingell slept soundly at the noise of this battle, although he might have heard even the shouts of the Russian militia. He seconded the attack of Wittgenstein during that night as little as Wittgenstein had seconded his the day before. It was not until Wittgenstein had finished on the right side, until the bridge of Polotsk was broken down, and Saint Cyr, with all his force on the left bank, and then fully able to cope with Steingell, that the latter began to put himself in motion. But De Wrede, with 6000 French, surprised him in his first movement, beat him back several leagues into the woods which he had quitted, and took or killed 2000 of his men.

CHAPTER II

FRENCH ERRORS

THOSE three days were days of glory. Wittgenstein was repulsed, Steingell defeated, and ten thousand Russians, with six generals, killed or put *hors-du-combat*. But Saint Cyr was wounded, the offensive was lost, confidence, joy, and plenty reigned in the enemy's camp, despondency and scarcity in ours; it was necessary to fall back. The army required a commander: De Wrede pretended to be so, but the French generals refused even to enter into concert with that Bavarian, from a knowledge of his character, and a belief that it was impossible to go on harmoniously with him. Owing to their jarring pretensions Saint Cyr, although wounded, was obliged to retain the command of these two corps.

Immediately after, he gave orders to retreat on Smoliantzy by all the roads leading to that place. He himself kept in the centre, regulating the march of the different columns by that of each other. This was a mode of retreat completely contrary to that which Napoleon had just adopted.

Saint Cyr's object was to find more provisions, to march with greater freedom, and more concert; in short, to avoid that confusion which is so common in the march of numerous columns, when troops, artillery, and baggage are crowded together on the same road. He succeeded. Ten thousand French,

Swiss, and Croats, with fifty thousand Russians at their heels, retired slowly in four columns, without allowing themselves to be broken, and kept Wittgenstein and Steingell from advancing more than three marches in eight days.

By retreating in this manner towards the south, they covered the right flank of the road from Orcha to Borizoff, by which the emperor was returning from Moscow. One column only, that of the left, met with a check. It was that of De Wrede and his fifteen hundred Bavarians, augmented with a brigade of French cavalry, which he retained with him in spite of Saint Cyr's orders. He marched at his own pleasure; his wounded pride would no longer suffer him to yield obedience to others; but it cost him the whole of his baggage. Afterwards, under pretence of better serving the common cause by covering the line of operations from Wilna to Witepsk, which the emperor had abandoned, he separated himself from the second corps, retreated by Glubokoë on Vileika, and made himself useless.

The discontent of De Wrede had existed ever since the 19th of August. He fancied that he had contributed so great a part to the victory of the 18th, that he thought it was made too little of in the report of the following day. This feeling had rankled in his mind, and was increased by repeated complaints, and by the instigation of a brother, who, it was said, was serving in the Austrian army. Added to this, it was believed, that at the last period of the retreat, the Saxon general Thielmann had drawn him into his plans for the liberation of Germany.

This defection was scarcely felt at the time. The duke of Belluno, with 25,000 men, hastened from Smolensk, and, on the 31st of October, effected a junction with Saint Cyr in front of Smoliantzy, at the very moment that Wittgenstein, ignorant of this junction, and relying on his superior strength, had crossed the Lukolmlia, imprudently engaged himself in defiles at his rear, and attacked our outposts. It only required a simultaneous effort of the two French corps to have destroyed his army completely. The generals and soldiers of the second corps were burning with ardour; but at the moment that victory was in their hearts, and when, believing it before their eyes, they only waited for the signal to engage, Victor gave orders to retreat.

Whether this prudence, which was then considered unseasonable, arose from his unacquaintance with a country which he then saw for the first time, or from his distrust of soldiers whom he had not yet tried, we know not. It is possible that he did not feel himself justified in risking a battle, the loss of which would certainly have involved that of the grand army and its leader.

After falling back behind the Lukolmlia, and keeping on the defensive the whole of the day, he took advantage of the night to gain Sienno. The Russian general then became sensible of the peril of his position; it was so critical, that he only took advantage of our retrograde movement, and the discouragement which it occasioned, to effect his retreat.

The officers who gave us these details added, that ever since that time Wittgenstein seemed to think of nothing but retaking Witepsk, and keeping on the defensive. He probably thought it too rash to turn the Berezina at its sources, in order to join Tchitchakoff; for a vague rumour had already reached us of the march of this army from the south upon Minsk and Borizoff, and of the defection of Schwartzenberg.

It was at Mikalewska, on the 6th of November, that unfortunate day when he had just received information of Mallet's conspiracy, that Napoleon was informed of the junction of the second and the ninth corps, and of the unfortunate engagement at Czazniki. Irritated at the intelligence, he sent orders to the duke of Belluno immediately to drive Wittgenstein behind the Dwina, as the safety of the army depended upon it. He did not conceal from the marshal that he had arrived at Smolensk with an army harassed to death and his cavalry entirely dismounted.

Thus, therefore, the days of good fortune were passed, and from all quarters nothing but disastrous intelligence arrived. On one side Polotsk, the Dwina, and Witepsk lost, and

Wittgenstein already within four days' march of Borizoff; on the other, towards Elnia, Baraguay d'Hilliers defeated. That general had allowed the enemy to cut off the brigade of Augereau, and to take the magazines and the Elnia road, by the possession of which Kutusoff was now enabled to anticipate us at Krasnoë, as he had done at Viazma.

At the same time, at one hundred leagues in advance of us, Schwartzenberg informed the emperor, that he was covering Warsaw; in other words, that he had uncovered Minsk and Borizoff, the magazine, and the retreat of the grand army, and that probably the emperor of Austria would deliver up his son-in-law to Russia.

At the same moment, in our rear and our centre, Prince Eugene was conquered by the Wop; the draught-horses which had been waiting for us at Smolensk were devoured by the soldiers; those of Mortier carried off in a forage; the cattle at Krasnoë captured; the army exhibiting frightful symptoms of disease; and at Paris the period of conspiracies appeared to have returned; in short, every thing seemed to combine to overwhelm Napoleon.

The daily reports which he received of the state of each corps of the army were like so many bills of mortality; in these he saw his army, which had conquered Moscow, reduced from an hundred and eighty thousand men, to thirty thousand men still capable of fighting. To this mass of calamities, he could only oppose an inert resistance, an impassible firmness, and an unshaken attitude. His countenance remained the same; he changed none of his habits, nothing in the form of his orders; in reading them, you would have supposed that he had still several armies under his command. He did not even expedite his march. Irritated only at the prudence of marshal Victor, he repeated his orders to him to attack Wittgenstein, and thereby remove the danger which menaced his retreat. As to Baraguay d'Hilliers, whom an officer had just accused, he had him brought before him, and sent him off to Berlin, where that general, overwhelmed by the fatigues of the retreat, and sinking under the weight of chagrin, died before he had an opportunity of making his defence.

The unshaken firmness which the emperor preserved was the only attitude which became so great a spirit, and so irreparable a misfortune. But it appears surprising, that he should have allowed fortune to strip him of every thing, rather than sacrifice a part to save the rest. It was at first without his orders that the commanders of corps burnt the baggage and destroyed their artillery; he only allowed it to be done. If he afterwards gave similar instructions, they were absolutely extorted from him; he seemed as if he was tenacious, above every thing, that no action of his should confess his defeat; either from a feeling that he thus respected his misfortunes, and by his inflexibility set the example of inflexible courage to those around him, or from that proud feeling of men who have been long fortunate, which precipitates their downfall.

Smolensk, however, which was twice fatal to the army, was a place of rest for some. During the respite which this afforded to their sufferings, these were asking each other, "how it happened, that at Moscow every thing had been forgotten; why there was so much useless baggage; why so many soldiers had already died of hunger and cold, under the weight of their knapsacks, which were loaded with gold, instead of food and raiment; and, above all, if three and thirty days' rest had not allowed sufficient time to make snow-shoes for the artillery, cavalry, and draught-horses, which would have made their march more sure and rapid?

"If that had been done, we should not have lost our best men at Viazma, at the Wop, at the Dnieper, and along the whole road; in short, even now, Kutusoff, Wittgenstein, and perhaps Tchitchakoff, would not have had time to prepare more fatal days for us.

"But, why, in the absence of orders from Napoleon, had not that precaution been taken by the commanders, all of them kings, princes, and marshals? Had not the winter in Russia been foreseen? Was it that Napoleon, accustomed to the active intelligence of his soldiers, had reckoned too much upon their foresight? Had the recollection of the campaign in Poland, during a winter as mild as that of our own climate, deceived him as well as an unclouded sun, whose countenance, during the whole of the month of October, had astonished even the Russians themselves? What spirit of infatuation was it that had seized the whole army as well as its leader? What had every one been reckoning upon? as even supposing that at Moscow the hope of peace had dazzled us all, it was always necessary to return, and nothing had been prepared, even for a pacific journey homeward!"

The greater number could not account for this general infatuation, otherwise than by their own carelessness, and because in armies, as well as in despotic governments, it is the office of one to think for all; in this case that one was alone regarded as responsible, and misfortune, which authorises distrust, led every one to condemn him. It had been already remarked, that in this important fault, in this forgetfulness, so little to be expected in an active genius during so long and unoccupied a residence, there was something of that spirit of error, "the fatal forerunner of the fall of kings!"

Napoleon had been at Smolensk for five days. It was known that Ney had received orders to arrive there as late as possible,[1] and Eugene to halt for two days at Doukhowtchina. "Then it was not the necessity of waiting for the army of Italy which detained him! To what then must we attribute this delay, when famine, disease, and the winter, and three hostile armies were gradually surrounding us?

"While we had been penetrating to the heart of the Russian Colossus, had not his arms remained advanced and extended towards the Baltic and the Black Sea? was he likely to leave them motionless now, when, instead of striking him mortal blows, we had been struck ourselves? Was not the fatal moment arrived when this Colossus was about to surround us with his threatening arms? Could we imagine that we had either tied them up, or paralysed them, by opposing to them the Austrians in the south, and the Prussians in the north? Was it not rather a method of rendering the Poles and the French, who were mixed with these dangerous allies, entirely useless!

"But without going far in search of causes of uneasiness, was the emperor ignorant of the joy of the Russians, when three months before he stopped to attack Smolensk, instead of marching to the right to Elnia, where he would have cut off the enemy's army from a retreat upon their capital? Now that the war had returned back to the same spots, would the Russians, whose movements are much more free than ours were then, imitate our error? Would they keep in our rear when they could so easily place themselves before us, on the line of our retreat?

"Was Napoleon unwilling to allow that Kutusoff's attack might be bolder and more skilful than his own had been? Were the circumstances still the same? Was not every thing favourable to the Russians during their retreat, and, on the contrary, had not every thing become unfavourable to us in ours? Would not the cutting off of Augereau and his brigade upon that road open his eyes? What business had we in the burnt and ravaged Smolensk, but to take a supply of provisions and proceed rapidly onwards?

"But the emperor no doubt fancied that by dating his despatches five days from that city, he would give to his disorderly flight the appearance of a slow and glorious retreat![2] This was the reason of his ordering the destruction of the towers which surround Smolensk, from the wish, as he expressed it, of not being again stopped short by its walls! as if there was any idea of our returning to a place, which we did not even know whether we should ever get out of.

"Will any one believe that he wished to give time to the artillerymen to get their horses rough shod? as if he could expect any labour from workmen emaciated with hunger and long marches; from poor wretches who hardly found the day long enough to procure provisions and dress them, whose forges were thrown away or damaged, and who besides wanted the indispensable materials for a labour so considerable.

"But perhaps he wished to allow himself time to drive on before him, out of danger and clear of the ranks, the troublesome crowd of soldiers, who had become useless, to rally the better sort, and to re-organise the army? as if it were possible to convey any orders whatever to men so scattered about, or to rally them, without lodgings, or distribution of provisions to *bivouacs*; in short, to think of re-organisation for corps of dying soldiers, all of whom had no longer any thing to adhere to, and whose union the least touch would dissolve."

Such, around Napoleon, were the conversations of his officers; or rather their secret reflections: for their devotion to him remained entire for two whole years longer, in the midst of the greatest calamities, and of the general revolt of nations.

The emperor, however, made an effort which was not altogether fruitless; namely, to rally under one commander, all that remained of the cavalry: of thirty-seven thousand cavalry which were present at the passage of the Niemen, there were now only eight hundred left on horseback. He gave the command of them to Latour-Maubourg; whether from the esteem felt for him, or from fatigue, no one objected to it.

As to Latour-Maubourg, he received the honour or the charge without expressing either pleasure or regret. He was a character of peculiar stamp; always ready without forwardness, calm and active, remarkable for his extreme purity of morals, simple and unostentatious; in other respects, unaffected and sincere in his relations with others, and attaching the idea of glory only to actions, and not to words. He always marched with the same order and moderation in the midst of the most immoderate disorder; and yet, what does honour to the age, he attained to the highest distinctions as quickly and as rapidly as any who could be named.

This feeble re-organisation, the distribution of a part of the provisions, the plunder of the rest, the repose which the emperor and his guard were enabled to take, the destruction of part of the artillery and baggage, and finally, the expediting a number of orders, were nearly all the benefits which were derived from that fatal delay. In other respects, all the misfortunes happened which had been foreseen. A few hundred men were rallied only for a moment. The explosion of the mines scarcely blew up the outside of some of the walls, and was only of use on the last day, in driving out of the town the stragglers whom we had been unable to set in motion.

The soldiers who had totally lost heart, the women, and several thousand sick and wounded, were here abandoned. This was when Augereau's disaster near Elnia made it but too evident that Kutusoff, now become the pursuer, did not confine himself to the high road; that he was marching from Viazma by Elnia, direct upon Krasnoë; finally, when we ought to have foreseen that we should be obliged to cut our way through the Russian army, it was only on the 14th of November that the grand army (or rather thirty-six thousand troops) commenced its march.

The old and young guard had not more than from nine to ten thousand infantry, and two thousand cavalry; Davoust and the first corps, from eight to nine thousand; Ney and the third corps, five to six thousand; Prince Eugene and the arm of Italy, five thousand; Poniatowski, eight hundred; Junot and the Westphalians, seven hundred; Latour-Maubourg and the rest of the cavalry, fifteen hundred; there might also be about one thousand light horse, and five hundred dismounted cavalry, whom we had succeeded in collecting together.

This army had left Moscow one hundred thousand strong; in five-and-twenty days it had been reduced to thirty-six thousand men. The artillery had already lost three hundred and fifty of their cannon, and yet these feeble remains were always divided into eight armies, which were encumbered with sixty thousand unarmed stragglers, and a long train of cannon and baggage.

Whether it was the encumbrance of so many men and carriages, or a mistaken sense of security, which led the emperor to order a day's interval between the departure of each marshal, is uncertain; most probably it was the latter. Be that as it may, he, Eugene, Davoust, and Ney only quitted Smolensk in succession; Ney was not to leave it till the 16th or 17th. He had orders to make the artillery saw the trunnions off the cannon left behind, and bury them; to destroy the ammunition, to drive all the stragglers before him, and to blow up the towers which surrounded the city.

Kutusoff, meanwhile, was waiting for us at some leagues' distance, and preparing to cut in pieces successively those remnants of corps thus extended and parcelled out.

1. This is erroneous. A letter of Napoleon, to Berthier, proves that Ney was "to march as rapidly as possible, that what remained of the fine weather might not be thrown away."—*Ed.*

2. "It is necessary," says general Gourgaud, "to repeat that the emperor halted no longer at Smolensk than was necessary to rally the stragglers, send off the sick and wounded, turn to account the resources of the city, and prevent the retreat from degenerating into a rout, which would have been the case if he had marched constantly without stopping."—*Ed.*

CHAPTER III

SMOLENSK TO KRASNOË

IT was on the 14th of November, about five in the morning, that the imperial column at last quitted Smolensk. Its march was still firm, but gloomy and silent as night, like the mute and discoloured aspect of the country through which it was advancing.

This silence was only interrupted by the cracking of the whips applied to the horses, and by short and violent imprecations when they met with ravines, and when upon these icy declivities, men, horses, and artillery were rolling in obscurity one over the other. The first day they advanced five leagues. The artillery of the guard took twenty-two hours to get over that ground.

Nevertheless, this first column arrived, without any great loss of men, at Korythnia, which Junot had passed with his Westphalian corps, now reduced to seven hundred men. A vanguard had pushed on as far as Krasnoë. The wounded and disbanded men were on the point of reaching Liady. Korythnia is five leagues from Smolensk; Krasnoë five leagues from Korythnia; Liady four leagues from Krasnoë. The Borysthenes flows at two leagues on the right of the high road from Korythnia to Krasnoë.

Near Korythnia another road, that from Elnia to Krasnoë, runs close to the high-road. That very day Kutusoff advanced upon that road with ninety thousand men, which completely covered it; his march was parallel with that of Napoleon, whom he soon outstripped; on the cross-roads he sent forward several vanguards to intercept our retreat.

One of these, said to be commanded by Ostermann, made its appearance at Korythnia at the same time with Napoleon, and was driven back.

A second, consisting of twenty thousand men, commanded by Miloradowitch, took a position three leagues in advance of us, towards Merlino and Nikoulina, behind a ravine which skirts the left side of the great road; and there, lying in ambush on the flank of our retreat, it awaited our passage.

At the same time a third reached Krasnoë, which it surprised during the night, but was driven out by Sebastiani, who had just arrived there.

Finally, a fourth, pushed still more in advance, got between Krasnoë and Liady, and carried off, upon the high road, several generals and other officers who were marching singly.

Kutusoff, at the same time, with the bulk of his army, advanced, and took a position in rear of these vanguards, and within reach of them all, and felicitated himself on the success of his manœuvres, which would have inevitably failed, owing to his tardiness, had it not been for our want of foresight; for this was a contest of errors, in which ours being the greatest, we narrowly escaped total destruction. Having made these dispositions, the Russian commander must have believed that the French army was entirely in his power; but this belief saved us. Kutusoff was wanting to himself at the moment of action; his old age executed only half and badly the plans which it had combined wisely.

During the time that all these masses were arranging themselves round Napoleon, he remained perfectly tranquil in a miserable hut, the only one left standing in Korythnia, apparently quite unconscious of all these movements of troops, artillery, and cavalry, which were surrounding him in all directions; at least he sent no orders to the three corps which had halted at Smolensk to expedite their march, and he himself waited for day-light to proceed.

His column was advancing without precaution, preceded by a crowd of stragglers, all eager to reach Krasnoë, when at two leagues from that place, a row of Cossacks extending from the heights on our left across the great road, appeared before them. Seized with astonishment, these stragglers halted; they had looked for nothing of the kind, and at first were inclined to believe that relentless fate had traced upon the snow between them and Europe, that long, black, and motionless line as the fatal term assigned to their hopes.

Some of them, stupified and rendered insensible by the misery of their situation, with their eyes mentally fixed on home, and pursuing mechanically and obstinately that direction, would listen to no warning, and were about to surrender; the others collected together; on both sides there was a pause, in order to consider each other's force. Several officers, who then came up, put these disbanded soldiers in some degree of order; seven or eight riflemen, whom they sent forward, were sufficient to break through that threatening curtain.

The French were smiling at the audacity of this idle demonstration, when all at once, from the heights on their left, an enemy's battery began firing. Its bullets crossed the road; at the same time thirty squadrons showed themselves on the same side, threatening the Westphalian corps which was advancing, the commander of which was so confused, that he made no disposition to meet their attack.

A wounded officer, unknown to these Germans, and who was there by mere chance, called out to them with an indignant voice, and immediately assumed their command. The men obeyed him as they would their own leader. In this case of pressing danger the differences of convention disappeared. The man really superior having shown himself, acted as a rallying point to the crowd, who grouped themselves around him, while the general-in-chief remained mute and confounded, receiving with docility the impulse the other had given, and acknowledging his superiority, which, after the danger was over, he disputed, but of which he did not, as too often happens, seek to revenge himself.

This wounded officer was Excelmans! In this action he was every thing, general, officer, soldier, even an artilleryman, for he actually laid hold of a cannon that had been abandoned, loaded and pointed it, and made it once more be of use against our enemies. As to the commander of the Westphalians, after this campaign, his premature and melancholy end makes us presume that excessive fatigue, and the consequences of some severe wounds, had already affected him mortally.

On seeing this leading column marching in such good order, the enemy confined itself to attacking it with their bullets, which it despised, and soon left behind it. When it came to the turn of the grenadiers of the old guard to pass through this fire, they closed their ranks around Napoleon like a moveable fortress, proud of having to protect him. Their band of music expressed this pride. When the danger was greatest, they played the well-known air, *"Où peut-on être mieux qu'au sein de sa famille?"* (Where can we be happier than in the bosom of our family?) But the emperor, whom nothing escaped, stopped them with an exclamation, "Rather play, *Veillons au salut de l'Empire!"* (Let us watch for the safety of the empire!) words much better suited to his pre-occupation, and to the general situation.

At the same time, the enemy's fire becoming troublesome, he gave orders to silence it, and in two hours he reached Krasnoë. The sight of Sebastiani, and of the first grenadiers who preceded him, had been sufficient to drive away the enemy's infantry. Napoleon entered in a state of great anxiety, from not knowing what corps had been attacking him, his cavalry being too weak to enable them to get him information, out of reach of the high-road. He left Mortier and the young guard a league behind him, in this way stretching out from too great a distance a hand too feeble to assist his army, and determined to wait for it.

The passage of his column had not been sanguinary, but it could not conquer the ground as it did the enemy; the road was hilly; at every eminence cannon were obliged to be left behind without being spiked, and baggage, which was plundered before it was abandoned. The Russians from the heights saw the whole interior of the army, its weaknesses, it deformities, its most shameful parts: in short, all that is generally concealed with the greatest care.

Notwithstanding, it appeared as if Miloradowitch, from his elevated position, was satisfied with merely insulting the passage of the emperor, and of that old guard which had been so long the terror of Europe. He did not dare to gather up its fragments until it had passed by; but then he became bold, concentrated his forces, and descending from the heights, took up a strong position with twenty thousand men, quite across the high road; by this movement he separated Eugene, Davoust, and Ney from the emperor, and closed the road to Europe against these three leaders.

CHAPTER IV

PRINCE EUGENE'S RETREAT

WHILE Miloradowitch was making these preparations, Eugene was using all his efforts at Smolensk to collect his scattered troops; with great difficulty he tore them from the plunder of the magazines, and he did not succeed in rallying eight thousand men until late on the 15th of November. He was obliged to promise them supplies of provisions, and to show them the road to Lithuania, in order to induce them to resume their march. Night compelled him to halt at three leagues' distance from Smolensk; half his soldiers had already left their ranks. Next morning he continued his march, with all that the cold of the night and of death had not fixed round their bivouacs.

The noise of the cannon which had been heard the day before had ceased; the royal column was advancing with difficulty, adding its own fragments to those which it encountered. At its head, the viceroy and the chief of his staff, buried in their own melancholy reflections, gave the reins to their horses. Insensibly they left their troop behind them, without being aware of it; for the road was strewed with stragglers and men marching at their pleasure, the idea of keeping whom in order had been abandoned.

In this way they advanced to within two leagues of Krasnoë, but then a singular movement which was passing before them attracted their absent looks. Several of the disbanded soldiers had suddenly halted; those who followed as they came up, formed a group with them; others who had advanced farther fell back upon the first; they crowded together; a mass was soon formed. The viceroy was surprised, and looked about him; he perceived that he had got the start of his main body by an hour's march; that he had about him only fifteen hundred men of all ranks, of all nations, without organisation, without leaders, without order, without arms ready or fit for an engagement—at this moment he was summoned to surrender.

This summons was answered by a general cry of indignation! But the Russian flag of truce, who presented himself singly, insisted: "Napoleon and his guard," said he to them, "have been beaten; you are surrounded by twenty thousand Russians: you have no means of safety but in accepting honourable conditions, and these Miloradowitch proposes to you."

At these words, Guyon, one of the generals whose soldiers were either all dead or dispersed, rushed from the crowd, and with a loud voice called out, "Return immediately to whence you came, and tell him who sent you, that if he has twenty thousand men, we have eighty thousand!" The Russian, confounded, immediately retired.

All this happened in the twinkling of an eye; in a moment after the hills on the left of the road were spouting out lightning and volumes of smoke; showers of shells and grape shot swept the high road, and threatening advancing columns showed their bayonets.

The viceroy hesitated for a moment; it grieved him to quit that unfortunate troop, but at last leaving his chief of the staff with them, he returned back to his divisions, in order to bring them forward to the combat, to make them get beyond the obstacle before it became insurmountable, or to perish; for with the pride derived from a crown and so many victories, it was not to be expected that he could ever admit the thought of surrender.

Meanwhile, Guilleminot summoned about him the officers who, in this crowd, were mingled with the soldiers. Several generals, colonels, and a great number of officers immediately sprung forward and surrounded him; they concerted together, and accepting him for their leader, they distributed into platoons all the men who had hitherto formed but one mass, and whom in that state they had found it impossible to excite.

This organisation took place under a sharp fire. Several superior officers went and placed themselves proudly in the ranks, and became once more common soldiers. From a different species of pride, some marines of the guard insisted on being commanded by one of their own officers, while each of the other platoons was commanded by a general. Hitherto the emperor himself had been their colonel; now they were on the point of perishing they maintained their privilege, which nothing could make them forget, and which was respected accordingly.

These brave men, in this order, proceeded on their march to Krasnoë; and they had already got beyond the batteries of Miloradowitch, when the latter rushing with his columns upon their flank, hemmed them in so closely, as to compel them to turn about, and seek a position in which they could defend themselves. To the eternal glory of these warriors, these fifteen hundred French and Italians, who were as one to ten, it should be told, that with nothing in their favour but a determined countenance and very few fire-arms in a state fit for use, they kept their enemies at a respectful distance upwards of an hour.

But as there was still no appearance of the viceroy and the rest of his divisions, a longer resistance was evidently impossible. They were again and again summoned to lay down their arms. During these short pauses they heard the cannon rolling at a distance in their front and in their rear. Thus, therefore, "the whole army was attacked at once, and from Smolensk to Krasnoë it was but one engagement! If we wanted assistance, there could be none expected by waiting for it; we must go and look for it; but on which side? At Krasnoë it was impossible; we were too far from it; there was every reason to believe that our troops were fighting there. It would besides become a matter of necessity for us to retreat; and we were too near the Russians under Miloradowitch, who were calling to us from their ranks to lay down our arms, to venture to turn our backs upon them. It would therefore be a much better plan, as our faces were now turned towards Smolensk, and as Prince Eugene was on that side, to form ourselves into one compact mass, keep all its movements well combined, and rushing headlong, to re-enter Russia by cutting our way through these Russians, and rejoin the viceroy; then to return together, to overthrow Miloradowitch, and at last reach Krasnoë."

To this proposition of their leader, there was a loud and unanimous cry of assent. Instantly the column formed into a mass, and rushed into the midst of ten thousand hostile muskets and cannon. The Russians, at first seized with astonishment, opened their ranks and allowed this handful of warriors, almost disarmed, to advance into the middle of them. Then, when they comprehended their purpose, either from pity or admiration, the enemy's battalions, which lined both sides of the road, called out to our men to halt; they entreated and conjured them to surrender; but the only answer they received was a more determined march, a stern silence, and the point of the bayonet. The whole of the enemy's fire was then poured upon them at once, at the distance of a few yards, and the half of this heroic column was stretched wounded or lifeless on the ground.

The remainder proceeded without a single man quitting the body of his troop, which no Russian was bold enough to venture near. Few of these unfortunate men again saw the viceroy and their advancing divisions. Then only they separated; they ran and threw themselves into these feeble ranks, which were opened to receive and protect them.

For more than an hour the Russian cannon had been thinning them. While one half of their forces had been pursuing Guilleminot, and compelling him to retreat, Miloradowitch, with the other half, had stopped Prince Eugene. His right rested on a wood, which was protected by heights entirely covered with cannon; his left touched the high road, but more in the rear. This disposition dictated that of Eugene. The royal column, by degrees, as it came up, deployed on the right of the road, its right more forward than its left. The viceroy thus placed obliquely between him and the enemy the high road, the possession of which was the subject of contest. Each of the two armies occupied it by its left.

The Russians, placed in a position so offensive, kept entirely on the defensive; their bullets alone attacked Eugene. A cannonade was kept up on both sides; on theirs most destructive, on ours almost ineffective. Tired out with this firing, Eugene formed his resolution; he called the 14th French division, drew it up on the left of the great road, pointed out to it the woody height on which the enemy rested, and which formed his principal strength; *that* was the decisive point, the centre of the action, and to make the rest fall, *that* must be carried. He did not expect it would; but that effort would draw the attention and the strength of the enemy on that side, the right of the great road would remain free, and he would endeavour to take proper advantage of it.

Three hundred soldiers, formed into three troops, were all that could be found willing to mount to this assault. These devoted men advanced resolutely against hostile thousands in a formidable position. A battery of the Italian guard advanced to protect them, but the Russian batteries immediately demolished it, and their cavalry took possession of it.

In spite of the grape-shot which was mowing them rapidly down, the three hundred French kept moving on, and had actually reached the enemy's position, when suddenly from both sides of the wood two masses of cavalry rushed forth, bore down upon, overwhelmed and massacred them. Not one escaped; and with them perished all remains of discipline and courage in their division.

It was at that moment that general Guilleminot again made his appearance. That in a position so critical, Prince Eugene, with four thousand enfeebled troops, the remnant of forty-two thousand and upwards, should not have despaired, that he should still have exhibited a bold countenance, may be conceived, from the known character of that commander; but that the sight of our disaster and the ardour of success should not have urged the Russians to more than indecisive efforts, and that they should have allowed the night to put an end to the battle, is with us, to this day, a matter of astonishment. Victory was so new to them, that even when they held it in their hands, they knew not how to profit by it; they delayed its completion until the next day.

The viceroy saw that the greater part of the Russians, attracted by his demonstrations, had collected on the left of the road, and he only waited until night, the sure ally of the weakest, had chained all their movements. Then it was, that leaving his fires burning on that side, to deceive the enemy, he quitted it, and marching across the fields, he turned, and silently got beyond the left of Miloradowitch's position, while that general, too certain of his victory, was dreaming of the glory of receiving, next morning, the sword of the son of Napoleon.

In the midst of this perilous march, there was an awful moment. At the most critical instant, when these soldiers, the remnants of so many battles, were stealing along the side of the Russian army, holding their breath and the noise of their steps—when their all depended on a look or a cry of alarm—the moon all at once coming out of a thick cloud appeared to light their movements. At that moment a Russian sentinel called out to them to halt, and demanded who they were. They gave themselves up for lost! But Klisky, a Pole, ran up to this Russian, and speaking to him in his own language, said to him with the greatest composure, in a low tone of voice, "Be silent, fellow! don't you see that we belong to the corps of Ouwaroff, and that we are going on a secret expedition?" The Russian, outwitted, held his tongue.

But the Cossacks were galloping up every moment to the flanks of the column, as if to reconnoitre it, and then return to the body of their troop. Their squadrons advanced several times as if they were about to charge; but they did no more, either from doubt as to what they saw, for they were still deceived, or from prudence, as the column frequently halted, and presented a determined front to them.

At last, after two hours' most anxious march, they again reached the high road, and the viceroy was actually in Krasnoë on the 17th of November, when Miloradowitch, descending from his heights in order to seize him, found the field of battle occupied only by a few stragglers, whom no effort could induce the night before to quit their fires.

CHAPTER V

BATTLE OF KRASNOË

THE emperor on his side had waited for the viceroy during the whole of the preceding day. The noise of his engagement had irritated him. An effort to break through the enemy, in order to join him, had been ineffectually attempted; and when night came on without his making his appearance, the uneasiness of his adopted father was at its height. "Eugene and the army of Italy, and this long day of baffled expectation, had they then terminated together?" Only one hope remained to Napoleon; and that was, that the viceroy, driven back towards Smolensk, had there joined Davoust and Ney, and that the following day they would, with united forces, attempt a decisive effort.

In his anxiety, the emperor assembled the marshals who remained with him. These were Berthier, Bessières, Mortier, and Lefebvre; these were saved; they had cleared the obstacle; they had only to continue their retreat through Lithuania, which was open to them; but would they abandon their companions in the midst of the Russian army? No, certainly; and they determined once more to enter Russia, either to deliver or to perish with them.

When this resolution was taken, Napoleon coolly prepared the dispositions to carry it into effect. He was not at all shaken by the great movements which the enemy were evidently making around him. He saw that Kutusoff was advancing in order to surround and take him prisoner in Krasnoë. The very night before, he had learned that Ojarowski, with a vanguard of Russian infantry, had got beyond him, and taken a position at Maliewo, in a village in the rear on his left. Irritated, instead of being depressed, by misfortune, he called his aide-de-camp Rapp, and told him, "that he must set out immediately, and proceed during the darkness to attack that body of infantry with the bayonet; that this was the first time of its exhibiting so much audacity, and that he was determined to make it repent it, in such a way, that it should never again dare to approach so near to his head-quarters." Then instantly recalling him, he continued, "But, no! let Roguet and his division go alone! As for thee, remain where thou art, I don't wish thee to be killed here, I shall have occasion for thee at Dantzic."

Rapp, while he was carrying this order to Roguet, could not help feeling astonished, that his leader, surrounded by eighty thousand enemies, whom he was going to attack next day with nine thousand, should have so little doubt about his safety, as to be thinking of what he should have to do at Dantzic, a city from which he was separated by the winter, two other hostile armies, famine, and a hundred and eighty leagues.

The nocturnal attack on Chirkowa and Maliewo was successful. Roguet formed his idea of the enemy's position by the direction of their fires; they occupied two villages, connected by a causeway, which was defended by a ravine. He disposed his troop into three columns of attack; those on the right and left were to advance silently, as close as possible to the enemy; then at the signal to charge, which he himself would give them from the centre, they were to rush into the midst of the enemy without firing a shot, and make use only of their bayonets.

Immediately the two wings of the young guard commenced the action. While the Russians, taken by surprise, and not knowing on which side to defend themselves, were wavering from their right to their left, Roguet, with his column, rushed suddenly upon their centre and into the midst of their camp, into which he entered pell-mell with them. Thus divided and thrown into confusion, they had barely time to throw the best part of their great and small arms into a neighbouring lake, and to set fire to their tents, the flames arising from which, instead of saving them, only gave light to their destruction.

This check stopped the movement of the Russian army for four-and-twenty hours, put it in the emperor's power to remain at Krasnoë, and enabled Eugene to rejoin him during the following night. He was received by Napoleon with the greatest joy; but the emperor's uneasiness respecting Davoust and Ney became shortly after proportionably greater.

Around us the camp of the Russians presented a spectacle similar to what it had done at Winkowo, Malo-Yaroslawetz, and Viazma. Every evening close to the general's tent, the relics of the Russian saints, surrounded by an immense number of wax tapers, were exposed to the adoration of the soldiers. While each of these was, according to custom, giving proofs of his devotion by an endless repetition of crossings and genuflections, the priests were addressing them with fanatical exhortations, which would appear barbarous and absurd to every civilised nation.

In spite, however, of the great influence of such means, of the number of the Russians, and of our weakness, Kutusoff, who was only at two leagues' distance from Miloradowitch, while the latter was beating Prince Eugene, remained immoveable. During the following night, Beningsen, urged on by the ardent Wilson, in vain attempted to animate the old Russian. Elevating the faults of his age into virtues, he applied the names of wisdom, humanity, and prudence, to his dilatoriness and strange circumspection he was resolved to finish as he had begun. For if we may be allowed to compare small things with great, his renown had been established on a principle directly contrary to that of Napoleon, fortune having made the one, and the other having created his fortune.

He made a boast of "advancing only by short marches; of allowing his soldiers to rest every third day: he would blush, and halt immediately, if they wanted bread or spirits for a single moment." Then, with great self-gratulation, he pretended that "all the way from Viazma, he had been escorting the French army as his prisoners: chastising them whenever they wished to halt, or strike out of the high road; that it was useless to run any risks with captives; that the Cossacks, a vanguard, and an army of artillery, were quite sufficient to finish them, and make them pass successively under the yoke; and that in this plan, he was admirably seconded by Napoleon himself. Why should he seek to *purchase* of Fortune what she was so generously *giving* him? Was not the term of Napoleon's destiny already irrevocably marked? it was in the marshes of the Berezina that this meteor would be extinguished, this colossus overthrown, in the midst of Wittgenstein, Tchitchakoff, and himself, and in the presence of the assembled Russian armies. As for himself, he would have the glory of delivering him up to them, enfeebled, disarmed, and dying; and to him that glory was sufficient."

To this discourse the English officer, still more active and eager, replied only by entreating the field-marshal "to leave his head-quarters only for a few moments, and advance upon the heights; there he would see that the last moments of Napoleon was already come. Would he allow him even to get beyond the frontiers of Russia Proper, which loudly called for the sacrifice of this great victim? Nothing remained but to strike the blow; let him only give the order, ore charge would be sufficient, and in two hours the face of Europe would be entirely changed!"

Then, gradually getting warmer at the coolness with which Kutusoff listened to him, Wilson, for the third time, threatened him with the general indignation. "Already, in his army, at the sight of the straggling, mutilated and dying column, which was about to escape from him, he might hear the Cossacks exclaiming, what a shame it was to allow these skeletons to escape in this manner from their tombs!" But Kutusoff, whom old age, that misfortune without hope, rendered indifferent, became angry at the attempts made to rouse him, and by a short and violent answer, shut the indignant Englishman's mouth.

It is asserted that the report of a spy had represented to him Krasnoë as filled with an enormous mass of the imperial guard, and that the old marshal was afraid of compromising his reputation by attacking it. But the sight of our distress emboldened Beningsen; this chief of the staff prevailed upon Strogonoff, Gallitzin, and Miloradowitch, with a force of more than fifty thousand Russians, and one hundred pieces of cannon, to venture to attack at daylight, in spite of Kutusoff, fourteen thousand famished, enfeebled, and half-frozen French and Italians.

This was a danger, the imminence of which Napoleon fully comprehended. He might have escaped from it; daylight had not yet appeared. He was at liberty to avoid this fatal engagement; he might have gained Orcha and Borizoff, by rapid marches along with Eugene and his guard; there he could have rallied his forces with thirty thousand French under Victor and Oudinôt, with the corps of Dombrowski, Regnier, and Schwartzenberg, and with all his depôts, and he might again, the following year, have made his appearance as formidable as ever.

On the 17th, before daylight, he issued his orders, armed himself, and going out on foot, at the head of his old guard, began his march. But it was not towards Poland, his ally, that it was directed, nor towards France, where he would be still received as the head of a new dynasty, and the emperor of the West. His words on taking up his sword on this occasion were, "I have sufficiently acted the Emperor; it is time I should become the general." He turned back into the midst of eighty thousand enemies, plunged into the thickest of them, in order to draw all their efforts against himself, to make a diversion in favour of Davoust and Ney, and to wrest them from a country the gates of which had closed them in.

Daylight at last appeared, exhibiting on one side the Russian battalions and batteries, which on three sides, in front, on our right, and in our rear, bounded the horizon, and on the other, Napoleon with his six thousand guards advancing with a firm step, and proceeding to take his place in the middle of that terrible circle. At the same time Mortier, a few yards in front of his emperor, displayed in the face of the whole Russian army, the five thousand men which still remained to him.

Their object was to defend the right flank of the high road from Krasnoë to the great ravine in the direction of Stachowa. A battalion of *chasseurs* of the old guard, formed in a square like a fortress, was planted close to the high road, and acted as a support to the left wing of our young soldiers. On their right, in the snowy plains which surrounded Krasnoë, the remains of the cavalry of the guard, a few cannon, and the four hundred cavalry of Latour-Maubourg (as, since they left Smolensk, the cold had killed or dispersed five hundred of them,) occupied the place of the battalions and batteries which the French army no longer possessed.

The artillery of the duke of Treviso was reinforced by a battery commanded by Drouot; one of those men who are endowed with the whole strength of virtue, who think that duty embraces every thing, and are capable of making the noblest sacrifices simply and without the least effort.

Claparède remained at Krasnoë, where, with a few soldiers, he protected the wounded, the baggage, and the retreat. Prince Eugene continued his retreat towards Liady. His engagement of the preceding day and his night march had entirely broken up his corps; his divisions only retained sufficient unity to drag themselves along, in order to perish, but not to fight.

Meantime Roguet had been recalled to the field of battle from Maliewo. The enemy kept pushing columns through that village, and was extending more and more beyond our right in order to surround us. The battle then commenced. But what kind of battle? The emperor had here no sudden illumination to trust to, no flashes of momentary inspiration, none of these great strokes so unforeseen from their boldness, which ravish for tune, extort a victory, and by which he has so often disconcerted, stunned, and crushed his enemies. All *their* movements were now free, all *ours* enchained, and this genius of attack was reduced to defend himself.

Here therefore it became perfectly evident that renown is not a vain shadow, that she is real strength, and doubly powerful by the inflexible pride which she imparts to her favourites, and the timid precautions which she suggests to such as venture to attack her. The Russians had only to march forward without manœuvring, even without firing; their mass was quite sufficient of itself to crush Napoleon and all his feeble troops: but they did not dare to come to close quarters with him. They were awed by the presence of the conqueror of Egypt and of Europe. The Pyramids, Marengo, Austerlitz, Friedland, an army of victories, seemed to rise between him and the whole of the Russians. We might also fancy that, in the eyes of that submissive and superstitious people, a renown so extraordinary appeared like something supernatural; that they regarded it as beyond their reach; that they believed they could only attack and demolish it from a distance; and in short, that against that old guard, that living fortress, that column of granite, as it had been styled by its leader, human efforts were impotent, and that cannon alone could demolish it

These made wide and deep breaches in the ranks of Roguet and the young guard, but they killed without vanquishing. These young soldiers, one half of whom had never before been in an engagement, received the shock of death during three hours without retreating one step, without making a single movement to escape it, and without being able to return it, their artillery having been broken, and the Russians keeping beyond the reach of their musketry.

But every instant strengthened the enemy and weakened Napoleon. The noise of artillery as well as Claparède apprised him, that in the rear of Krasnoë and his army, Beningsen was proceeding to take possession of the road to Liady, and cut off his retreat. The east, the west, and the south were sparkling with the enemy's fires; one side only remained open, that of the north and the Dnieper, towards an eminence, at the foot of which were the high road and the emperor. We fancied we saw the enemy covering this eminence with his cannon: in that situation they were just over Napoleon's head, and might have crushed him at a few yards' distance. He was apprised of his danger, cast his eyes for an instant upon it, and uttered merely these words, "Very well, let a battalion of my *chasseurs* take possession of it!" Immediately afterwards, without paying farther attention to it, his whole looks and attention reverted to the perilous situation of Mortier.

Then at last Davoust made his appearance, forcing his way through a swarm of Cossacks, whom he drove away by a precipitate march. At the sight of Krasnoë, this marshal's troops disbanded themselves, and ran across the fields to get beyond the right of the enemy's line, in the rear of which they had come up. Davoust and his generals could only rally them at Krasnoë.

The first corps was thus preserved, but we learned at the same time, that our rear-guard could no longer defend itself at Krasnoë; that Ney was probably still at Smolensk, and that we must give up waiting for him any longer. Napoleon, however, still hesitated; he could not determine on making this great sacrifice.

But at last, as all were likely to perish, his resolution was fixed. He called Mortier, and squeezing his hand sorrowfully, told him, "that he had not a moment to lose; that the enemy were overwhelming him in all directions; that Kutusoff might already reach Liady, perhaps Orcha, and the last elbow of the Borysthenes before him; that he would therefore proceed thither rapidly with his old guard, in order to occupy that passage. Davoust would relieve Mortier; but both of them must endeavour to hold out in Krasnoë until night, after which they must come and rejoin him." Then with his heart full of Ney's misfortune, and of despair at abandoning him, he withdrew slowly from the field of battle, traversed Krasnoë, where he again halted, and then cleared his way to Liady.

Mortier was anxious to obey, but at that moment the Dutch troops of the guard lost, along with a third part of their number, an important post which they were defending, which the enemy immediately after covered with his artillery. Roguet, feeling the destructive effect of its fire, fancied he was able to extinguish it. A regiment which he sent against the Russian battery was repulsed; a second (the 1st of the *voltigeurs*) got into the middle of the Russians, and stood firm against two charges of their cavalry. It continued to advance, torn to pieces by their grape-shot, when a third charge overwhelmed it. Fifty soldiers and eleven officers were all of it that Roguet was able to preserve.

That general had lost the half of his men. It was now two o'clock, and his unshaken fortitude still kept the Russians in astonishment, when at last, emboldened by the emperor's departure, they began to press upon him so closely, that the young guard was nearly hemmed in, and very soon in a situation in which it could neither hold out nor retreat.

Fortunately, some platoons which Davoust had rallied, and the appearance of another troop of his stragglers, attracted the enemy's attention. Mortier availed himself of it. He gave orders to the three thousand men he had still remaining to retreat slowly in the face of their fifty thousand enemies. "Do you hear, soldiers?" cried General Laborde, "the marshal orders ordinary time! Ordinary time, soldiers!" And this brave and unfortunate troop, dragging with them some of their wounded, under a shower of balls and grape-shot, retired as slowly from this field of carnage, as they would have done from a field of manœuvre.

CHAPTER VI

DESPAIR AND DISORGANISATION

AS soon as Mortier had succeeded in placing Krasnoë between him and Beningsen, he was in safety. The communication between that town and Liady was only interrupted by the fire of the enemy's batteries, which flanked the left side of the great road. Colbert and Latour-Maubourg kept them in check upon their heights. In the course of this march a most singular accident occurred. A howitzer shell entered the body of a horse, burst there, and blew him to pieces without wounding his rider, who fell upon his legs, and went on.

The emperor, meanwhile, halted at Liady, four leagues from the field of battle. When night came on, he learned that Mortier, who he thought was in his rear, had got before him. Melancholy and uneasy, he sent for him, and with an agitated voice, said to him, "that he had certainly fought gloriously, and suffered greatly. But why had he placed his emperor between him and the enemy? Why had he exposed him to be cut off?"

The marshal had got the start of Napoleon without being aware of it. He explained, "that he had at first left Davoust in Krasnoë again endeavouring to rally his troops, and that he himself had halted not far from that: but that the first corps, having been driven back upon him, had obliged him to retrograde. That besides, Kutusoff did not follow up his victory with vigour, and appeared to hang upon our flank with all his army with no other view than to feast his eyes with our distress, and gather up our fragments."

Next day the march was continued with hesitation. The impatient stragglers took the lead, and all of them got the start of Napoleon; he was on foot, with a stick in his hand, walking with difficulty and repugnance, and halting every quarter of an hour, as if unwilling to tear himself from that old Russia, whose frontier he was then passing, and in which he had left his unfortunate companion in arms.

In the evening he reached Dombrowna, a wooden town, and inhabited as well as Liady; a novel sight for an army, which had for three months seen nothing but ruins. We had at last emerged from old Russia, and her deserts of snow and ashes, and were entering into a friendly and inhabited country, whose language we understood. The weather just then became milder, a thaw began, and we received some provisions.

Thus the winter, the enemy, solitude, and, with some, famine and bivouacs, all ceased at once; but it was too late. The emperor saw that his army was destroyed; every moment the name of Ney escaped from his lips, with exclamations of grief. That night particularly he was heard groaning and exclaiming, "that the misery of his poor soldiers cut him to the heart, and yet that he could not succour them without fixing himself in some place: but where was it possible for him to rest, without ammunition, provisions, or artillery? He was no longer strong enough to halt; he must reach Minsk as quickly as possible."

He had hardly spoken the words, when a Polish officer arrived with the news, that Minsk itself, his magazine, his retreat, his only hope, had just fallen into the hands of the Russians, Tchitchakoff having entered it on the 16th. Napoleon, at first, was mute and overpowered at this last blow; but immediately afterwards, elevating himself in proportion to his danger, he coolly replied, "Very well! we have now nothing to do, but to clear ourselves a passage with our bayonets."

But in order to reach this new enemy, who had escaped from Schwartzenberg, or whom Schwartzenberg had perhaps allowed to pass, (for we knew nothing of the circumstances,) and to escape from Kutusoff and Wittgenstein, we must cross the Berezina at Borizoff. With that view Napoleon (on the 19th of November, from Dombrowna) sent orders to Dombrowski to give up all idea of fighting Hoertel, and proceed with all haste to occupy that passage. He wrote to the duke of Reggio, to march rapidly to the same point, and to hasten to recover Minsk; the duke of Belluno would cover his march. After giving these orders, his agitation was appeased, and his mind, worn out with suffering, sunk into depression.

It was still far from daylight, when a singular noise drew him out of his lethargy. Some say that shots were at first heard, which had been fired by our own people, in order to draw out of the houses such as had taken shelter in them, that they might take their places; others assert, that from a disorderly practice, too common in our bivouacs, of vociferating to each other, the name of *Hausanne*, a grenadier, being suddenly called out in the midst of a profound silence, was mistaken for the alert cry of *aux armes*, which announced a surprise by the enemy.

Whatever might be the cause, every one immediately saw, or fancied he saw, the Cossacks, and a great noise of war and of terror surrounded Napoleon. Without disturbing himself, he said to Rapp, "Go and see, it is no doubt some rascally Cossacks, determined to disturb our rest!" But it became very soon a complete tumult of men running to fight or to flee, and who, meeting in the dark, mistook each other for enemies.

Napoleon for a moment imagined that a serious attack had been made. As an embanked stream of water ran through the town, he inquired if the remaining artillery had been placed behind that ravine, and being informed that the precaution had been neglected; he himself immediately ran to the bridge, and caused his cannon to be hurried over to the other side.

He then returned to his old guard, and stopping in front of each battalion: "Grenadiers!" said he to them, "we are retreating without being conquered by the enemy, let us not be vanquished by ourselves! Set an example to the army! Several of you have already deserted your eagles, and even thrown away your arms. I have no wish to have recourse to military laws to put a stop to this disorder, but appeal entirely to yourselves! Do justice among yourselves. To your own honour I commit the support of your discipline!"

The other troops he harangued in a similar style. These few words were quite sufficient to the old grenadiers, who probably had no occasion for them. The others received them with acclamation, but an hour afterwards, when the march was resumed, they were quite forgotten. As to his rear-guard, throwing the greatest part of the blame of this hot alarm upon it, he sent an angry message to Davoust on the subject.

At Orcha we found rather an abundant supply of provisions, a bridge equipage of sixty boats, with all its appurtenances, which were entirely burnt, and thirty-six pieces of cannon, with their horses, which were distributed between Davoust, Eugene, and Latour-Maubourg.

Here for the first time we again met with the officers and gendarmes, who had been sent for the purpose of stopping on the two bridges of the Dnieper the crowd of stragglers, and making them rejoin their columns. But those eagles, which formerly promised every thing, were now looked upon as of fatal omen, and deserted accordingly.

Disorder was already regularly organised, and had enlisted in its ranks men who showed their ability in its service. When an immense crowd had been collected, these wretches called out "the Cossacks!" with a view to quicken the march of those who preceded them, and to increase the tumult. They then took advantage of it, to carry off the provisions and cloaks of those whom they had thrown off their guard.

The gendarmes, who again saw this army for the first time since its disaster, were astonished at the sight of such misery, terrified at the great confusion, and became discouraged. This friendly frontier was entered tumultuously; it would have been given up to pillage, had it not been for the guard, and a few hundred men who remained with Prince Eugene.

Napoleon entered Orcha with six thousand guards, the remains of thirty-five thousand! Eugene, with eighteen hundred soldiers, the remains of forty-two thousand! Davoust, with four thousand, the remains of seventy thousand!

This marshal had lost every thing, was actually without linen, and emaciated with hunger. He seized upon a loaf which was offered him by one of his comrades, and voraciously devoured it. A handkerchief was given him to wipe his face, which was covered with rime. He exclaimed, "that none but men of iron constitutions could support such trials, that it was physically impossible to resist them; that there were limits to human strength, the utmost of which had been exceeded."

He it was who at first supported the retreat as far as Viazma. He was still, according to his custom, halting at all the defiles, and remaining there the very last, sending every one to his ranks, and constantly struggling with the disorder. He urged his soldiers to insult and strip of their booty such of their comrades as threw away their arms, the only means of retaining the first and punishing the last. Nevertheless, his methodical and severe genius, so much out of its element in that scene of universal confusion, has been accused of being too much intimidated at it.

The emperor made fruitless attempts to check this despondency. When alone, he was heard compassionating the sufferings of his soldiers; but in their presence, even upon that point, he wished to appear inflexible. He issued a proclamation, "ordering every one to return to their ranks; if they did not, he would strip the officers of their commissions and put the soldiers to death."

A threat like this produced neither good nor bad impression upon men who had become insensible, or were reduced to despair, fleeing, not from danger, but from suffering, and less apprehensive of the *death* with which they were threatened than of the *life* that was offered to them.

But Napoleon's confidence increased with his peril; in his eyes, and in the midst of these deserts of mud and ice, this handful of men was still the grand army! and himself the conqueror of Europe! and there was no infatuation in this firmness; we were certain of it, when in this very town, we saw him burning with his own hands every thing belonging to him, which might serve as trophies to the enemy, in the event of his fall.

There also were unfortunately consumed all the documents which he had collected in order to write the history of his life, for such was his intention when he set out for this fatal war.[1] He had then determined to halt as a threatening conqueror on the borders of the Dwina and the Borysthenes, to which he now returned as a disarmed fugitive. At that time he regarded the *ennui* of six winter months, which he would have been detained on these rivers, as his greatest enemy, and to overcome it, this second Cæsar intended there to have dictated his Commentaries.

1. This is not correct. Napoleon had no documents of the kind with him. Nor did he intend to write the history of his campaigns till after a general pacification had taken place.—*Ed.*

CHAPTER VII

COUNCIL AT ORCHA

EVERY thing, however, was now changed; two hostile armies were cutting off his retreat. The question to determine was, through which of them he must attempt to force his way and as he knew nothing of the Lithuanian forests into which he was about to penetrate, he summoned such of his officers as had passed through them, in order to reach him.

The emperor began by telling them, that "too much familiarity with great victories was frequently the precursor of great disasters, but that recrimination was now out of the question." He then mentioned the capture of Minsk, and after admitting the skilfulness of Kutusoff's persevering manœuvres on his right flank, declared "that he meant to abandon his line of operations on Minsk,[1] unite with the dukes of Belluno and Reggio, cut his way through Wittgenstein's army, and regain Wilna by turning the sources of the Berezina."

Jomini combated this plan. That Swiss general described the position of Wittgenstein as a series of long defiles, in which his resistance might be either obstinate or flexible, but in either way sufficiently long to consummate our destruction. He added, that in this season, and in such a state of disorder, a change of route would complete the destruction of the army; that it would lose itself in the cross-roads of these barren and marshy forests; he maintained that the high road alone could keep it in any degree of union. Borizoff, and its bridge over the Berezina, were still open; and it would be sufficient to reach it.

He then stated that he knew of a road to the right of that town, constructed on wooden bridges, and passing across the marshes of Lithuania.[2] This was the only road, by his account, by which the army could reach Wilna by Zembin and Malodeczno, leaving Minsk on the left, the road to which was a day's journey longer, its fifty broken bridges rendering a passage impracticable and Tchitchakoff being in possession of it. In this manner we should pass between the two hostile armies, avoiding them both.

The emperor was staggered; but as his pride revolted at the appearance of avoiding an engagement, and he was anxious to signalise his departure from Russia by a victory, he sent for general Dode, of the engineers. As soon as he saw him he called out to him, "Whether shall we retreat by Zembin, or go and beat Wittgenstein at Smoliantzy?" and knowing that Dode had just come from the latter position, he asked him if it was assailable?

His reply was, that Wittgenstein occupied a height which entirely commanded that miry country; that it would be necessary for us to tack about, within his sight and within his reach, by following the windings and turnings of the road, in order to ascend to the Russian camp; that thus our column of attack would be long exposed to their fire, first its left and then its right flank; that this position was therefore unapproachable in front, and that to turn it, it would be necessary to retrograde towards Witepsk, and take too long a circuit.

Disappointed in this last hope of glory, Napoleon then decided for Borizoff. He ordered general Eblé to proceed with eight companies of sappers and pontonniers to secure the passage of the Berezina, and general Jomini to act as his guide.[3] But he said at the same time, "that it was cruel to retreat without fighting, to have the appearance of flight. If he had any magazine, any point of support, which would allow him to halt, he would still prove to Europe that he still knew how to fight and to conquer."

All these illusions were now destroyed. At Smolensk, where he arrived first, and from which he was the first to depart, he had rather been informed of than witnessed his disaster. At Krasnoë, where our miseries had successively been enrolled before his eyes, the peril had diverted his attention from them; but at Orcha he could contemplate, at once and leisurely, the full extent of his misfortunes.

At Smolensk, thirty-six thousand combatants, one hundred and fifty cannon, the army-chest, and the hope of life and breathing at liberty on the other side of the Berezina, still remained; here, there were scarcely ten thousand soldiers, almost without clothing or shoes, entangled amidst a crowd of dying men, with a few cannon, and a pillaged army-chest.

In five days, every evil had been aggravated; destruction and disorganisation had made frightful progress; Minsk had been taken. He had no longer to look for rest and abundance on the other side of the Berezina, but fresh contests with a new enemy. Finally, the defection of Austria from his alliance seemed to be declared, and perhaps it was a signal given to all Europe.

Napoleon was even uncertain whether he should reach Borizoff in time to ward the new peril, which Schwartzenberg's hesitation seemed to have prepared for him. We have seen that a third Russian army, that of Wittgenstein, menaced, on his right, the interval which separated him from that town that he had sent the duke of Belluno against him, and had ordered that marshal to retrieve the opportunity he had lost on the 1st of November, and to resume the offensive.

In obedience to these orders, on the 14th of November, the very day that Napoleon quitted Smolensk, the dukes of Belluno and of Reggio had attacked and driven back the out-posts of Wittgenstein towards Smoliantzy, preparing, by this engagement, for a battle which they agreed should take place on the following day.

The French were thirty-thousand against forty thousand; there, as well as at Viazma, the soldiers were sufficiently numerous, if they had not had too many leaders.

The two marshals disagreed. Victor wished to manœuvre on the enemy's left wing, to overthrow Wittgenstein with the two French corps, and march by Botscheikowo on Kamen, and from Kamen by Pouichna on Berezino. Oudinôt warmly disapproved of this plan, saying that it would separate them from the grand army, which required their assistance.

In consequence, as one of the leaders wished to manœuvre, and the other to attack in front, they did neither. Oudinôt retired during the night to Czereïa; and Victor, discovering this retreat at day-break, was compelled to follow him.

He halted within a day's march of the Lukolm, near Sienno, where Wittgenstein did not much disturb him; but the duke of Reggio having at last received the order dated from Dombrowna, which directed him to recover Minsk, Victor was about to be left alone before the Russian general. It was possible that the latter would then become aware of his superiority: and the emperor, who at Orcha, on the 20th of November, saw his rear-guard lost, his left flank menaced by Kutusoff, and his advance column stopt at the Berezina by the army of Volhynia, learned that Wittgenstein and forty-thousand more enemies, far from being beaten and repulsed, were ready to fall upon his right, and that he had no time to lose.

But Napoleon was long before he could determine to quit the Borysthenes. It appeared to him that this was like a second abandonment of the unfortunate Ney, and casting off for ever his intrepid companion in arms. There, as he had done at Liady and Dombrowna, he was calling every hour of the day and night, and sending to inquire if no tidings had been heard of that marshal; but not a trace of his existence had transpired through the Russian army; four days this mortal silence had lasted, and yet the emperor still continued to hope.

At last, being compelled, on the 20th of November, to quit Orcha, he still left there Eugene, Mortier, and Davoust, and halted at two leagues from thence, inquiring for Ney, and still expecting him. The same feeling of grief pervaded the whole army, of which Orcha then contained the remains. As soon as the most pressing wants allowed a moment's rest, the thoughts and looks of every one were directed towards the Russian bank. They listened for any warlike noise which might announce the arrival of Ney, or rather his last sighs; but nothing was to be seen but enemies who were already menacing the bridges of the Borysthenes! One of the three leaders then wished to destroy them, but the others refused their consent, on the ground, that this would be again separating them from their companion in arms, and a confession that they despaired of saving him, an idea to which, from their dread of so great a misfortune, they could not reconcile themselves.

But with the fourth day all hope at last vanished. Night only brought with it a wearisome repose. They blamed themselves for Ney's misfortune, forgetting that it was utterly impossible to wait longer for the third corps in the plains of Krasnoë, where they must have fought for another twenty-eight hours, when they had merely strength and ammunition left for one.

Already, as is the case in all cruel losses, they began to treasure up recollections. Davoust was the last who had quitted the unfortunate marshal, and Mortier and the viceroy were inquiring of him what were his last words! At the first reports of the cannonade opened on the 15th on Napoleon, Ney was anxious immediately to evacuate Smolensk in the suite of the viceroy; Davoust refused, pleading the orders of the emperor, and the obligation to destroy the ramparts of the town. The two chiefs became warm, and Davoust persisting to remain until the following day, Ney, who had been appointed to bring up the rear, was compelled to wait for him.

It is true, that on the 16th, Davoust sent to warn him of his danger; but Ney, either from a change of opinion, or from an angry feeling against Davoust, then returned him for answer, "that all the Cossacks in the universe should not prevent him from executing his instructions."

After exhausting these recollections and all their conjectures, they again relapsed into a more gloomy silence, when suddenly they heard the steps of several horses, and then the joyful cry, "Marshal Ney is safe! here are some Polish cavalry come to announce his approach!" One of his officers then galloped in, and informed them that the marshal was advancing on the right bank of the Borysthenes, and had sent him to ask for assistance.

Night had just set in: Davoust, Eugene, and Mortier had only its short duration to revive and animate the soldiers, who had hitherto always bivouacked. For the first time since they left Moscow, these poor fellows had received a sufficient quantum of provisions; they were about to prepare them and to take their rest, warm and under cover: how was it possible to make them resume their arms, and turn them from their asylums during that night of rest, whose inexpressible sweets they had just begun to taste? Who could persuade them to interrupt it, to retrace their steps, and return once more into the darkness and frozen deserts of Russia.

Eugene and Mortier disputed the honour of this sacrifice, and the first only carried it in right of his superior rank. Shelter and the distribution of provisions had effected that which threats had failed to do. The stragglers were rallied, the viceroy again found himself at the head of four thousand men; all were ready to march at the idea of Ney's danger; but it was their last effort.

They proceeded in the darkness, by unknown roads, and had marched two leagues at random, halting every few minutes to listen. Their anxiety was already increased. Had they lost their way? were they too late? had their misfortunate comrades fallen? was it the victorious Russian army they were about to meet? In this uncertainty, Prince Eugene directed some cannon shot to be fired. Immediately after they fancied they heard signals of distress on that sea of snow; they proceeded from the third corps, which, having lost all its artillery, answered the cannon of the fourth by some volleys of platoon firing.

The two corps were thus directed towards their meeting. Ney and Eugene were the first to recognise each other; they ran up, Eugene more precipitately, and threw themselves into each other's arms. Eugene wept, Ney let some angry words escape him. The first was delighted, melted, and elevated by the warlike heroism which his chivalrous heroism had just saved! The latter, still heated from the combat, irritated at the dangers which the honour of the army had run in his person, and blaming Davoust, whom he wrongfully accused of having deserted him.

Some hours afterwards, when the latter wished to excuse himself, he could draw nothing from Ney but a severe look, and these words, "Monsieur le Maréchal, I have no reproaches to make to you; God is our witness and your judge!"

When the two corps had fairly recognised each other, they no longer preserved their ranks. Soldiers, officers, generals, all ran towards each other. Those of Eugene shook hands with those of Ney; they touched them with a joyful mixture of astonishment and curiosity, and pressed them to their bosoms with the tenderest compassion. The refreshments and brandy which they had just received they lavished upon them; they overwhelmed them with questions. They then all proceeded together in company, towards Orcha, all impatient, Eugene's soldiers to hear, and Ney's to tell their story.

1. The letters of Napoleon prove that, at this moment, he did *not* design to abandon his line of operations on Minsk.—*Ed.*

2. This road was well known to all the Polish officers on the staff of Napoleon's army.—*Ed.*

3. It was not till Napoleon arrived at Bobz, five days later than the date here assigned, that he despatched Eblé on this mission.—*Ed.*

CHAPTER VIII

NEY'S RETREAT FROM SMOLENSK

THEY stated, that on the 17th of November they had quitted Smolensk with twelve cannon, six thousand infantry, and three hundred cavalry, leaving there five thousand sick at the mercy of the enemy; and that had it not been for the noise of Platoff's cannon, and the explosion of the mines, their marshal would never have been able to bring away from the ruins of that city seven thousand unarmed stragglers who had taken shelter in them. They dwelt upon the attentions which their leader had shown to the wounded, and to the women and their children, proving upon this occasion that the bravest was also the most humane.

At the gates of the city an unnatural action struck them with a degree of horror which was still undiminished. A mother had abandoned her little son, only five years old; in spite of his cries and tears, she had driven him away from her sledge which was too heavily laden. She herself cried out with a distracted air, "that he had never seen France! that *he* would not regret it! as for *her*, *she* knew France! *she* was resolved to see France once more!" Twice did Ney himself replace the unfortunate child in the arms of his mother, twice did she cast him off on the frozen snow.

This solitary crime, amidst a thousand instances of the most devoted and sublime tenderness, they did not leave unpunished.

The unnatural mother was herself abandoned to the same snow from which her infant was snatched, and entrusted to another mother; this little orphan was exhibited in their ranks; he was afterwards seen at the Berezina, then at Wilna, even at Kowno, and finally escaped from all the horrors of the retreat.

The officers of Ney continued, in answer to the pressing questions of those of Eugene; they depicted themselves advancing towards Krasnoë, with their marshal at their head, completely across our immense wrecks, dragging after them one afflicted multitude, and preceded by another, whose steps were quickened by hunger.

They described how they found the bottom of each ravine filled with helmets, hussar-caps, trunks broken open, scattered garments, carriages and cannon, some overturned, others with the horses still harnessed, and the poor animals worn out, expiring, and half devoured.

How, near Korythnia, at the end of their first day's march, a violent cannonading and the whistling of several bullets over their heads, had led them to imagine that a battle had just commenced. This discharge appeared to proceed from before and quite close to them, even upon the road, and yet they could not get sight of a single enemy. Ricard and his division advanced with a view to discover them, but they only found, in a turn of the road, two French batteries abandoned, with their ammunition, and in a neighbouring field a horde of wretched Cossacks, who immediately fled, terrified at their audacity in setting fire to them, and at the noise they had made.

Ney's officers here interrupted their narrative to inquire in their turn what had passed? What was the cause of the general discouragement? Why had the cannon been abandoned to the enemy untouched? Had they not had time to spike them, or at least to spoil their ammunition?

In continuation, they said they had hitherto only discovered the traces of a disastrous march. But next morning there was a complete change, and they confessed their unlucky presentiments when they arrived at that field of snow reddened with blood, sprinkled with broken cannon and mutilated corpses. The dead bodies still marked the ranks and places of battle; they pointed them out to each other. *There* had been the fourteenth division; *there* were still to be seen, on the broken plates of their caps, the numbers of its regiments. *There* had been the Italian guard; there were its dead, whose uniforms were still distinguishable! But where were its living remnants? Vainly did they interrogate that field of blood, these lifeless forms, the motionless and frozen silence of the desert and the grave! they could neither penetrate the fate of their companions, nor that which awaited themselves.

Ney hurried them rapidly over all these ruins, and they had advanced without impediment to a part of the road, where it descends into a deep ravine, from which it rises into a broad and level height. It was that of Katova, and the same field of battle, where, three months before, in their triumphant march, they had beat Newerowskoi, and saluted Napoleon with the cannon which they had taken the day before from his enemies. They said they recollected the situation, notwithstanding the different appearance given to it by the snow.

Mortier's officers here exclaimed, "that it was in that very position that the emperor and they had waited for them on the 17th, fighting all the time." Very well, replied those of Ney, Kutusoff, or rather Miloradowitch, had taken Napoleon's place, for the old Russian general had not yet quitted Dobroé.

Their disbanded men were already retrograding, pointing to the snowy plains completely black with the enemy's troops, when a Russian, detaching himself from their army, descended the hill; he presented himself alone to their marshal, and either from an affectation of extreme politeness, respect for the misfortune of their leader, or dread of the effects of his despair, covered with honeyed words the summons to surrender.

It was Kutusoff who had sent him. "That field-marshal would not have presumed to make so cruel a proposal to so great a general, to a warrior so renowned, if there remained a single chance of safety for him. But there were eighty thousand

Russians before and around him, and if he had any doubt of it, Kutusoff offered to let him send a person to go through his ranks, and count his forces."

The Russian had not finished his speech, when suddenly forty discharges of grape shot, proceeding from the right of his army, and cutting our ranks to pieces, struck him with amazement, and interrupted what he had to say. At the same moment a French officer darted forward, seized, and was about to kill him as a traitor, when Ney checking this fury, called to him angrily, "A marshal never surrenders; there is no parleying under an enemy's fire; you are my prisoner." The unfortunate officer was disarmed, and placed in a situation of exposure to the fire of his own army. He was not released until we reached Kowno, after twenty-six days' captivity, sharing all our miseries, at liberty to escape, but restrained by his parole.

At the same time the enemy's fire became still hotter, and, as the narrators said, all the hills, which but an instant before looked cold and silent, became like so many volcanoes in eruption, but that Ney became still more elevated at it: then with a burst of enthusiasm that seemed to return every time they had occasion to mention his name in their narrative, they added, that in the midst of all this fire, that ardent man seemed to breathe an element exclusively his own.

Kutusoff had not deceived him. On the one side, there were eighty thousand men in complete ranks, full, deep, well-fed, and in double lines, a numerous cavalry, an immense artillery occupying a formidable position, in short, every thing, and fortune to boot, which alone is equal to all the rest. On the other side, five thousand soldiers, a straggling and dismembered column, a wavering and languishing march, arms defective and dirty, the greatest part mute and tottering in enfeebled hands.

And yet the French leader had no thought of yielding, nor even of dying, but of penetrating and cutting his way through the enemy; and that without the least idea that he was attempting a sublime effort. Alone, and looking no where for support, while all were supported by him, he followed the impulse of a strong natural temperament, and the pride of a conqueror, whom the habit of gaining improbable victories had impressed with the belief that every thing was possible.

But what most astonished them, was, that they had been all so docile; for all had shown themselves worthy of him; and they added, that it was there they clearly saw that it is not merely great obstinacy, great designs, or great temerity, which constitute greatness, but principally the power of influencing and supporting others.

Ricard and his fifteen hundred soldiers were in front. Ney impelled them against the enemy, and prepared the rest of his army to follow them. That division descended with the road into the ravine, but ascending from it, was driven back, overwhelmed by the first Russian line.

The marshal, without being intimidated, or allowing others to be so, collected the survivors, placed them in reserve, and proceeded forward in their place; Ledru, Razout, and Marchand seconded him. He ordered four hundred Illyrians to take the enemy on their left flank, and with three thousand men he himself mounted in front to the assault. He made no harangue; he marched at their head, setting the example, which in a hero is the most eloquent of all oratorical movements, and the most imperious of all orders. All followed him. They attacked, penetrated, and overturned the first Russian line, and without halting were precipitating themselves upon the second; but before they could reach it, a volley of artillery and grape shot poured down upon them. In an instant Ney saw all his generals wounded, the greatest part of his soldiers killed; their ranks were empty, their shapeless column whirled round, tottered, fell back, and drew him along with it.

Ney found that he had attempted an impossibility, and he waited until the flight of his men had once more placed the ravine between them and the enemy, that ravine which was now his sole resource; there, equally hopeless and fearless he halted and rallied them. He drew up two thousand men against eighty thousand; he returned the fire of two hundred cannon with six pieces, and made fortune blush that she should ever betray such courage.

She it was, doubtless, who then struck Kutusoff with inertness. To their infinite surprise, they saw this Russian Fabius running into extremes, like all imitators, persisting in what he called his humanity and prudence, remaining upon his heights with his pompous virtues, without allowing himself, or daring to conquer, as if he was astonished at his own superiority. Seeing that Napoleon had been conquered by his rashness, he pushed his horror of that fault to the very extreme of the opposite vice.

It required, however, but a transport of indignation in any one of the Russian corps to have completely extinguished us; but all were afraid to make a decisive movement; they remained clinging to their soil with the immobility of slaves, as if they had no boldness but in their watchword, or energy but in their obedience. This discipline, which formed their glory in *their* retreat, was their disgrace in *ours*.

They were for a long time uncertain, not knowing what enemy they were fighting with; for they had imagined that Ney had retreated from Smolensk by the right bank of the Dnieper; they were mistaken, as is frequently the case, from supposing that their enemy had done what he ought to have done.

At the same time, the Illyrians had returned completely in disorder; they had had a most singular adventure. In their advance to the left flank of the enemy's position, these four hundred men had met with five thousand Russians returning from a partial engagement, with a French eagle, and several of our soldiers prisoners.

These two hostile troops, the one returning to its position, the other going to attack it, advanced in the same direction, side by side, measuring each other with their eyes, but neither of them venturing to commence the engagement. They marched so close to each other, that from the middle of the Russian ranks the French prisoners stretched out their arms towards their friends, conjuring them to come and deliver them. The latter called out to them to come to them, and they would receive and defend them; but no one moved on either side. Just then Ney was overthrown, and they retreated along with him.

Kutusoff, however, relying more on his artillery than his soldiers, sought only to conquer at a distance. His fire so completely commanded all the ground occupied by the French, that the same bullet which prostrated a man in the first rank, proceeded to deal destruction in the last of the train of carriages, among the women who had fled from Moscow.

Under this murderous hail, Ney's soldiers remained astonished, motionless, looking at their chief, waiting his decision to be satisfied that they were lost, hoping they knew not why, or rather, according to the remark of one of their officers, because in the midst of this extreme peril they saw his spirit calm and tranquil, like a thing which is in its place. His countenance became silent and thoughtful; he was watching the enemy's army, which, becoming more suspicious since the successful artifice of Prince Eugene, extended itself to a great distance on his flanks, in order to shut him out from all means of preservation.

The approach of night began to render objects indistinct; winter, which in that sole point was favourable to our retreat, brought it on quickly. Ney had been waiting for it, but the advantage he took of the respite was to order his men to return towards Smolensk. They all said that at these words they remained frozen with astonishment. Even his aide-de-camp could not believe his ears; he remained silent like one who did not understand what he heard, and looked at his general with amazement. But the marshal having repeated the same order in a brief and imperious tone, they recognised a resolution taken, a resource discovered that self-confidence which inspires others with the same quality, and a spirit which overrules its situation, however perilous that may be. They immediately obeyed, and without hesitation turned their backs on their own army, on Napoleon, and on France! They returned once more into that fatal Russia. Their retrograde march lasted an hour; they passed again over the field of battle marked by the remains of the army of Italy; there they halted, and their marshal, who had remained alone in the rear-guard, then rejoined them.

Their eyes followed his every movement. What was he going to do; and whatever might be his plan, whither would he direct his steps, without a guide, in an unknown country? But he, with his warlike instinct, halted on the edge of a ravine of such depth, as to make it obvious that a rivulet ran through it. He made them clear away the snow and break the ice; then consulting his map, he exclaimed, "That this was one of the streams which flowed into the Dnieper! this must be our guide, and we must follow it; it would lead us to that river, which we must cross, and on the other side we should be safe!" He immediately proceeded in that direction.

However at a little distance from the high road, which he had abandoned, he again halted in a village, the name of which they knew not, but believed it was either Fomina, or Danikowa. There he rallied his troops, and made them light their fires, as if he intended to take up his quarters in it for the night. Some Cossacks who followed him took that for granted, and no doubt sent immediately to apprise Kutusoff of the spot where, next day, a French marshal would surrender his arms to him; for shortly after the noise of their cannon was again heard.

Ney listened: "Is this Davoust at last," he exclaimed, "who has recollected me?" and he listened a second time. But there were regular intervals between the firing; it was a salvo. Being then fully satisfied that the Russian army was triumphing by anticipation over his captivity, he swore he would give the lie to their joy, and immediately resumed his march.

At the same time his Poles ransacked the country. A lame peasant was the only inhabitant they had discovered; this was an unlooked-for piece of good fortune. He informed them that they were within the distance of a league of the Dnieper, but that it was not fordable there, and could not yet be frozen over. "It will be so," was the marshal's remark; but when it was observed to him that the thaw had just commenced, he added, "that it did not signify, we must pass, as there was no other resource."

At last, about eight o'clock, after passing through a village, the ravine terminated, and the lame Russian, who walked first, halted and pointed to the river. They imagined that this must have been between Syrokorenia and Gusinoé. Ney, and those immediately behind him, ran up to it. They found the river sufficiently frozen to bear their weight, the course of the flakes which it bore along to that point, being counteracted by a sudden turn in its banks, was there suspended; the winter had completely frozen it over only in that single spot; both above and below it, its surface was still moveable.

This observation was sufficient to make their first sensation of joy give way to uneasiness. This hostile river might only offer them a treacherous appearance. One officer devoted himself for the rest; he crossed to the other side with great difficulty. He returned, and reported that the men, and perhaps some of the horses, might pass over, but that the rest must be abandoned, and there was no time to lose, as the ice was beginning to give way in consequence of the thaw.

But in this nocturnal and silent march across fields, of a column composed of weakened and wounded men, and women with their children, they had been unable to keep close enough, to prevent their extending, separating, and losing the traces of each other in the darkness. Ney perceived that only a part of his people had come up; nevertheless, he might have still surmounted the obstacle, thereby secured his own safety, and waited on the other side. The idea never once entered his mind; some one proposed it to him, but he rejected it instantly. He allowed three hours for the rallying; and without suffering himself to be agitated by impatience, or the danger of waiting so long, he wrapped himself up in his cloak, and passed these three dangerous hours in a profound sleep on the bank of the river. So much did he possess of the temperament of great men, a strong mind in a robust body, and that vigorous health, without which no man can ever expect to be a hero.

CHAPTER IX

NEY'S ARRIVAL AT ORCHA

AT last, about midnight, the passage began; but the first persons who ventured on the ice, called out that the ice was bending under them, that it was sinking, that they were up to their knees in water; immediately after which, that frail support was heard splitting with frightful cracks, which were prolonged in the distance, as in the breaking up of a frost. All halted in consternation.

Ney ordered them to pass only one at a time; they proceeded with caution, not knowing sometimes in the darkness, if they were putting their feet on the flakes or into a chasm; for there were paces where they were obliged to clear large crevices, and jump from one piece of ice to another, at the risk of falling between them and disappearing for ever. The first hesitated, but those who were behind kept calling to them to make haste.

When at last, after several of these dreadful panics, they reached the opposite bank and fancied themselves saved, a perpendicular steep, entirely covered with rime, again opposed their landing. Many were thrown back upon the ice, which they broke in their fall, or which bruised them. By their account, this Russian river and its banks appeared only to have contributed with regret, by surprise, and as it were by compulsion, to their escape.

But what affected them with the greatest horror in their relation, was the trouble and distraction of the females and the sick, when it became necessary to abandon, along with the baggage, the remains of their fortune, their provisions, and, in short, their whole resources against the present and the future. They saw them stripping themselves, selecting, throwing away, taking up again, and falling with exhaustion and grief upon the frozen bank of the river. They seemed to shudder again at the recollection of the horrible sight of so many men scattered over that abyss, the continual noise of persons falling, the cries of such as sunk in, and, above all, of the wailing and despair of the wounded, who, from their carts, which durst not venture on this weak support, stretched out their hands to their companions, and entreated not to be left behind.

Their leader then determined to attempt the passage of several wagons, loaded with these poor creatures; but in the middle of the river the ice sunk down and separated. Then were heard on the opposite bank, proceeding from the gulf, first cries of anguish long and piercing, then stifled and feeble groans, and last of all an awful silence. All had disappeared!

Ney was looking steadfastly at the abyss with an air of consternation, when through the darkness he imagined he saw an object still moving; it turned out to be one of those unfortunate persons, an officer named Briqueville, whom a deep wound in the groin had disabled from standing upright. A large piece of ice had borne him up. He was soon distinctly seen, dragging himself from one piece to another on his knees and hands, and on his getting near enough to the side, the marshal himself caught hold of and saved him.

The losses since the preceding day amounted to four thousand stragglers and three thousand soldiers, either dead or missing; the cannon and the whole of the baggage were lost; there remained to Ney scarcely three thousand soldiers, and about as many disbanded men. Finally, when all these sacrifices were consummated, and all that had been able to cross the river were collected, they resumed their march, and the vanquished river became once more their friend and their guide.

They proceeded at random and uncertain, when one of them happening to fall, recognised a beaten road; it was but too much so, for those who were marching first, stooping and using their hands, as well as their eyes, halted in alarm, exclaiming, "that they saw the marks quite fresh of a great number of cannon and horses." They had, therefore, only avoided one hostile army to fail into the midst of another; at a time when they could scarcely walk, they must be again obliged to fight! The war was therefore everywhere! But Ney made them push on, and without disturbing himself, continued to follow these menacing traces.

They brought them to a village called Gusinoé, into which they entered suddenly, and seized every thing; they found in it all that they had been in want of since they left Moscow, inhabitants, provisions, repose, warm dwellings, and a hundred Cossacks, who only awoke to find themselves prisoners. Their reports, and the necessity of taking some refreshment to enable him to proceed, detained the marshal there a few minutes.

About ten o'clock, they reached two other villages, and were resting themselves there, when suddenly the surrounding forests appeared to be filled with movements. They had scarcely time to call to each other, to look about, and to concentrate themselves in the village which was nearest to the Borysthenes, when thousands of Cossacks came pouring out from between the trees, and surrounded the unfortunate troop with their lances and their cannon.

These were Platoff, and all his hordes, who were following the right bank of the Dnieper. They might have burnt the village, discovered the weakness of Ney's force, and exterminated it; but for three hours they remained motionless, without even firing; for what reason is not known. The account since given by themselves is, that they had no orders; that at that moment their leader was not in a state to give any: and that in Russia no one dares to take upon himself a responsibility that does not belong to him.

The bold countenance of Ney kept them in check. He himself and a few soldiers were sufficient; he even ordered the rest of his people to continue their repast till night came on. He then caused the order to be circulated to decamp in silence, to give notice to each other in a low tone of voice, and to march as compact as possible. Afterwards, they all began their march together; but their very first step was like a signal given to the enemy, who immediately discharged the whole of his artillery at them: all his squadrons also put themselves in movement at once.

At the noise occasioned by this, the disarmed stragglers, of whom there were yet between three and four thousand, took the alarm. This flock of men wandered here and there; the great mass of them kept running about in uncertainty, sometimes attempting to throw themselves into the ranks of the soldiers, who drove them back. Ney contrived to keep them between him and the Russians, whose fire was principally absorbed by these useless beings. The most timid, therefore, in this instance, served as a covering to the bravest.

At the same time that the marshal made a rampart of those poor wretches to cover his right flank, he regained the banks of the Dnieper, and by that covered his left flank; he marched on thus between the two, proceeding from wood to wood, from one undulation of the ground to another, taking advantage of all the windings, and of the least accidents of the soil. Whenever he ventured to any distance from the river, which he was frequently obliged to do, Platoff then surrounded him on all sides.

In this manner, for two days and a distance of twenty leagues, did six thousand Cossacks keep constantly buzzing about the flanks of their column, now reduced to fifteen hundred men in arms, keeping it in a state of siege, disappearing before its sallies, and returning again instantly like their Scythian ancestors; but with this fatal difference, that they managed their cannon mounted on sledges, and discharged their bullets in their flight, with the same agility which their forefathers exhibited in the management of their bows and the discharge of their arrows.

The night brought some relief, and at first they plunged into the darkness with a degree of joy; but then, if any one halted for a moment to bid a last adieu to some worn-out or wounded comrade, who sunk to rise no more, he ran the risk of losing the traces of his column. Under such circumstances there were many cruel moments, and not a few instances of despair. At last, however, the enemy slackened his pursuit.

This unfortunate column was proceeding more tranquilly, groping its way through a thick wood, when all at once, a few paces .before it, a brilliant light and several discharges of cannon flashed in the faces of the men in the first rank. Seized with terror, they fancied that there was an end of them, that they were cut off, that their last day was now come, and they fell down terrified; those who were behind got entangled among them, and were brought to the ground. Ney, who saw that all was lost, rushed forward, ordered the charge to be beat, as if he had foreseen the attack, called out, "Comrades, now is your time: forward! We have them!" At these words, his soldiers, who but a minute before were in consternation, and fancied themselves surprised, believed they were about to surprise their foes; from being vanquished, they rose up conquerors; they rushed upon the enemy, who had already disappeared, and whose precipitate flight through the forest they heard at a distance.

They passed quickly through this wood; but, about ten o'clock at night, they met with a small river embanked in a deep ravine, which they were obliged to cross one by one, as they had done the Dnieper. Intent on the pursuit of these poor fellows, the Cossacks again got sight of them, and tried to take advantage of that moment: but Ney, by a few discharges of his musketry, again repulsed them. They surmounted this obstacle with difficulty, and in an hour after reached a large village, where hunger and exhaustion compelled them to halt for two hours longer.

The next day, the 19th of November, from midnight till ten o'clock in the morning, they kept marching on, without meeting any other enemy than a hilly country; but about that time Platoff's columns again made their appearance, and Ney halted and faced them, under the protection of the skirts of a wood. As long as the day lasted, his soldiers were obliged to resign themselves to see the enemy's bullets overturning the trees which served to shelter them, and furrowing their bivouacs; for they had now nothing but small arms, which could not keep the Cossack artillery at a sufficient distance.

On the return of night, the marshal gave the usual signal, and they proceeded on their march to Orcha. During the preceding day, he had already despatched thither Pchébendowski with fifty horsemen, to demand assistance; they must already have arrived there, unless the enemy had already gained possession of that town.

Ney's officers concluded their narrative by saying, that during the rest of their march, they had met with several formidable obstacles, but that they did not think them worth relating. They continued, however, speaking enthusiastically of their marshal, and making us sharers of their admiration of him for even his equals had no idea of being jealous of him. He had been too much regretted, and his preservation had excited too agreeable emotions, to allow envy to have any part in them; besides, Ney had placed himself completely beyond its reach. As to himself, in all this heroism, he had gone so little beyond his natural disposition, that had it not been for the éclat of his glory in the eyes, the gestures, and the acclamations of every one, he would never have imagined that he had performed a sublime action.

And this was not an enthusiasm of surprise. Each of the latter days had had its remarkable men; amongst others, that of the 16th had Eugene, that of the 17th had Mortier; but after this time, Ney was universally proclaimed the hero of the retreat.

The distance between Smolensk and Orcha is hardly five days' march. In that short passage, what a harvest of glory had been reaped! how little space and time are required to establish an immortal renown! Of what nature then are those great inspirations, that invisible and impalpable germ of great devotedness, produced in a few moments, issuing from a single heart, and which must fill time and space.

When Napoleon, who was two leagues farther on, heard that Ney had again made his appearance, he leaped and shouted for joy, and exclaimed, "I have then saved, my eagles! I would have given three hundred millions from my treasury, sooner than have lost such a man."

BOOK XI

CHAPTER I

CRITICISM OF THE CAMPAIGN

THE army had thus for the third and last time repassed the Dnieper, a river half Russian and half Polish, but of Muscovite origin. It runs from east to west as far as Orcha, where it appears as if it would penetrate into Poland; but there the heights of Lithuania oppose its farther progress, and compel it to turn abruptly towards the south, and to become the frontier of the two countries.

Kutusoff and his eighty thousand Russians halted before this feeble obstacle. Hitherto they had been rather the spectators than the authors of our calamities; we saw them no more; our army was delivered from the punishment of their joy.

In this war, and as always happens, the character of Kutusoff availed him more than his talents. So long as it was necessary to deceive and to temporise, his crafty spirit, his indolence, and his great age, acted of themselves; he was the creature of circumstances, which he ceased to be as soon as it became necessary to march rapidly, to pursue, to anticipate, and to attack.

But after passing Smolensk, Platoff passed over to the right flank of the road, in order to join Wittgenstein. The war was then entirely transferred to that side.

On the 22nd of November, the army had a disagreeable march from Orcha to Borizoff, on a wide road, (skirted by a double row of large birch trees,) in which the snow had melted, and through a deep and liquid mud. The weakest were drowned in it; it detained and delivered to the Cossacks such of our wounded as, under the idea of a continuance of the frost, had exchanged their wagons for sledges.

In the midst of this gradual decay, an action was witnessed exhibiting the antique energy. Two marines of the guard were cut off from their column by a band of Cossacks, who seemed determined to take them. One became discouraged and wished to surrender; the other continued to fight, and called out to him, that if he was coward enough to do so, he would certainly shoot him. In fact, seeing his companion throw away his musket, and stretching out his arms to the enemy, he brought him to the ground just as he fell into the hands of the Cossacks; then profiting by their surprise, he quickly reloaded his musket, with which he threatened the most forward. He kept them thus at bay, retreated from tree to tree, gained ground upon them, and succeeded in rejoining his troop.

It was during the early part of the march to Borizoff, that the news of the fall of Minsk became generally known in the army. The leaders themselves began then to look around them with consternation; their imagination, tormented with such a long continuance of frightful spectacles, gave them glimpses of a still more fatal futurity. In their private conversation, several exclaimed, that, "like Charles XII. in the Ukraine, Napoleon had carried his army to Moscow only to destroy it."

Others would not agree in attributing the calamities we at present suffered to that incursion. Without wishing to excuse the sacrifices to which we had submitted, in the hope of terminating the war by a single campaign, they asserted, "that that hope had been well founded; that in pushing his line of operation as far as Moscow, Napoleon had given to that lengthened column a base sufficiently broad and solid."

They showed "the trace of this base marked out by the Dwina, the Dnieper, the Ula, and the Berezina, from Riga to Bobruisk; they said that Macdonald, Saint Cyr and De Wrede,

Victor and Dombrowski, were there waiting for them; there were thus, including Schwartzenberg, and even Augereau, (who protected the interval between the Elbe and the Niemen with fifty thousand men,) nearly two hundred and eighty thousand soldiers on the defensive, who, from the north to the south, supported the attack of one hundred and fifty thousand men upon the east; and from thence they argued, that this *point* upon Moscow, however hazardous it might appear, had been both sufficiently prepared, and was worthy of the genius of Napoleon, and that its success was possible; in fact, its failure had been entirely occasioned by errors in detail."

They then brought to mind our useless waste of lives before Smolensk, Junot's inaction at Valoutina, and they maintained, "that in spite of all these losses, Russia would have been completely conquered on the field of battle of the Moskwa, if marshal Ney's first successes had been followed up.

"Even at last, although the expedition had failed in a military point of view, by the indecision of that day, and politically by the burning of Moscow, the army might still have returned from it safe and sound. From the time of our entrance into that capital, had not the Russian general and the Russian winter allowed us, the one forty, and the other fifty days, to recover ourselves, and to make our retreat?"

Deploring then the rash obstinacy of the stay at Moscow, and the fatal hesitation at Malo-Yaroslawetz, they proceeded to reckon up their losses. Since their departure from Moscow, they had lost all their baggage, five hundred cannon, thirty-one eagles, twenty-seven generals, forty thousand prisoners, sixty thousand dead; all that remained were forty thousand unarmed stragglers, and eight thousand effective soldiers.

Last of all, when their column of attack had been destroyed, they asked, "by what fatality it had happened, that its remains, when collected at its base, which had been vigorously supported, were left without knowing where to halt, or to take fresh breath? Why could they not even concentrate themselves at Minsk and at Wilna, behind the marshes of the Berezina, and there keep back the enemy, at least for some time, take advantage of the winter, and recruit themselves?

"But no, all is lost by another side, by the fault of entrusting an Austrian to guard the magazines, and cover the retreat of all these brave armies, and not placing a military leader at Wilna or Minsk, with a force sufficient either to supply the insufficiency of the Austrian army to meet the combined armies of Moldavia and Volhynia, or to prevent its betraying us."

Those who made such complaints were not unaware of the presence of the duke of Bassano at Wilna; but notwithstanding the talents of that minister, and the great confidence the emperor placed in him, they considered that being a stranger to the art of war, and overloaded with the cares of a great administration, and of every thing political, the direction of military affairs should not have been left to him.[1] Such, however, were the complaints of those whose sufferings left them the leisure necessary for observation. That a fault had been committed, it was impossible to doubt; but to say how it might have been avoided, to appreciate properly the motives which had occasioned it, in so great a crisis, and in the presence of so great a man, is more than any one would venture to undertake. Who is there besides who does not know, that in these hazardous and gigantic enterprises, every thing becomes a fault when the object of them has failed?

Although the treachery of Schwartzenberg was by no means so evident, it is certain, that, with the exception of the three French generals who were with him, the whole of the grand army considered it as beyond a doubt. They said, "that Walpole's only object at Vienna was to act as a secret agent of England; that he and Metternich had composed between them the perfidious instructions which were sent to Schwartzenberg. Hence it was, that ever since the 20th of September, the day when the arrival of Tchitchakoff and the battle of Lutsk closed the victorious career of Schwartzenberg, that marshal had repassed the Bug, and covered Warsaw by uncovering Minsk; hence his perseverance in that false manœuvre: hence, after a feeble effort towards Brezck-litowsky on the 10th of October, his neglect to avail himself of Tchitchakoff's inaction by getting between him and Minsk, and hence his losing his time in military promenades, and in insignificant marches towards Briansk, Bialystock, and Volkowitz.

"He had thus allowed the admiral to take rest, and rally his sixty thousand men, to divide them into two, to leave one half with Sacken to oppose him, and to set out on the 27th of October with the other half to take possession of Minsk and of Borizoff, of the magazine and the passage of Napoleon, and of his winter quarters. Then only did Schwartzenberg put himself in the rear of this hostile movement, instead of anticipating it, as he had orders to do, leaving Regnier in the presence of Sacken, and marching so slowly, that from the very first the admiral had got five marches the start of him.

"On the 14th of November, at Volkowitz, Sacken attacked Regnier, separated him from the Austrians, and pressed him so closely, that he was obliged to call Schwartzenberg to his aid. Immediately, the latter, as if he had been expecting the summons, retrograded, leaving Minsk to its fate. It is true that he released Regnier, that he beat Sacken, and destroyed half his army, pursuing him as far as the Bug; but on the 16th of November, the very day of his victory, Minsk was taken by Tchitchakoff: this was a double victory for Austria. Thus all appearances were preserved; the new field-marshal satisfied the wishes of his government, which was equally the enemy of the Russians whom he had just weakened on one side, and of Napoleon, whom on the other he had betrayed to them."

Such was the language of almost the whole of the grand army; its leader was silent, either because he expected no more zeal on the part of an ally, or from policy, or because he believed that Schwartzenberg had acted with sufficient honour, in sending him the sort of notice which he did six weeks before, when he was at Moscow. However, he did address some reproaches to the field-marshal. To these the latter replied, by complaining bitterly, first, of the double and contradictory instructions which he had received, to cover Warsaw and Minsk at the same time; and second, of the false news which had been transmitted to him by the duke of Bassano.

He said, "that minister had constantly represented to him that the grand army was retreating safe and sound, in good order, and always formidable. Why had he been trifled with, by sending him bulletins made to deceive the idlers of the capital? His only reason for not making greater efforts to join the grand army was, because he believed that it was fully able to protect itself."

He also alleged his own weakness. "How could it be expected that with twenty thousand men he could so long keep sixty thousand in check? In that situation, if Tchitchakoff stole a few marches on him, was it at all wonderful? Had he then hesitated to follow him, to leave Gallicia, his point of departure, his magazines, and his depôt? If he ceased his pursuit, it was only because Regnier and Durutte, the two French generals, summoned him in the most urgent manner to come to their assistance. Both they and he had reason to expect that Maret, Oudinôt, or Victor, would provide for the safety of Minsk."

1. "These reproaches," says M. Gourgaud, "are groundless. The duke of Bassano was at Wilna with his chancery and the diplomatic body, which could not follow the army. He managed there the business of his department, and at the same time exercised a paramount influence in the government of the country. The orders relative to military operations did not pass through his office; the prince of Neufchatel (Berthier) always forwarded them direct to those generals who were acting out of the sphere which recived its impulse immediately from the emperor."—*Ed.*

CHAPTER II

NAPOLEON'S DISTRESS

IN fact, we had scarcely any right to accuse others of treachery, when we had betrayed ourselves, for all had failed in their duty in the time of need.

At Wilna, they appeared to have had no suspicion of the real state of affairs; and at a time when the garrisons, the depôts, the marching battalions, and the divisions of Durutte, Loison, and Dombrowski, between the Berezina and the Vistula, might have formed at Minsk an army of thirty thousand men, three thousand men, headed by a general of no reputation, were the only forces which Tchitchakoff found there to oppose him. It was a known fact that this handful of young soldiers was exposed in front of a river, into which they were precipitated by the admiral, whereas, if they had been placed on the other side, that obstacle would have protected them for some time.

For thus, as frequently happens, the faults of the general plan had led to faults of detail. The governor of Minsk had been negligently chosen. He was, it was said, one of those men who undertake every thing, who promise every thing, and who do nothing. On the 16th of November, he lost that capital, and with it four thousand seven hundred sick, the warlike ammunition, and two million rations of provisions. It was five days since the news of this loss had reached Dombrowna, and the news of a still greater calamity came on the heels of it.

This same governor had retreated towards Borizoff. There he neglected to inform Oudinôt, who was only at the distance of two marches, to come to his assistance; and failed to support Dombrowski, who made a hasty march thither from Bobruisk and Igumen. The latter did not arrive, however, in the night of the 20th and 21st, at the *tête-du-pont* until after the enemy had taken possession of it; notwithstanding, he expelled Tchitchakoff's vanguard, took possession of it, and defended himself gallantly there until the evening of the 21st; but being then overpowered by the fire of the Russian artillery, which took him in the flank, and attacked by a force more than double his own, he was driven across the river, and out of the town, as far as the Moscow road.

This disaster was wholly unexpected by Napoleon: he supposed that he had completely prepared against it by the instructions he had sent to Victor from Moscow, on the 6th of October. These instructions "anticipated a warm attack from Wittgenstein or Tchitchakoff: they recommend Victor to keep within reach of Polotsk and of Minsk; to have a prudent, discreet, and intelligent officer about Schwartzenberg; to keep up a regular correspondence with Minsk, and to send other agents in different directions."

But Wittgenstein having made his attack before Tchitchakoff, the nearer and more pressing danger had occupied every one's attention; the wise instructions of the 6th of October had not been repeated by Napoleon and they appeared to have been entirely forgotten by his lieutenant. Finally, when the emperor learned at Dombrowna the loss of Minsk, he had no idea that Borizoff was in such imminent danger, as when he passed the next day through Orcha, he had the whole of his bridge equipage burnt.[1]

His correspondence also of the 20th of November with Victor attested his security; it supposed that Oudinôt would have nearly arrived on the 25th at Borizoff, while that place had been taken possession of by Tchitchakoff on the 21st.

It was on the day immediately subsequent to that fatal catastrophe, at the distance of three marches from Borizoff, and upon the high road, that an officer arrived and announced to Napoleon this fresh disaster. The emperor, striking the ground with his stick, and darting a furious look to heaven, pronounced these words, "Is it then written above that we shall now commit nothing but faults?"

Meanwhile marshal Oudinôt, who was already marching towards Minsk, totally ignorant of what had happened, halted on the 21st between Bobr and Kroupki, where in the middle of the night general Brownikowski arrived to announce to him his own defeat, as well as that of general Dombrowski; that Borizoff was taken, and that the Russians were following close at his heels.

On the 22nd the marshal marched to meet them, and rallied the remains of Dombrowski's force.

On the 23rd, at three leagues on the other side of Borizoff, he came in contact with the Russian vanguard, which he overthrew, taking from it nine hundred men and fifteen hundred carriages, and drove back by the united force of his artillery, infantry, and cavalry, as far as the Berezina; but the remains of Lambert's force, on repassing Borizoff and that river, destroyed the bridge.

Napoleon was then at Toloczina: he made them describe to him the position of Borizoff. They assured him that at that point the Berezina was not merely a river but a lake of moving ice; that the bridge was three hundred fathoms in length; that it had been irreparably destroyed and the passage by it rendered henceforth impracticable.

At that moment arrived a general of engineers, who had just returned from the duke of Belluno's corps. Napoleon interrogated him; the general declared "that he saw no means of escape but through the middle of Wittgenstein's army." The emperor replied, "that he must find a direction in which he could turn his back to all the enemy's generals, to Kutusoff, to Wittgenstein, to Tchitchakoff;" and he pointed with his finger on the map to the course of the Berezina below Borizoff; it was there he wished to cross the river. But the general objected to him the presence of Tchitchakoff on the right bank; the emperor then pointed to another passage below the first, and then to a third, still nearer to the Dnieper. Recollecting, however, that he was then approaching the country of the Cossacks he stopped short, and exclaimed, "Oh yes! Pultawa! that is like Charles XII.!"

In fact, every disaster which Napoleon could anticipate had occurred; the melancholy conformity, therefore, of his situation with that of the Swedish conqueror, threw his mind into such a state of agitation, that his health became still more seriously affected than it had been at Malo-Yaroslawetz. Among the expressions he made use of, loud enough to be overheard, was this: "See what happens when we heap faults on faults!"

Nevertheless, these first movements were the only ones that escaped him, and the valet-de-chambre who assisted him was the only person that witnessed his agitation. Duroc, Daru, and Berthier, all said, that they knew nothing of it, that they saw him unshaken; this was very true, humanly speaking, as he retained sufficient command over himself to avoid betraying his anxiety, and as the strength of man is most frequently shown in concealing his weakness.

A remarkable conversation, which was overheard the same night, will show better than any thing else how critical was his position, and how well he bore it. The night was far advanced; Napoleon had gone to bed. Duroc and Daru, who remained in his chamber, fancying that he was asleep, were giving way, in whispers, to the most gloomy conjectures; he overheard them, however, and the words "prisoner of state" coming to his ear, "How;" exclaimed he, "do you believe they would dare?" Daru after his surprise, immediately answered, "that if we were compelled to surrender, we must be prepared for every thing; that he had no reliance on an enemy's generosity; that we all knew too well that great state policy considered itself identified with morality, and was regulated by no law." "But

France," said the emperor, "what would France say?" "Oh, as to France," continued Daru, "we are at liberty to make a thousand conjectures more or less disagreeable, but none of us can know what will take place there." And he then added, "that for the sake of the emperor's chief officers, as well as the emperor himself, the most fortunate thing would be, if by the air or otherwise, as the earth was closed upon us, the emperor could reach France, from whence he could much more certainly provide for their safety, than by remaining among them!" "Then I suppose I am in your way?" replied the emperor, smiling. "Yes, Sire." "And you have no wish to be a prisoner of state?" Daru replied in the same tone, "that it was enough for him to be a prisoner of war." On which the emperor remained for some time in a profound silence; then with a more serious air: "Are all the reports of my ministers burnt?" "Sire, hitherto you would not allow that to be done." "Very well, go and destroy them; for it must be confessed we are in a most melancholy position." This was the sole avowal which it extorted from him, and on that idea he went to sleep, knowing, when it was necessary, how to postpone every thing to the next day.

His orders displayed equal firmness. Oudinôt had just sent to inform him of his determination to overthrow Lambert: this he approved of, and he also urged him to make himself master of a passage, either above or below Borizoff. He was desirous that by the 24th this passage should be fixed on and the preparations begun, and that he should be apprised of it, in order to make his march correspond. Far from thinking of making his escape through the midst of these three hostile armies, his only idea now was that of beating Tchitchakoff, and retaking Minsk.

It is true, that eight hours afterwards, in a second letter to the duke of Reggio, he resigned himself to cross the Berezina near Veselowo, and to retreat directly upon Wilna, by Vileika, avoiding the Russian admiral.

But on the 24th he learned that the passage could only be attempted near Studzianka: that at that spot the river was only fifty-four fathoms wide, and six feet deep; that they would land on the other side, in a marsh, under the fire of a commanding position strongly occupied by the enemy.

1. The bridge-equipage was burned that the horses belonging to it might be appropriated to the artillery which was at Orcha. It would have been difficult to get it to Borizoff, and, besides, Napoleon did not expect that Borizoff would be so hastily abandoned, as it was, to the enemy.—*Ed.*

CHAPTER III

PASSAGE THROUGH
THE FOREST OF MINSK

ALL hope of passing between the Russian armies was thus lost; driven by the armies of Kutusoff and Wittgenstein upon the Berezina, there was no alternative but to cross that river in the teeth of the army of Tchitchakoff, which lined its banks.

Ever since the 23rd, Napoleon had been preparing for it as for a desperate action. And first he had the eagles of all the corps brought in, and burnt.[1] He rallied into two battalions, eighteen hundred dismounted cavalry of his guard, of whom only eleven hundred and fifty-four were armed with muskets and carabines.

The cavalry of the army of Moscow was so completely destroyed, that Latour-Maubourg had not now remaining under his command more than two hundred and fifty men on horseback. The emperor collected around his person all the officers of that arm who were still mounted; he styled this troop, consisting of about five hundred officers, his *sacred squadron*. Grouchy and Sebastiani commanded it; generals of divisions served in it as captains.

Napoleon ordered further, that all the useless carriages should be burnt; that no officer should retain more than one; that half the wagons and carriages of all the corps should also be burnt, and that the horses should be given to the artillery of the guard.

The officers of that arm had orders to take all the draught-cattle within their reach, even the horses of the emperor himself, sooner than abandon a single cannon, or ammunition wagon.

After giving these orders, he plunged into the gloomy and immense forest of Minsk, in which a few hamlets and wretched habitations have scarcely cleared a few open spots. The noise of Wittgenstein's artillery filled it with its echo. That Russian general came rushing from the north upon the right flank of our expiring column; he brought back with him the winter which had quitted us at the same time with Kutusoff; the news of his threatening march quickened our steps. From forty to fifty thousand men, women, and children, glided through this forest as precipitately as their weakness and the slipperiness of the ground, from the frost beginning again to set in, would allow.

These forced marches, commenced before day-light, and which did not finish at its close, dispersed all that had remained together. They lost themselves in the darkness of these great forests and long nights. They halted at night and resumed their march in the morning, in darkness, at random, and without hearing the signal; the dissolution of the remains of the corps was then completed; all were mixed and confounded together.

In this last stage of weakness and confusion, as we were approaching Borizoff, we heard loud cries before us. Some rushed forward, fancying it was an attack. It was Victor's army, which had been feebly driven back by Wittgenstein to the right side of our road, where it remained waiting for the emperor to pass by. Still quite complete and full of animation, it received the emperor, as soon as he made his appearance, with the customary, but now long-forgotten, acclamations.

Of our disasters it had heard nothing: they had been carefully concealed even from its leaders. When therefore, instead of that grand column which had conquered Moscow, its soldiers perceived behind Napoleon only a train of spectres covered with rags, with female pelisses, pieces of carpet, or dirty cloaks, half burnt and riddled by the fires, and with nothing on their feet but rags of all sorts, their consternation was extreme. They looked terrified at the sight of those unfortunate soldiers, as they defiled before them, with lean carcasses, faces black with dirt, and hideous bristly beards, unarmed, shameless, marching confusedly, with their heads bent, their eyes fixed on the ground and silent, like a troop of captives.

But what astonished them more than all, was to see the number of colonels and generals scattered about and insulated, who seemed only occupied about themselves, and thinking of nothing but saving the wrecks of their property, or their persons; they were marching pell-mell with the soldiers, who did not notice them, to whom they had no longer any commands to give, and of whom they had nothing to expect, all ties between them being broken, and all distinction of ranks obliterated by the common misery.

The soldiers of Victor and Oudinôt could not believe their eyes. Moved with compassion their officers, with tears in their eyes, detained such of their companions as they recognised in the crowd. They first supplied them with clothes and provisions, and asked them where were their corps? And when the others pointed them out, seeing, instead of so many thousand men, only a weak platoon of officers and non-commissioned officers round a commanding officer, their eyes still kept on the look out.

The sight of so great a disaster struck the second and the ninth corps with discouragement from the very first day. Disorder, the most contagious of all evils, attacked them; for it would seem as if order was an effort against nature. And yet the unarmed, and even the dying, although they were now fully aware that they had to fight their way across a river, and through a fresh enemy, never doubted of their being victorious.

It was now merely the shadow of an army, but it was the shadow of the grand army. It felt conscious that nature alone had vanquished it. The sight of its emperor revived it, it had been long accustomed to look to him, not for its means of support, but solely to lead it to victory. This was its first unfortunate campaign, and it had had so many fortunate ones!

it only required to be able to follow him. He alone, who had elevated his soldiers so high, and now sunk them so low, was yet able to save them. He was still, therefore, cherished in the heart of his army, like hope in the heart of man.

Thus, amid so many beings who might have reproached him with their misfortunes, he marched on without the least fear, speaking to one and all without affectation, certain of being respected as long as glory could command our respect. Knowing perfectly that he belonged to us, as much as we to him, his renown being a species of national property, we should have sooner turned our arms against ourselves, (which was the case with many,) than against him, and it was a minor suicide.

Some of them fell and died at his feet, and, though they were in the most frightful delirium, their sufferings never gave its wanderings the turn of reproach, but of entreaty. And in fact did not he share the common danger? Which of them all risked so much as he? Who suffered the greatest loss in this disaster?

If any imprecations were uttered, it was not in his presence: it seemed, that of all misfortunes, that of incurring his displeasure was still the greatest; so rooted was their confidence in, and submission to that man who had subjected the world to them: whose genius, hitherto uniformly victorious and infallible, had assumed the place of their freewill, and who having so long in his hands the hook of pensions, of rank, and of history, had found wherewithal to satisfy not only covetous spirits, but also every generous heart.

1. "This fact," says general Gourgaud, "is not true. Even supposing the emperor to have such an idea, it could not have been executed; for the eagles were made of copper. How, besides, is it possible to suppose that, at the moment when that prince was rallying the stragglers, distributing muskets, carabines, and ammunition to them, and when, by the junction of the corps of Oudinôt and Victor with those which had been at Moscow, he was at the head of 50,000 men, with

a formidable artillery; how, I repeat, can we suppose that he would adopt such a measure, which would have served only as a signal of disorganisation, and would, in fact, have been equivalent to crying out "*Sauve qui peut.*"—*Ed.*

CHAPTER IV

AT THE BEREZINA

WE were now approaching the most critical moment; Victor was in the rear with 15,000 men; Oudinôt in front with 5000, and already close to the Berezina; the emperor between them, with 7,000 men, 40,000 stragglers, and an enormous quantity of baggage and artillery, the greatest part of which belonged to the second and the ninth corps.

On the 25th, as he was about to reach the Berezina, he appeared to linger on his march. He halted every instant on the high road, waiting for night to conceal his arrival from the enemy, and to allow the duke of Reggio time to evacuate Borizoff.

This marshal, when he entered that town upon the 23rd, found the bridge, which was 300 fathoms in length, destroyed at three different points, and that the vicinity of the enemy rendered it impossible to repair it. He had learned that on his left, two miles lower down the river, there was, near Oukoholda, a deep and unsafe ford; that at the distance of a mile above Borizoff, namely at Stadhoff, there was another, but of difficult approach. Finally, he had ascertained within the last two days, that at Studzianka, two leagues above Stadhoff, there was a third passage;—for the knowledge of this he was indebted to Corbineau's brigade.

This was the same brigade which the Bavarian general, De Wrede, had taken from the second corps, in his march to Smoliantzy. He had retained it until he reached Dokszitzi, from whence he sent it back to the second corps by way of Borizoff. When Corbineau arrived there, he found Tchitchakoff already in possession of it, and was compelled to make his retreat by ascending the Berezina, and concealing his force in the forests which border it. Not knowing at what point to cross the river, he accidentally saw a Lithuanian peasant, whose horse seemed to be quite wet, as if he had just come out of it. He laid hold of this man, and made him his guide; he got up behind him, and crossed the river at a ford opposite to Studzianka. He immediately rejoined Oudinôt, and informed him of the discovery he had made.

As Napoleon's intention was to retreat directly upon Wilna, the marshal saw at once that this passage was the most direct, as well as the least dangerous. It was also observed, that even if our infantry and artillery should be too closely pressed by Wittgenstein and Kutusoff, and prevented from crossing the river on bridges, there was at least a certainty, from the ford having been tried, that the emperor and the cavalry would be able to pass; that all would not then be lost, both peace and war, as if Napoleon himself remained in the enemy's hands. The marshal therefore did not hesitate. In the night of the 23rd, the general of artillery, a company of pontoniers, a regiment of infantry, and the brigade Corbineau, took possession of Studzianka.

At the same time the other two passages were reconnoitred and found to be strongly watched. The object, therefore, was to deceive and displace the enemy. As force could do nothing, recourse was had to stratagem; in furtherance of which, on the 24th, three hundred men and several hundred stragglers were sent towards Oukoholda, with instructions to collect there, with as much noise as possible, all the necessary materials for the construction of a bridge; the whole division of the cuirassiers was also made to promenade on that side within view of the enemy.

In addition to this, major-general Lorenc had several Jews sought out and brought to him; he interrogated them with great apparent minuteness relative to that ford, and the roads leading from it to Minsk. Then, affecting to be mightily pleased with their answers, and to be satisfied that there was no better passage to be found, he detained some of these rascals as guides, and had the others conveyed beyond our outposts. But to make still more sure of the latter *not* keeping their word with him, he made them swear that they would return to meet us, in the direction of the lower Berezina, in order to inform us of the enemy's movements.

While these attempts were making to draw Tchitchakoff's attention entirely to the left, the means of effecting a passage were secretly preparing at Studzianka. It was only on the 25th, at five in the evening, that Eblé arrived there, followed only by two field forges, two wagons of coal, six covered wagons of utensils and nails, and some companies of pontoniers. At Smolensk he had made each workman provide himself with a tool and some cramp-irons.

But the tressels, which had been made the day before, out of the beams of the Polish cabins, were found to be too weak. The work was all to do over again, It was found to be quite impossible to finish the bridge during the night; it could only be fixed during the following day, the 26th, in full daylight, and under the enemy's fire; but there was no room for hesitation.

On the first approach of that decisive night, Oudinôt ceded to Napoleon the occupation of Borizoff, and went to take position with the rest of his corps, at Studzianka. They marched in the most profound obscurity, without making the least noise, and mutually recommending to each other the deepest silence.

By eight o'clock at night Oudinôt and Dombrowski had taken possession of the heights commanding the passage, while general Eblé descended from them. That general placed himself on the borders of the river, with his pontoniers and a wagon-load of the irons of abandoned wheels, which at all hazards he made into cramp-irons. He had sacrificed every thing to preserve that feeble resource, and it saved the army.

At the close of the night of the 25th he made them sink the first tressel in the muddy bed of the river. But to crown our misfortunes, the rising of the waters had made the traces of the ford entirely disappear. It required the most incredible efforts on the part of our unfortunate sappers, who were plunged in the water up to their mouths, and had to contend with the floating pieces of ice which were carried along by the stream. Many of them perished from the cold, or were drowned by the ice flakes, which a violent wind drove against them.[1]

They had every thing to conquer but the enemy. The rigour of the atmosphere was just at the degree necessary to render the passage of the river more difficult, without suspending its course, or sufficiently consolidating the moving ground upon which we were about to venture. On this occasion the winter showed itself more hostile to us than even the Russians themselves. The latter were wanting to their season, which never failed them.

The French laboured during the whole night by the light of the enemy's fires, which shone on the heights of the opposite bank, and within reach of the artillery and musketry of Tchaplitz's division. The latter, having no longer any doubt of our intentions, sent to apprise his commander-in-chief.

1. This duty was performed by the pontoniers, and not by the sappers.—*Ed.*

CHAPTER V

PREPARATIONS FOR CROSSING

THE presence of a hostile division deprived us of all hope of deceiving the Russian admiral. We expected every instant to hear the whole fire of his artillery directed upon our workmen; and even if he did not discover them until daylight, their labours would not then be sufficiently advanced; and the opposite bank, being low and marshy, was too much commanded by Tchaplitz's positions to make it at all possible for us to force a passage.

When he quitted Borizoff, therefore, at ten o'clock at night, Napoleon imagined that he was setting out for a most desperate contest. He took up his quarters for the night, with the 6,400 guards which still remained to him, at Staroi-Borizoff, a chateau belonging to prince Radzivil, situated on the right of the road from Borizoff to Studzianka, and equi-distant from these two points.

He passed the remainder of that night on his feet, going out every moment, either to listen, or to repair to the passage where his destiny was accomplishing; for the magnitude of his anxieties so completely filled his hours, that as each revolved he fancied that it was morning. Several times he was reminded of his mistake by his attendants.

Darkness had scarcely disappeared when he joined Oudinôt. The sight of danger tranquillised him, as it always did; but on seeing the Russian fires and their position, his most determined generals, such as Rapp, Mortier, and Ney, exclaimed, "that if the emperor escaped from this danger, they must absolutely believe in the influence of his star!" Murat himself thought it was now time to think of nothing but saving Napoleon. Some of the Poles proposed it to him.

The emperor was waiting for the approach of daylight in one of the houses on the borders of the river, on a steep bank which was crowned with Oudinôt's artillery. Murat obtained access to him; he declared to his brother-in-law, "that he looked upon the passage as impracticable; he urged him to save his person while it was yet time. He informed him that he might, without any danger, cross the Berezina a few leagues above Studzianka; that in five days he would reach Wilna; that some brave and determined Poles, perfectly acquainted with all the roads, had offered themselves for his guards, and to be responsible for his safety."

But Napoleon rejected this proposition as an infamous plan, as a cowardly flight, and was indignant that any one should dare to think for a moment that he would abandon his army, so long as it was in danger. He was not, however, at all displeased with Murat, probably because that prince had afforded him an opportunity of showing his firmness, or rather because he saw nothing in his proposal but a mark of devotion, and because the first quality in the eyes of sovereigns is attachment to their persons.

At that moment the appearance of daylight made the Russian bivouac fires grow pale and disappear. Our troops stood to their arms, the artillerymen placed themselves by their pieces, the generals were observing, and the looks of all were steadily directed to the opposite bank, preserving that silence which betokens great expectation, and is the forerunner of great danger.

Since the evening before, every blow struck by our pontoniers, echoing among the woody heights, must, we concluded, have attracted the whole attention of the enemy. The first dawn of the 26th was therefore expected to display to us his battalions and artillery, drawn up in front of the weak scaffolding, to the construction of which Eblé had yet to devote eight hours more. Doubtless they were only waiting for daylight to enable them to point their cannon with better aim. When day appeared, we saw their fires abandoned, the bank deserted, and upon the heights thirty pieces of artillery in full retreat. A single bullet of theirs would have been sufficient to annihilate the only plank of safety, which we were about to fix, in order to unite the two banks; but that artillery gradually retreated, as our batteries were placed.

Farther off, we perceived the rear of a long column, which was moving off towards Borizoff without ever looking behind it; one regiment of infantry, however, and twelve cannon remained, but without taking up any position; we also saw a horde of Cossacks wandering about the skirts of the wood: they formed the rear-guard of Tchaplitz's division, six thousand strong, which was thus retiring, as if for the purpose of delivering up the passage to us.

The French at first could hardly venture to believe their eyes. At last, transported with joy, they clapped their hands, and uttered loud shouts. Rapp and Oudinôt rushed precipitately into the house where the emperor was. "Sire," they said to him, "the enemy has just raised his camp, and quitted his position!"—"It is not possible!" he replied; but Ney and Murat just then hurried in and confirmed this report. Napoleon immediately darted out; he looked, and could just see the last files of Tchaplitz's column getting farther off and disappearing in the woods. Transported with joy, he exclaimed, "I have outwitted the admiral!"

During this first movement, two of the enemy's pieces re-appeared, and fired. An order was given to remove them by a discharge of our artillery.

One salvo was enough; it was an act of imprudence which was not repeated, for fear of its recalling Tchaplitz. The bridge was as yet scarcely begun; it was eight o'clock, and the first tressels were only then fixing.

The emperor, however, impatient to get possession of the opposite bank, pointed it out to the bravest. Jacqueminot, aide-de-camp to the duke of Reggio, and the Lithuanian count Predziecski, were the first who threw themselves into the river and in spite of the pieces of ice, which cut and bled the chests and sides of their horses, they succeeded in reaching the other side. Sourd, chief of a squadron, and fifty chasseurs of the 7th, each carrying a voltigeur *en croupe*, followed them, as well as two frail rafts which transported four hundred men in twenty trips. The emperor having expressed a wish to have a prisoner to interrogate, Jacqueminot, who overheard him, had scarcely crossed the river, when he saw one of Tchaplitz's soldiers; he rushed after, attacked, and disarmed him; then seizing and placing him on his saddle bow, he brought him through the river and the ice to Napoleon.

About one o'clock the bank was entirely cleared of the Cossacks, and the bridge for the infantry finished. The division Legrand crossed it rapidly with its cannon, the men shouting "Vive l'Empereur!" in the presence of their sovereign, who was himself actively pressing the passage of the artillery, and encouraging his brave soldiers by his voice and example.

He exclaimed, when he saw them fairly in possession of the opposite bank, "Behold my star again appear!" for he was a believer in fatality, like all conquerors, those men, who, having the largest accounts with Fortune, are fully aware how much they are indebted to her, and who, moreover, having no intermediate power between themselves and Heaven, feel themselves more immediately under its protection.

CHAPTER VI

THE CROSSING AT STUDZIANKA

AT that moment, a Lithuanian nobleman, disguised as a peasant, arrived from Wilna with the news of Schwartzenberg's victory over Sacken. Napoleon appeared pleased in giving publicity to this intelligence, with the addition, that "Schwartzenberg had immediately returned upon the heels of Tchitchakoff, and that he was coming to our assistance." A conjecture, to which the disappearance of Tchaplitz gave considerable probability.

Meantime, as the first bridge which was just finished had only been made for the infantry, a second was begun immediately after, a hundred fathoms higher up, for the artillery and baggage, which was not finished until four o'clock in the afternoon. During that interval, the duke of Reggio, with the rest of the second corps, and Dombrowski's division, followed general Legrand to the other side; they formed about seven thousand men.

The marshal's first care was to secure the road to Zembin, by a detachment which chased some Cossacks from it; to push the enemy towards Borizoff, and to keep him as far back as possible from the passage of Studzianka.

Tchaplitz, in obedience to the admiral's orders, proceeded as far as Stakhowa, a village close to Borizoff; he then turned back, and encountered the first troops of Oudinôt, commanded by Albert. Both sides halted. The French, finding themselves rather too far off from their main body, only wanted to gain time, and the Russian general waited for orders.

Tchitchakoff had found himself in one of those difficult situations, in which prepossession, being compelled to fluctuate in uncertainty between several points at once, has no sooner determined and fixed upon one side, than it removes and gets overturned upon another.

His march from Minsk to Borizoff in three columns, not only by the high road, but by the roads of Antonopolia, Logoïsk, and Zembin, showed that his whole attention was at first directed to that part of the Berezina, above Borizoff. Feeling himself then so strong upon his left, he felt only that his right was weakened, and, in consequence, his anxiety was entirely transferred to that side.

The error which led him into that false direction had also other foundations. Kutusoff's instructions directed his responsibility to that point. Hoertel, who commanded twelve thousand men near Bobruisk, refused to quit his cantonments, to follow Dombrowski, and to come and defend that part of the river. He alleged, as his justification for refusal, the danger of a distemper among the cattle, a pretext unheard of and improbable, but perfectly true, as Tchitchakoff himself admitted.

The admiral adds further, that information sent to him by Wittgenstein directed his anxiety towards the Lower Berezina, as well as the supposition, natural enough, that the presence of that general on the right flank of the grand army, and above Borizoff, would push Napoleon below that town.

The recollection of the passage of Charles XII. and of Davoust at Berezino, might also be another of his motives. By taking that direction, Napoleon would not only escape Wittgenstein, but he might retake Minsk, and form a junction with Schwartzenberg. This last was a serious consideration with Tchitchakoff, Minsk being his conquest, and Schwartzenberg his first adversary. Lastly, and principally, Oudinôt's deceptious demonstration near Oukoholda, and probably the report of the Jews, determined him.

The admiral, completely deceived, had therefore resolved, on the evening of the 25th, to descend the Berezina, at the very moment that Napoleon had determined to re-ascend it. It might almost be said that the French emperor dictated the Russian general's resolution, the time for adopting it, the precise moment, and every detail of its execution. Both started at the same time from Borizoff, Napoleon for Studzianka, Tchitchakoff for Szabaszawiczy, turning their backs to each other as if by mutual agreement, and the admiral recalling all the troops which he had above Borizoff, with the exception of a small body of light troops, and without even taking the precaution of breaking up the roads.

Notwithstanding, at Szabaszawiczy he was not more than five or six leagues from the passage which was effectuating. On the morning of the 26th he must have been informed of it. The bridge of Borizoff was only three hours' march from the point of attack. He had left fifteen thousand men before that bridge; he might therefore have returned in person to that point, rejoined Tchaplitz at Stakhowa, on the same day made an attack, or at least made preparations for it, and on the following day, the 27th, overthrown with eighteen thousand men the seven thousand soldiers of Oudindôt and Dombrowski;[1] and finally resumed, in front of the emperor and of Studzianka, the position which Tchaplitz had quitted the day before.

But great errors are seldom repaired with the same readiness with which they are committed; either because it is in our nature to be at first doubtful of them, and that no one is disposed to admit them until they are completely certain; or because they confuse, and, in the distrust of our own judgment, we hesitate, and require the support of other opinions.

Thus it was, that the admiral lost the remainder of the 26th and the whole of the 27th in consultations, in feeling his way, and in preparations. The presence of Napoleon and his grand army, of the weakness of which it was impossible for him to have any idea, dazzled him. He saw the emperor every where; before his right, in the simulated preparations for a passage; opposite his centre at Borizoff, because in fact the arrival of the successive portions of our army filled that place with movements; and finally, at Studzianka before his left, where the emperor really was.

On the 27th, so little had he recovered from his error that he made his chasseurs reconnoitre and attack Borizoff; they crossed over upon the beams of the burnt bridge, but were repulsed by the soldiers of Partouneaux's division.

On the same day, while the Russian general was thus irresolute, Napoleon, with about five thousand guards, and Ney's corps, now reduced to six hundred men, crossed the Berezina about two o'clock in the afternoon; he posted himself in reserve to Oudinôt, and secured the outlet from the bridges against Tchitchakoff's future efforts.

He had been preceded by a crowd of baggage and stragglers. Numbers of them continued to cross the river after him as long as day-light lasted. The army of Victor, at the same time, succeeded the guard in its position on the heights of Studzianka.

1. "It would not only," says general Gourgaud, "have been the 7,000 soldiers of Oudinôt with whom Tchitchakoff would have had to encounter, but also the imperial guard, and the corps of Eugene, Ney, and Davoust, which would have formed a mass of forces much more considerable than those of the admiral."—*Ed.*

CHAPTER VII

DEFEAT OF
PARTOUNEAUX'S DIVISION

HITHERTO all had gone on well. But Victor, in passing through Borizoff, had left there Partouneaux with his division. That general had orders to stop the enemy in the rear of that town, to drive before him the numerous stragglers who had taken shelter in it, and to rejoin Victor before the close of the day. It was the first time that Partouneaux had seen the disorder of the grand army. He was anxious, like Davoust at the beginning of the retreat, to hide the traces of it from the Cossacks of Kutusoff, who were at his heels. This fruitless attempt, the attacks of Platoff by the high road of Orcha, and those of Tchitchakoff by the burnt bridge of Borizoff, detained him in that place until the close of the day.

He was preparing to quit it, when an order reached him from the emperor himself, to remain there all night. Napoleon's idea, no doubt, was, in that manner to direct the whole attention of the three Russian generals upon Borizoff, and that Partouneaux, by keeping them in check at that point, would allow him sufficient time to operate the passage of the whole army.

But Wittgenstein left Platoff to pursue the French army along the high road, and directed his own march more to the right. He debouched the same evening on the heights which border the Berezina, between Borizoff and Studzianka, intercepted the road between these two points, and captured all that were found there. A crowd of stragglers, who were driven back on Partouneaux apprised him that he was separated from the rest of the army.

Partouneanx did not hesitate: although he had no more than three cannon with him, and three thousand five hundred soldiers, he determined to cut his way through, made his dispositions accordingly, and began his march. He had at first to march along a slippery road, crowded with baggage and runaways; with a violent wind blowing directly in his face, and in a dark and icy-cold night. To these obstacles were shortly added the fire of several thousand enemies, who lined the heights upon his right. As long as he was only attacked in flank, he proceeded; but shortly after, he had to meet it in front from numberless troops well posted, whose bullets traversed his column through and through.

This unfortunate division then got entangled in a deep-hollow; a long file of five or six hundred carriages embarrassed all its movements; seven thousand terrified stragglers, howling with terror and despair, rushed into the midst of its feeble lines. They broke through them, caused its platoons to waver, and were every moment involving in their disorder fresh soldiers, who got disheartened. It became necessary to retreat in order to rally, and take a better position, but in falling back, they encountered Platoff's cavalry.

Half of our combatants had already perished, and the fifteen hundred soldiers who remained found themselves surrounded by three armies and by a river.

In this situation, a flag of truce came, in the name of Wittgenstein and fifty thousand men, to order the French to surrender. Partouneaux rejected the summons. He recalled into his ranks such of his stragglers as yet retained their arms; he wished to make a last effort, and to clear a sanguinary passage to the bridge of Studzianka; but these men, who were formerly so brave, were now so degraded by their miseries that they would no longer make use of their arms.

At the same time, the general of his vanguard apprised him that the bridges of Studzianka were burnt; an aide-de-camp, named Rochex, who had just brought the report, pretended that he had seen them burning. Partouneaux believed this false intelligence, for, in regard to calamities, misfortune is credulous.

He concluded that he was abandoned and sacrificed; and as the night, the incumbrances, and the necessity of facing the enemy on three sides, separated his weak brigades, he desired each of them to be told to try and steal off, under favour of the darkness, along the flanks of the enemy. He himself, with one of these brigades, now reduced to four hundred men, ascended the steep and woody heights on his right, with the hope of passing through Wittgenstein's army in the darkness, of escaping him, and rejoining Victor; or, at all events, of getting round by the sources of the Berezina.

But at every point where he attempted to pass, he encountered the enemy's fires, and was obliged to turn again; he wandered about for several hours quite at random, in plains of snow, in the midst of a violent hurricane. At every step he saw his soldiers transfixed by the cold, emaciated with hunger and fatigue, falling half dead into the hands of the Russian cavalry, who pursued him without intermission.

This unfortunate general was still struggling with the heavens, with men, and with his own despair, when he felt even the earth give way under his feet. In fact, being deceived by the snow, he had fallen into a lake, which was not frozen sufficiently hard to bear him, and in which he would have been drowned. Then only he yielded, and gave up his arms.

While this catastrophe was accomplishing, his other three brigades, being more and more hemmed in upon the road, lost all power of movement. They delayed their surrender till the next morning, first by fighting, and then by parleying; they then all fell in their turn; a common misfortune again united them with their general.

Of the whole division, a single battalion only escaped: it had been left the last in Borizoff. It quitted it in the midst of the

Russians of Platoff and of Tchitchakoff, who were effecting in that town, and at that very moment, the junction of the armies of Moscow and of Moldavia. This battalion, being alone and separated from its division, might have been expected to be the first to fall, but that very circumstance saved it. Several long trains of equipages and disbanded soldiers were flying towards Studzianka in different directions; drawn aside by one of these crowds, mistaking his road, and leaving on his right that which had been taken by the army, the leader of this battalion glided to the borders of the river, followed all its windings and turnings, and protected by the combat of his less fortunate comrades, by the darkness, and the very difficulties of the ground, moved off in silence, escaped from the enemy, and brought to Victor the confirmation of Partouneaux's surrender.

When Napoleon heard the news, he was struck with grief, and exclaimed, "How unfortunate it was, that when all appeared to be saved, as if miraculously, this *defection* had happened, to spoil all!"[1] The expression was improper, but grief extorted it from him, either because he anticipated that Victor, being thus weakened, would be unable to hold out long enough next day; or because he had made it a point of honour to leave nothing during the whole of his retreat in the hands of the enemy, but stragglers, and no armed and organised corps. In fact, this division was the first and the only one which laid down its arms.

1. It is denied that Napoleon used the expression which is here attributed to him.—*Ed.*

CHAPTER VIII

A CONCERTED RUSSIAN ATTACK

THIS success encouraged Wittgenstein. At the same time, after two days feeling his way, the report of a prisoner, and the recapture of Borizoff by Platoff, had opened Tchitchakoff's eyes. From that moment the three Russian armies of the north, east, and south, felt themselves united; their commanders had mutual communications. Wittgenstein and Tchitchakoff were jealous of each other, but they detested us still more; hatred, and not friendship, was their bond of union. These generals were therefore prepared to attack in conjunction the bridges of Studzianka, on both sides of the river.

This was on the 28th of November, The grand army had had two days and two nights to effect its passage; it ought to have been too late for the Russians. But the French were in a state of complete disorder, and materials were deficient for two bridges. Twice, during the night of the 26th, the one for the carriages broke down, and the passage had been retarded by it for seven hours: it broke a third time on the 27th, about four in the afternoon. On the other hand, the stragglers, who had been dispersed in the woods and surrounding villages, had not taken advantage of the first night, and on the 27th, when daylight appeared, they all presented themselves at once in order to cross the bridges.

This was particularly the case when the guard, by whose movements they regulated themselves, began its march. Its departure was like a signal; they rushed in from all parts, and crowded upon the bank. Instantly there was seen a deep, broad, and confused mass of men, horses, and chariots, besieging the narrow entrance of the bridge, and overwhelming it. The first, pushed forward by those behind them, and driven back by the guards and pontoniers, or stopped by the river, were crushed, trodden under foot, or precipitated among the floating ices of the Berezina. From this immense and horrible rabble-rout there arose at times a confused buzzing noise, at others a loud clamour, mingled with groans and dreadful imprecations.

The efforts of Napoleon and his lieutenants to save these desperate men, by establishing order among them, were for a long time completely fruitless. The disorder was so great, that about two o'clock, when the emperor presented himself in his turn, it was necessary to employ force to open a passage for him. A corps of grenadiers of the guard, and Latour-Maubourg, out of pure compassion, declined clearing themselves a way through these poor wretches.

The imperial head-quarters were established at the hamlet of Zaniwki, which is situated in the midst of the woods, within a league of Studzianka. Eblé had just then made a survey of the baggage with which the bank was covered; he apprised the emperor that six days would not be sufficient to enable so many carriages to pass over. Ney, who was present, immediately called out, "that in that case they had better be burnt immediately." But Berthier, instigated by the demon of courts, opposed this; he assured the emperor that the army was far from being reduced to that extremity, and the emperor was led to believe him, from a preference for the opinion which flattered him the most, and from a wish to spare so many men, of whose misfortunes he reproached himself as the cause, and whose provisions and little all these carriages contained.

In the night of the 27th the disorder ceased by the effect of an opposite disorder. The bridges were abandoned, and the village of Studzianka attracted all these stragglers; in an instant, it was pulled to pieces, disappeared, and was converted into an infinite number of bivouacs. Cold and hunger kept these wretched people fixed around them; it was found impossible to tear them from them. The whole of that night was again lost for their passage.

Meantime Victor, with six thousand men, was defending them against Wittgenstein. But with the first dawn of the 28th, when they saw that marshal preparing for a battle, when they heard the cannon of Wittgenstein thundering over their heads, and that of Tchitchakoff rumbling at the same time on the opposite bank, they all rose at once, descended from the heights, precipitated themselves tumultuously, and returned to besiege the bridges.

Their terror was not without foundation; the last day of numbers of these unfortunate persons was come. Wittgenstein and Platoff, with forty thousand Russians of the armies of the north and east, attacked the heights on the left bank, which Victor, with his small force, defended. On the right bank, Tchitchakoff, with his twenty-seven thousand Russians of the army of the south, debouched from Stakhowa against Oudinôt, Ney, and Dombrowski. These three could hardly reckon eight thousand men in their ranks,[1] which were supported by the sacred squadron, as well as by the old and young guard, which then consisted of three thousand eight hundred infantry and nine hundred cavalry.

The two Russian armies attempted to possess themselves at once of the two outlets from the bridges, and of all who had been unable to push forward beyond the marshes of Zembin. More than sixty thousand men, well clothed, well fed, and completely armed, attacked eighteen thousand, half-naked, badly-armed, dying of hunger, separated by a river, surrounded by morasses, and additionally encumbered with more than fifty thousand stragglers, sick or wounded, and by an enormous mass of baggage. During the last two days, the cold and misery had been such that the old guard had lost one-third, and the young guard one-half, of their effective men.

This fact, and the calamity which had overtaken Partouneaux's division, sufficiently explain the frightful diminution of Victor's corps; and yet that marshal kept Wittgenstein in check during the whole of that day, the 28th. As to Tchitchakoff, he was beaten. Marshal Ney, with his eight thousand French, Swiss, and Poles, was a match for twenty-seven thousand Russians.

The admiral's attack was tardy and feeble. His cannon cleared the road, but he durst not venture to follow his bullets, and penetrate by the chasm which they made in our ranks. Opposite to his right, however, the legion of the Vistula gave way to the attack of a strong column. Oudinôt, Albert, Dombrowski, Claparède, and Kosikowski were then wounded; some uneasiness began to be felt. But Ney hastened forward; he made Doumerc and his cavalry dash through the woods upon the flank of that Russian column; they broke through it, took two thousand prisoners, cut the rest to pieces; and by this vigorous charge decided the fate of the battle, which was dragging on in uncertainty. Tchitchakoff, thus defeated, was driven back into Stakhowa.

On our side, most of the generals of the second corps were wounded; for the fewer troops they had, the more they were obliged to expose their persons. Many officers on this occasion took the muskets and the places of their wounded men. Among the losses of the day, that of young Noailles, Berthier's aide-de-camp, was remarkable. He was struck dead by a ball. He was one of those meritorious but too ardent officers, who are incessantly exposing themselves, and are considered sufficiently rewarded by being employed.

During this combat, Napoleon, at the head of his guard, remained in reserve at Brilowa, covering the outlet of the bridges, between the two armies, but nearer to that of Victor. That marshal, although attacked in a very dangerous position, and by a force quadruple his own, lost very little ground. The right of his corps, mutilated by the capture of Partouneaux's division, was protected by the river, and supported by a battery which the emperor had erected on the opposite bank. His front was defended by a ravine, but his left was in the air, without support, and in a manner lost, in the elevated plain of Studzianka.

Wittgenstein's first attack was not made until ten o'clock in the morning of the 28th, across the road to Borizoff, and along the Berezina, which he endeavoured to ascend as far as the passage, but the French right wing attacked him, and kept him back for a considerable time, out of reach of the bridges. He then deployed and extended the engagement with the whole front of Victor, but without effect. One of his attacking columns attempted to cross the ravine, but it was attacked and destroyed.

At last, about the middle of the day, the Russian general discovered the point where his superiority lay: he outflanked the French left wing. Every thing would then have been lost, had it not been for a memorable effort of Fournier, and the devotion of Latour-Maubourg. That general was passing the bridges with his cavalry; he perceived the danger, and immediately retraced his steps. On his side, Fournier charged at the head of two regiments of Hesse and Baden; the Russian right wing, already victorious, was obliged to halt; it was attacking, but he forced it to defend itself, and the enemy's ranks were broken by a sanguinary charge.

Night came on before Wittgenstein's forty thousand men could make any impression on the six thousand of the duke of Belluno. That marshal remained in possession of the heights of Studzianka, and still preserved the bridges from the attacks of the Russian infantry, but he was unable to conceal them from the artillery of the left wing.

1. The three corps mentioned here were 14,700 strong.—*Ed.*

CHAPTER IX

DISASTER AT THE RIVER CROSSING

DURING the whole of that day, the situation of the ninth corps was so much more critical, as a weak and narrow bridge was its only means of retreat; in addition to which its avenues were obstructed by the baggage and the stragglers. By degrees, as the action got warmer, the terror of these poor wretches increased their disorder. First of all they were alarmed by the rumours of a serious engagement; then, by seeing the wounded returning from it; and last of all, by the batteries of the Russian left wing, some bullets from which began to fall among their confused mass.

They had all been already crowding one upon the other, and the immense multitude heaped upon the bank pell-mell with the horses and carriages, there formed a most alarming incumbrance. It was about the middle of the day that the first Russian bullets fell in the midst of this chaos; they were the signal of universal despair.

Then it was, as in all cases of extremity, that dispositions exhibited themselves without disguise, and actions were witnessed, some base, and others sublime. According to their different characters, some furious and determined, with sword in hand cleared for themselves a horrible passage. Others still more cruel, opened a way for their carriages by driving them without mercy over the crowds of unfortunate persons who stood in the way, whom they crushed to death. Their detestable avarice made them sacrifice their companions in misfortune to the preservation of their baggage. Others, seized with a disgusting terror, wept, supplicated, and sunk under the influence of that passion, which completed the exhaustion of their strength. Some were observed, (and these were principally the sick and wounded,) who, renouncing life, went aside and sat down resigned, looking with a fixed eye on the snow which was shortly to be their tomb.

Numbers of those who started first among this crowd of desperadoes missed the bridge, and attempted to scale it by the sides, but the greater part were pushed into the river. There were seen women in the midst of the ice, with their children in their arms, raising them by degrees as they felt themselves sinking, and even when completely immerged, their stiffened arms still held them above them.[1]

In the midst of this horrible disorder, the artillery bridge burst and broke down. The column, that was entangled in this narrow passage, in vain attempted to retrograde. The crowds which came behind, unaware of the calamity, and not hearing the cries of those before them, pushed them on, and threw them into the gulf, into which they were precipitated in their turn.

Every one then attempted to pass by the other bridge. A number of large ammunition wagons, heavy carriages, and cannon crowded to it from all parts. Directed by their drivers, and carried along rapidly over a rough and unequal declivity, in the midst of heaps of men, they ground to pieces the poor wretches who were unlucky enough to get between them; after which, the greater part, driving violently against each other and getting overturned, killed in their fall those who surrounded them. Whole rows of these desperate creatures being pushed against these obstacles, got entangled among them, were thrown down, and crushed to pieces by masses of other unfortunates who succeeded each other uninterruptedly.

Crowds of them were rolling in this way, one over the other; nothing was heard but cries of rage and suffering. In this frightful medley, those who were trodden and stifled under the feet of their companions, struggled to lay hold of them with their nails and teeth, but were repelled without mercy, like so many enemies.

Among them were wives and mothers, calling in vain, and in tones of distraction, for their husbands and their children, from whom they had been separated but a moment before, never more to be united: they stretched out their arms and entreated to be allowed to pass in order to rejoin them; but being carried backwards and forwards by the crowd, and overcome by the pressure, they sunk without being even remarked. Amidst the tremendous noise of a violent hurricane, the firing of cannon, the whistling of the storm and of the bullets, the explosion of shells, vociferations, groans, and the most frightful oaths, this infuriated and disorderly crowd heard not the cries of the victims whom it was swallowing up.

The more fortunate gained the bridge by scrambling over heaps of wounded, of women and children thrown down and half suffocated, and whom they again trod down in their attempts to reach it. When at last they got to the narrow defile, they fancied they were safe, but the fall of a horse, or the breaking or displacing of a plank again stopt all.

There was also, at the outlet of the bridge, on the other side, a morass, into which many horses and carriages had sunk, a circumstance which again embarrassed and retarded the clearance. Then it was, that in that column of desperadoes, crowded together on that single plank of safety, there arose a demoniacal struggle, in which the weakest and worst situated were thrown into the river by the strongest. The latter, without turning their heads, and hurried away by the instinct of self-preservation, pushed on toward the goal with fury, regardless of the imprecations of rage and despair, uttered by their companions or their officers, whom they had thus sacrificed.

But, on the other hand, how many noble instances of devotion! and why are time and space denied me to relate them? There were seen soldiers, and even officers, harnessing themselves to sledges, to snatch from that fatal bank their sick or wounded comrades. Farther off, and out of reach of the crowd, were seen soldiers motionless, watching over their dying officers, who had entrusted themselves to their care; in vain did the latter conjure them to think of nothing but their own preservation; they refused, and, sooner than abandon their leaders, were contented to take the chance of slavery or death.

Above the first passage, while the young Lauriston threw himself into the river, in order to execute the orders of his sovereign more promptly, a little boat, carrying a mother and her two children, was upset and sunk under the ice; an artilleryman, who was struggling like the others on the bridge to open a passage for himself, saw the accident; all at once, forgetting himself, he threw himself into the river, and by great exertion succeeded in saving one of the three victims. It was the youngest of the two children; the poor little thing kept calling for his mother with cries of despair, and the brave artilleryman was heard telling him, "not to cry; that he had not preserved him from the water merely to desert him on the bank; that he should want for nothing; that he would be his father, and his family."

The night of the 28th added to all these calamities. Its darkness was insufficient to conceal its victims from the artillery of the Russians. Amidst the snow, which covered every thing, the course of the river, the thorough black mass of men, horses, carriages, and the noise proceeding from them, were sufficient to enable the enemy's artillerymen to direct their fire.

About nine o'clock at night there was a still farther increase of desolation, when Victor commenced his retreat, and his divisions came and opened themselves a horrible breach through these unhappy wretches, whom they had till then been protecting. A rear-guard, however, having been left at Studzianka, the multitude, benumbed with cold, or too anxious to preserve their baggage, refused to avail themselves of the last night for passing to the opposite side. In vain were the carriages set fire to, in order to tear them from them. It was only the appearance of daylight, which brought them all at once, but too late, to the entrance of the bridge, which they again besieged. It was half-past eight in the morning, when Eblé, seeing the Russians approaching, at last set fire to it.

The disaster had reached its utmost bounds. A multitude of carriages and of cannon, several thousand men and women, and some children, were abandoned on the hostile bank. They were seen wandering in desolate troops on the borders of the river. Some threw themselves into it in order to swim across; others ventured themselves on the pieces of ice which were floating along: some there were also who threw themselves headlong into the flames of the burning bridge, which sunk under them; burnt and frozen at one and the same time, they perished under two opposite punishments. Shortly after, the bodies of all sorts were perceived collecting together and the ice against the tressels of the bridge. The rest awaited the Russians. Wittgenstein did not show himself upon the heights until an hour after Eblé's departure, and, without having gained a victory, reaped all the fruits of one.[2]

1. General Gourgaud states the number of women and children to have been small. There were, he says, "some suttlers' wives with the army, and very few children. On our return from Moscow several families, having accompanied us, the number was somewhat increased."—*Ed.*

2. The loss sustained by the French is attributed to the negligent manner in which were executed the orders given by Napoleon relative to the passage. "We have seen," says general Gourgaud, "that the corps of marshal Oudinôt occupied the point of passage two days previous to the arrival of the emperor, but that the tressels were so carelessly constructed, that it was necessary to do them over again. Had it not been for this circumstance, the passage would have been effected twenty-four hours earlier, and without loss." The prisoners who fell into the hands of the Russians, after the destruction of the bridge, are estimated at only 2000 stragglers, including sick and wounded, by the Russian colonel, Boutourlin.—*Ed.*

CHAPTER X

THE ROAD TO ZEMBIN

WHILE this catastrophe was accomplishing, the remains of the grand army on the opposite bank formed nothing but a shapeless mass, which unravelled itself confusedly as it took the road to Zembin. The whole of this country is a high and woody plain of great extent, where the waters, flowing in uncertainty between different inclinations of the ground, form one vast morass. Three consecutive bridges, of three hundred fathoms in length, are thrown over it; along these the army passed, with a mingled feeling of astonishment, fear, and delight.

These magnificent bridges, made of resinous fir, began at the distance of a few wersts from the passage. Tchaplitz had occupied them for several days. An *abatis* and heaps of bavins of combustible wood, already dry, were laid at their entrance, as if to remind him of the use he had to make of them. It would not have required more than the fire from one of the Cossacks' pipes to set these bridges on fire. In that case all our efforts and the passage of the Berezina would have been entirely useless. Caught between the morass and the river, in a narrow space, without provisions, without shelter, in the midst of a tremendous hurricane, the grand army and its emperor must have been compelled to surrender without striking a blow.

In this desperate situation, in which all France seemed destined to be taken prisoner in Russia, where every thing was against us and in favour of the Russians, the latter did nothing but by halves. Kutusoff did not reach the Dnieper, at Kopis, until the very day that Napoleon approached the Berezina. Wittgenstein allowed himself to be kept in check during the time that the former required for his passage. Tchitchakoff was defeated; and of eighty thousand men, Napoleon succeeded in saving sixty thousand.

He remained till the last moment on these melancholy banks, near the ruins of Brilowa, unsheltered and at the head of his guard, one-third of which was destroyed by the storm. During the day they stood to arms, and were drawn up in order of battle; at night, they bivouacked in a square round their leader; there the old grenadiers incessantly kept feeding their fires. They sat upon their knapsacks, with their elbows planted on their knees, and their hands supporting their head; slumbering in this manner doubled upon themselves, in order that one limb might warm the other, and that they should feel less the emptiness of their stomachs.

During these three days and three nights, spent in the midst of them, Napoleon, with his looks and his thoughts wandering on three sides at once, supported the second corps by his orders and his presence, protected the ninth corps and the passage with his artillery, and united his efforts with those of Eblé in saving as many fragments as possible from the wreck. He at last directed the remains to Zembin, to which Prince Eugene had preceded him.

It was remarked that he still gave orders to his marshals, who had no soldiers to command, to take up positions on that road, as if they had still armies at their beck. One of them made the observation to him with some degree of asperity, and was beginning an enumeration of his losses; but Napoleon, determined to reject all reports, lest they should degenerate into complaints, warmly interrupted him with these words: "why then do you wish to deprive me of my tranquillity?" and as the other was persisting, he shut his mouth at once by repeating, in a reproachful manner, "I ask you, sir, why do you wish to deprive me of my tranquillity?" An expression which, in his adversity, explained the attitude which he imposed upon himself, and that which he exacted of others.

Around him, during these mortal days, every bivouac was marked by a heap of dead bodies. There were collected men of all classes, of all ranks, of all ages; ministers, generals, administrators. Among them was remarked an elderly nobleman of the times long passed, when light and brilliant graces held sovereign sway. This general officer of sixty was seen sitting on the snow-covered trunk of a tree, occupying himself with unruffled gaiety every morning with the details of his toilette; in the midst of the hurricane, he had his hair elegantly dressed, and powdered with the greatest care, amusing himself in this manner with all the calamities, and with the fury of the combined elements which assailed him.[1]

Near him were officers of the scientific corps still finding subjects of discussion. Imbued with the spirit of an age which a few discoveries have encouraged to find explanations for every thing, the latter, amidst the acute sufferings which were inflicted upon them by the north wind, were endeavouring to ascertain the cause of its constant direction. According to them, since his departure for the antarctic pole, the sun, by warming the southern hemisphere, converted all its emanations into vapour, elevated them, and left on the surface of that zone a vacuum into which the vapours of ours, which were lower, on account of being less rarefied, rushed with violence. One after another, and from a similar cause, the Russian pole, completely surcharged with vapours which it had emanated, received, and cooled since the last spring, greedily followed that direction. It discharged itself of them by an impetuous and icy current, which swept the Russian territory quite bare, and stiffened or destroyed every thing which it encountered in its passage.

Several others of these officers remarked with curious attention the regular hexagonal crystallisation of each of the flakes of snow which covered their garments.

The phenomenon of parhelias, or simultaneous appearances of several images of the sun, reflected to their eyes by means of icicles suspended in the atmosphere, was also the subject of their observations, and occurred several times to divert their thoughts from their sufferings.

1. This officer was the count de Narbonne, who died governor of Torgau, in 1813. Notwithstanding his ludicrous attention to "the details of his toilette," he was a gallant and skilful soldier.—*Ed.*

CHAPTER XI

THE DISORDER OF THE FRENCH

ON the 29th the emperor quitted the banks of the Berezina, pushing on before him the crowd of disbanded soldiers, and marching with the ninth corps, which was already disorganised. The day before, the second and the ninth corps, and Dombrowski's division, presented a total of fourteen thousand men; and now, with the exception of about six thousand, the rest had no longer any form of division, brigade, or regiment.

Night, hunger, cold, the fall of a number of officers, the loss of the baggage on the other side of the river, the example of so many runaways, and the much more forbidding one of the wounded, who had been abandoned on both sides of the river, and were left rolling in despair on the snow, which was covered with their blood—every thing, in short, had contributed to discourage them; they were confounded in the mass of disbanded men who had come from Moscow.

The whole still formed sixty thousand men, but without the least order or unity. All marched pell-mell, cavalry, infantry, artillery, French and Germans; there was no longer either wing or centre. The artillery and carriages drove on through this disorderly crowd, with no other instructions than to proceed as quickly as possible.

On this causeway, sometimes narrow and sometimes hilly, many were crushed to death in crowding together through the defiles, after which there was a general dispersion to every point where either shelter or provisions were likely to be found. In this manner did Napoleon reach Kamen, where he slept, along with the prisoners made on the preceding day, who were put into a fold like sheep. These poor wretches, after devouring even the dead bodies of their fellows, almost all perished of cold and hunger.

On the 30th he reached Pleszczenitzy. Thither the duke of Reggio, after being wounded, had retired the day before, with about forty officers and soldiers. He fancied himself in safety, when all at once the Russian partisan, Landskoy, with one hundred and fifty hussars, four hundred Cossacks, and two cannon, penetrated into the village, and filled all its streets.

Oudinôt's feeble escort was dispersed. The marshal saw himself reduced to defend himself with only seventeen others, in a wooden house, but he did so with such audacity and success, that the enemy was panic-struck, quitted the village, and took position on a height, from which he attacked it with his cannon. The relentless destiny of this brave marshal so ordered it, that in this skirmish he was again wounded by a splinter of wood.

Two Westphalian battalions, which preceded the emperor, at last made their appearance and disengaged him, but not till late, and not until these Germans and the marshal's escort (who at first did not recognise each other as friends) had taken a long and anxious survey of each other.

On the 3rd of December, Napoleon arrived in the morning at Malodeczno, which was the last point where Tchitchakoff was likely to have got the start of him. Some provisions were found there, the forage was abundant, the day beautiful, the sun shining, and the cold bearable. There also the couriers, who had been so long in arrear, arrived all at once. The Poles were immediately directed forward to Warsaw through Olita, and the dismounted cavalry by Merecz to the Niemen; the rest of the army was to follow the high road, which they had again regained.

Up to that time, Napoleon seemed to have entertained no idea of quitting his army. But about the middle of that day, he suddenly informed Daru and Duroq of his determination to set off immediately for Paris.

Daru did not see the necessity of it. He objected "that the communication with France was again opened, and the most dangerous crisis passed; that at every retrograde step he would now be meeting the reinforcements sent him from Paris and from Germany." The emperor's reply was, "that he no longer felt himself sufficiently strong to leave Prussia between him and France. What necessity was there for his remaining at the head of a routed army? Murat and Eugene would be sufficient to direct it, and Ney to cover its retreat.

"His return to France was become indispensable, in order to secure her tranquillity, and to summon her to arms; to take measures there for keeping the Germans steady in their fidelity to him: and finally, to return with fresh and sufficient forces to the assistance of his grand army.

"But, in order to effect these objects, it was necessary that he should travel alone over four hundred leagues of the territories of his allies; and to do so without danger, that his resolution should be there unforeseen, his passage unknown, and the rumour of his disastrous retreat still uncertain; that he should precede the news of it, and anticipate the effect which it might produce on them, and all the defections to which it might give rise. He had, therefore, no time to lose, and the moment of his departure was now arrived."

He only hesitated in the choice of the leader whom he should leave in command of the army; he wavered between Murat and Eugene. He liked the prudence and devotedness of the latter; but Murat had greater celebrity, which would give him more weight. Eugene would remain with that monarch; his youth and inferior rank would be a security for his obedience, and his character for his zeal. He would set the example of these qualities to the other marshals.

Finally, Berthier, the channel to which they had been so long accustomed, of all the imperial orders and rewards, would remain with them; there would consequently be no change in the form or the organisation of the army; and this arrangement, at the same time that it would be a proof of the certainty of his speedy return, would serve both to keep the most impatient of his own officers in their duty, and the most ardent of his enemies in a salutary dread.

Such were the motives assigned by Napoleon. Caulaincourt immediately received orders to make secret preparations for departure. The rendezvous was fixed at Smorgoni, and the time, the night of the 5th of December.[1]

Although Daru was not to accompany Napoleon, who left him the heavy charge of the administration of the army, he listened in silence, having nothing to urge in reply to motives of such weight; but it was quite otherwise with Berthier. This enfeebled old man, who had for sixteen years never quitted the side of Napoleon, revolted at the idea of this separation.

The private scene which took place was most violent. The emperor was indignant at his resistance. In his rage he reproached him with all the favours with which he had loaded him; the army, he told him, stood in need of the reputation which he had made for him, and which was only a reflection of his own; but to cut the matter short, he allowed him four-and-twenty hours to decide; and if he then persisted in his disobedience, he might depart for his estates, where he should order him to remain, forbidding him ever again to enter Paris or his presence. Next day, the 4th of December, Berthier, excusing himself for his previous refusal by his advanced age and impaired health, resigned himself sorrowfully to his sovereign's pleasure.[2]

1. His quitting his army has subjected Napoleon to much unjust and absurd censure. A hostile historian, colonel Boutourlin, aide-de-camp to the emperor Alexander, has displayed more justice and good sense. "Various judgments," says he, "have been formed respecting this departure, and yet nothing would be more easy than to justify it. In

fact, Napoleon was not merely the general of the army which he left; and, since the fate of all France was dependent on his person, it is clear that, under the circumstances, his first duty was less to witness the death-throes of the remnant of his army than to watch over the safety of the great empire which he ruled. Now he could not perform that duty better than by going to Paris, that, by his presence, he might hasten the organisation of new armies, necessary to replace that which he had lost."—*Ed.*

2. The dispute arose from Berthier being adverse to the command of the army being conferred on Prince Eugene, which was Napoleon's original intention. Berthier was desirous that Murat should be its leader; and, unfortunately for Napoleon, Berthier carried his point.—*Ed.*

CHAPTER XII

PARTIAL ACTIONS
OF NEY AND MAISON

BUT at the very moment that Napoleon determined on his departure, the winter became terrible, as if the Russian atmosphere, seeing him about to escape from it, had redoubled its severity in order to overwhelm him and destroy us. On the 4th of December, when we reached Bienitza, the thermometer was at 26 degrees.

The emperor had left count Lobau and several hundred men of his old guard at Malodeczno, at which place the road to Zembin rejoins the high road from Minsk to Wilna. It was necessary to guard this point until the arrival of Victor, who in his turn would defend it until that of Ney.

For it was still to this marshal, and to the second corps commanded by Maison, that the rear-guard was entrusted. On the night of the 29th of November, when Napoleon quitted the banks of the Berezina, Ney, and the second and third corps, now reduced to three thousand soldiers, passed the long bridges leading to Zembin, leaving at their entrance Maison, and a few hundred men to defend and to burn them.

Tchitchakoff made a late but warm attack, and not only with musketry, but with the bayonet: but he was repulsed. Maison at the same time caused these long bridges to be loaded with the bavins, of which Tchaplitz, some days before, had neglected to make use. When every thing was ready, the enemy completely sickened of fighting, and night and the bivouacs well advanced, he rapidly passed the defile, and set fire to them. In a few minutes these long causeways were burnt to ashes, and fell into the morasses, which the frost had not yet rendered passable.

These quagmires stopped the enemy and compelled him to make a *detour.* During the following day, therefore, the march of Ney and of Maison was unmolested. But on the day after, the 1st of December, as they came in sight of Pleszczenitzy, lo and behold! the whole of the Russian cavalry were seen rushing forward impetuously, and pushing Doumerc and his cuirassiers on their right. In an instant they were attacked and overwhelmed on all sides.

At the same time, Maison saw that the village through which he had to retreat was entirely filled with stragglers. He sent to warn them to flee directly; but these unfortunate and famished wretches, not seeing the enemy, refused to leave their meals which they had just begun; Maison was driven back upon them into the village. Then only, at the sight of the enemy, and the noise of the shells, the whole of them started up at once, rushed out, and crowded and encumbered every part of the principal street.

Maison and his troop found themselves all at once in a manner lost in the midst of this terrified crowd, which pressed upon them, almost stifled them, and deprived them of the use of their arms. This general had no other remedy than to desire his men to remain close together and immoveable, and wait till the crowd had dispersed. The enemy's cavalry then came up with this mass, and got entangled with it, but it could only penetrate slowly and by cutting down. The crowd having at last dispersed, discovered to the Russians Maison and his soldiers waiting for them with a determined countenance. But in its flight, the crowd had drawn along with it a portion of our combatants. Maison, in an open plain, and with seven or eight hundred men against thousands of enemies, lost all hope of safety; he was already seeking only to gain a wood not far off, in order to sell their lives more dearly, when he saw coming out of it eighteen hundred Poles, a troop quite fresh, which Ney had met with and brought to his assistance. This reinforcement stopped the enemy, and secured the retreat as far as Malodeczno.

On the 4th of December, about four o'clock in the afternoon, Ney and Maison got within sight of that village, which Napoleon had quitted in the morning. Tchaplitz followed them close. Ney had now only six hundred men remaining with him. The weakness of his rear-guard, the approach of night, and the prospect of a place of shelter, excited the ardour of the Russian general; he made a warm attack. Ney and Maison, perfectly certain that they should die of cold on the high road, if they allowed themselves to be driven beyond that cantonment, preferred perishing in defending it.

They halted at its entrance, and as their artillery horses were dying, they gave up all idea of saving their cannon; determined, however, that it should do its duty for the last time in crushing the enemy, they formed every piece they possessed into a battery, and made a tremendous fire. Tchaplitz's attacking column was entirely broken by it, and halted. But that general, availing himself of his superior forces, diverted a part of them to another entrance, and his first troops had already crossed the inclosures of Malodeczno, when all at once, they there encountered a fresh enemy.

As good luck would have it, Victor, with about four thousand men, the remains of the ninth corps, still occupied this village. The fury on both sides was extreme; the first houses were several times taken and retaken. The combat on both sides was much less for glory than to keep or acquire a refuge against the destructive cold. It was not until half-past eleven at night that the Russians gave up the contest, and went from it half frozen, to seek for shelter in the surrounding villages.

The following day, December 5th, Ney and Maison had expected that the duke of Belluno would replace them at the rear-guard; but they found that that marshal had retired, according to his instructions, and that they were left alone in Malodeczno with only sixty men. All the rest had fled; the rigour of the climate had completely knocked up their soldiers, whom the Russians to the very last moment were unable to conquer; their arms fell from their hands, and they themselves fell at a few paces' distance from their arms.

Maison, who united great vigour of mind with a very strong constitution, was not intimidated; he continued his retreat to Bienitza, rallying at every step men who were incessantly escaping from him, but still continuing to give proofs of the existence of a rear-guard, with a few foot soldiers. This was all that was required; for the Russians themselves were frozen, and obliged to disperse before night into the neighbouring habitations, which they durst not quit until it was completely daylight. They then recommenced their pursuit of us, but without making any attack; for with the exception of some numbed efforts, the violence of the temperature was such as not to allow either party to halt with the view of making an attack, or of defending themselves.

In the mean time, Ney, being surprised at Victor's departure, went after him, overtook him, and tried to prevail upon him to halt, but the duke of Belluno, having orders to retreat, refused. Ney then wanted him to give up his soldiers, offering to take the command of them; but Victor would neither consent to do that, nor to take the rear-guard without express orders. In the altercation which arose in consequence between these two, the prince of the Moskwa gave way to his passion in a most violent manner, without producing any effect on the coolness of Victor. At last an order of the emperor arrived; Victor was instructed to support the retreat, and Ney was summoned to Smorgoni.

CHAPTER XIII

SMORGONI

NAPOLEON had just arrived there amidst a crowd of dying men, devoured with chagrin, but not allowing the least emotion to exhibit itself in his countenance, at the sight of these unhappy men's sufferings, who, on the other hand, had allowed no murmurs to escape them in his presence. It is true that a seditious movement was impossible; it would have required an additional effort, as the strength of every man was fully occupied in struggling with hunger, cold, and fatigue; it would have required union, agreement, and mutual understanding, while famine and so many evils separated and insulated them, by concentrating every man's feelings completely in himself. Far from exhausting themselves in provocations or complaints, they marched along silently, exerting all their efforts against a hostile atmosphere, and diverted from every other idea by a state of continual action and suffering. Their physical wants absorbed their whole moral strength; they thus lived mechanically in their sensations, continuing in their duty from recollection, from the impressions which they had received in better times, and in no slight degree from that sense of honour and love of glory which had been inspired by twenty years of victory, and the warmth of which still survived and struggled within them.

The authority of the commanders also remained complete and respected, because it had always been eminently paternal, and because the dangers, the triumphs, and the calamities, had always been shared in common. It was an unhappy family, the head of which was perhaps the most to be pitied. The emperor and the grand army, therefore, preserved towards each other a melancholy and noble silence; they were both too proud to utter complaints, and too experienced not to feel the inutility of them.

Meantime, however, Napoleon had entered precipitately into his last imperial head-quarters; he there finished his final instructions, as well as the 29th and last bulletin of his expiring army. Precautions were taken in his inner apartment, that nothing of what was about to take place there should transpire until the following day.

But the presentiment of a last misfortune seized his officers; all of them would have wished to follow him. Their hearts yearned after France, to be once more in the bosom of their families, and to flee from this horrible climate; but not one of them ventured to express a wish of the kind; duty and honour restrained them.

While they affected a tranquillity which they were far from tasting, the night and the moment which the emperor had fixed for declaring his resolution to the commanders of the army arrived. All the marshals were summoned. As they successively entered, he took each of them aside in private, and first of all gained their approbation of his plan, of some by his arguments, and of others by confidential effusions.[1]

Thus it was, that on perceiving Davoust, he ran forward to meet him, and asked him why it was that he never saw him, and if he had entirely deserted him? And upon Davoust's reply that he fancied he had incurred his displeasure, the emperor explained himself mildly, received his answers favourably, confided to him the road he meant to travel, and took his advice respecting its details.

His manner was kind and flattering to them all; afterwards, having assembled them at his table, he complimented them for their noble actions during the campaign. As to himself, the only confession he made of his temerity was couched in these words: "If I had been born on the throne, if I had been a Bourbon, it would have been easy for me not to have committed any faults."

When their entertainment was over, he made Prince Eugene read to them his twenty-ninth bulletin; after which, declaring aloud what he had already confided to each of them, he told them, "that he was about to depart that very night with Duroc, Caulaincourt, and Lobau, for Paris. That his presence there was indispensable for France as well as for the remains of his unfortunate army. It was there only he could take measures for keeping the Austrians and Prussians in check. These nations would certainly pause before they declared war against him, when they saw him at the head of the French nation, and a fresh army of twelve hundred thousand men."

He added, that "he had ordered Ney to proceed to Wilna, there to reorganise the army. That Rapp would second him, and afterwards go to Dantzic, Lauriston to Warsaw, and Narbonne to Berlin; that his household would remain with the army; but that it would be necessary to strike a blow at Wilna, and stop the enemy there. There they would find Loison, De Wrede, reinforcements, provisions, and ammunition of all sorts; afterwards they would go into winter-quarters on the other side of the Niemen; that he hoped the Russians would not pass the Vistula before his return."

In conclusion, "I leave the king of Naples to command the army. I hope that you will yield him the same obedience as you would to myself, and that the greatest harmony will prevail among you."

As it was now ten o'clock at night, he rose, affectionately, embraced them all, and departed.

1. This is denied by general Gourgaud.—*Ed.*

BOOK XII

CHAPTER I

NAPOLEON'S DEPARTURE FOR PARIS

COMRADES! I must confess that my spirit, discouraged, refused to penetrate farther into the recollection of so many horrors. Having arrived at the departure of Napoleon I had flattered myself that my task was completed. I had announced myself as the historian of that great epoch, when we were precipitated from the highest summit of glory to the deepest abyss of misfortune; but now that nothing remains for me to retrace but the most frightful miseries, why should we not spare ourselves, you the pain of reading them, and myself that of tasking a memory which has now only to rake up embers, nothing but disasters to reckon, and which can no longer write but upon tombs?

But as it was our fate to push bad as well as good fortune to the utmost verge of improbability, I will endeavour to keep the promise I have made you to the conclusion. Moreover, when the history of great men relates even their last moments, how can I conceal the last sighs of the grand army when it was expiring? Every thing connected with it appertains to renown, its dying groans as well as its cries of victory. Every thing in it was grand; it will be our lot to astonish future ages with our glory and our sorrow. Melancholy consolation! but the only one that remains to us; for doubt it not, comrades, the noise of so great a fall will echo in that futurity, in which great misfortunes immortalise as much as great glory.

Napoleon passed through the crowd of his officers, who were drawn up in an avenue as he passed, bidding them adieu merely by forced and melancholy smiles; their good wishes, equally silent, and expressed only by respectful gestures, he carried with him. He and Caulaincourt shut themselves up in a carriage; his Mameluke, and Wonsowitch, captain of his guard, occupied the box; Duroc and Lobau followed in a sledge.

His escort at first consisted only of Poles; afterwards of the Neapolitans of the royal guard. This corps consisted of between six and seven hundred men, when it left Wilna to meet the emperor; it perished entirely in that short passage; the winter was its only adversary. That very night the Russians surprised and afterwards abandoned Youpranoüi, (or, as others say, Osmiana,) a town through which the escort had to pass. Napoleon was within an hour of falling into that affray.

He met the duke of Bassano at Miedniki. His first words to him were, "that he had no longer an army; that for several days past he had been marching in the midst of a troop of disbanded men wandering to and fro in search of subsistence; that they might still be rallied by giving them bread, shoes, clothing, and arms; but that the duke's military administration had anticipated nothing, and his orders had not been executed." But upon Maret replying, by showing him a statement of the immense magazines collected at Wilna, he exclaimed, "that he gave him fresh life! that he would give him an order to transmit to Murat and Berthier to halt for eight days in that capital, there to rally the army, and infuse into it sufficient heart and strength to continue the retreat less deplorably."

The subsequent part of Napoleon's journey was effected without molestation. He went round Wilna by its suburbs, crossed Wilkowiski, where he exchanged his carriage for a sledge, stopped during the 10th at Warsaw, to ask the Poles for a levy of ten thousand Cossacks, to grant them some subsidies, and to promise them he would speedily return at the head of three hundred thousand men. From thence he rapidly crossed Silesia, visited Dresden, and its monarch, passed through Hanau and Mentz, and finally got to Paris, where he suddenly made his appearance on the 19th of December, two days after the appearance of his twenty-ninth bulletin.

From Malo-Yaroslawetz to Smorgoni, this master of Europe had been no more that the general of a dying and disbanded army. From Smorgoni to the Rhine, he was an unknown fugitive, travelling through a hostile country; beyond the Rhine he again found himself the master and the conqueror of Europe. A last breeze of the wind of prosperity once more swelled his sails.

Meanwhile, his generals, whom he left at Smorgoni, approved of his departure, and, far from being discouraged, placed all their hopes in it. The army had now only to flee, the road was open, and the Russian frontier at a very short distance. They were getting within reach of a reinforcement of eighteen thousand men, all fresh troops, of a great city, and immense magazines. Murat and Berthier, left to themselves, fancied themselves able to regulate the flight. But in the midst of the extreme disorder, it required a colossus for a rallying point, and he had just disappeared. In the great chasm which he left, Murat was scarcely perceptible.

It was then too clearly seen that a great man is not replaced; either because the pride of his followers can no longer stoop to obey another, or that having always thought of, foreseen, and ordered every thing himself, he had only formed good instruments, skilful lieutenants, but no commanders.

The very first night, a general refused to obey. The marshal who commanded the rear-guard was almost the only one who returned to the royal headquarters. Three thousand men of the old and young guard were still there. This was the whole of the grand army, and of that gigantic body there remained nothing but the head. But at the news of Napoleon's departure, these veterans, spoiled by the habit of being commanded only by the conqueror of Europe, being no longer supported by the honour of serving him, and scorning to act as guards to another, gave way in their turn, and voluntarily fell into disorder.

Most of the colonels of the army, who had hitherto been such subjects of admiration, and had marched on, with only four or five officers or soldiers around their eagle, preserving their place of battle, now followed no orders but their own; each of them fancied himself entrusted with his own safety, and looked only to himself for it. Men there were who marched two hundred leagues without even looking round. It was an almost general *sauve-qui-peut*.[1]

The emperor's disappearance and Murat's incapacity were not, however, the only causes of this dispersion; the principal certainly was the severity of the winter, which at that moment became extreme. It aggravated every thing, and seemed to have planted itself completely between Wilna and the army.

Till we arrived at Malodeczno, and up till the 4th of December, the day when it set upon us with such violence, the march, although painful, had been marked by a smaller number of deaths than before we reached the Berezina. This respite was partly owing to the vigorous efforts of Ney and Maison, which had kept the enemy in check, to the then milder temperance, to the supplies which were obtained from a less ravaged country, and, finally, to the circumstance that they were the strongest men who had escaped from the passage of the Berezina.

The partial organisation which had been introduced into the disorder was kept up. The mass of runaways kept on their way, divided into a number of petty associations of eight or ten men. Many of these bands still possessed a horse, which carried their provisions, and was himself finally destined to be converted to the same purpose. A covering of rags, some utensils, a knapsack, and a stick, formed the accoutrements and the armour of these poor fellows. They no longer possessed either the arms or the uniform of a soldier, nor the desire of combating any other enemies than hunger and cold; but they still retained perseverance, firmness, the habit of danger and suffering, and a spirit always ready, pliant, and quick in making the most of their situation. Finally, among the soldiers still under arms, the dread of a nickname, by which they themselves ridiculed their comrades who had fallen into disorder, retained some influence.

But after leaving Malodeczno, and the departure of Napoleon, when winter, with all its force, and doubled in severity, attacked each of us, there was a complete dissolution of all those associations against misfortune. It was no longer anything but a multitude of insulated and individual struggles. The best no longer respected themselves; nothing stopped them; no speaking looks detained them; misfortune was hopeless of assistance, and even of regret; discouragement had no longer judges to condemn, or witnesses to prove it; all were its victims.

Henceforward there was no longer fraternity in arms, there was an end to all society, to all ties; the excess of evils had brutified them. Hunger, devouring hunger, had reduced these unfortunate men, to the brutal instinct of self-preservation, all which constitutes the understanding of the most ferocious animals, and which is ready to sacrifice every thing to itself: a rough and barbarous nature seemed to have communicated to them all its fury. Like savages, the strongest despoiled the weakest; they rushed round the dying, and frequently waited not for their last breath. When a horse fell, you might have fancied you saw a famished pack of hounds; they surrounded him, they tore him to pieces, for which they quarrelled among themselves like ravenous dogs.

The greater number, however, preserved sufficient moral strength to consult their own safety without injuring others: but this was the last effort of their virtue. If either leader or comrade fell by their side, or under the wheels of the cannon, in vain did they call for assistance, in vain did they invoke the names of a common country, religion, and cause; they could not even obtain a passing look. The cold inflexibility of the climate had completely passed into their hearts; its rigour had contracted their feelings equally with their countenances. With the exception of a few of the commanders, all were absorbed by their sufferings, and terror left no room for compassion.

Thus it was that the same selfishness with which excessive prosperity has been reproached, was produced by the excess of misfortune, but much more excusable in the latter; the first being voluntary, and the last compulsive; the first a crime of the heart, and the other an impulse of instinct entirely physical; and certainly it was hazarding one's life to stop for an instant. In this universal shipwreck, the stretching forth one's hand to a dying leader or comrade was a wonderful act of generosity. The least movement of humanity became a sublime action.

There were a few, however, who stood firm against both heaven and earth; these protected and assisted the weakest; but these were indeed rare.

1. The fact General Gourgaud states to be as follows. "Marshal Ney, who had, in the rear-guard, some platoons composed of colonels and superior officers, having seen several of those officers swept away by a discharge of grape-shot, thought that their services were too dearly bought by the loss which a future army would sustain in their fall. He rightly believed, that it would be better to have a few hundred men less at this moment, and secure the future recomposition of the army, by saving from their over-devotedness, the colonels, superior officers, and others, who, having no longer any soldiers under them, persisted in combating along with the rear-guard. He therefore ordered all officers, who had no troops, to retire beyond the Niemen."—*Ed.*

CHAPTER II

THE SUFFERINGS OF THE ARMY

ON the 6th of December, the very day after Napoleon's departure, the sky exhibited a still more dreadful appearance. You might see icy particles floating in the air; the birds fell from it quite stiff and frozen. The atmosphere was motionless and silent; it seemed as if every thing which possessed life and movement in nature, the wind itself, had been seized, chained, and as it were frozen by an universal death. Not the least word or murmur was then heard: nothing but the gloomy silence of despair, and the tears which proclaimed it.

We flitted along in this empire of death like unhappy spirits. The dull and monotonous sound of our steps, the cracking of the snow, and the feeble groans of the dying, were the only interruptions to this vast and doleful silence. Anger and imprecations there were none, nor anything which indicated a remnant of warmth; scarcely did strength enough remain to utter a prayer; most of them even fell without complaining, either from weakness or resignation, or because people only complain when they look for kindness, and fancy they are pitied.

Such of our soldiers as had hitherto been the most persevering, here lost heart entirely. Sometimes the snow opened under their feet, but more frequently its glassy surface refusing them support, they slipped at every step, and marched from one fall to another. It seemed as if this hostile soil refused to carry them, that it escaped under their efforts, that it led them into snares, as if to embarrass and retard their march, and deliver them to the Russians in pursuit of them, or to their terrible climate.

And really, whenever they halted for a moment from exhaustion, the winter, laying his heavy and icy hand upon them, was ready to seize upon his prey. In vain did these poor unfortunates, feeling themselves benumbed, raise themselves, and already deprived of the power of speech and plunged into a stupor, proceed a few steps like automatons their blood freezing in their veins, like water in the current of rivulets, congealed their heart, and then flew back to their heads; these dying men then staggered as if they had been intoxicated. From their eyes, which were reddened and inflamed by the continual aspect of the snow, by the want of sleep, and the smoke of bivouacs, there flowed real tears of blood; their bosoms heaved heavy sighs; they looked at heaven, at us, and at the earth, with an eye dismayed, fixed, and wild; it expressed their farewell, and perhaps their reproaches to the barbarous nature which tortured them. They were not long before they fell upon their knees, and then upon their hands; their heads still wavered for a few minutes alternately to the right and left, and from their open mouth some agonising sounds escaped; at last it fell in its turn upon the snow, which it reddened immediately, with livid blood; and their sufferings were at an end.

Their comrades passed by them without moving a step out of their way, for fear of prolonging their journey, or even turning their head; for their beards and their hair were so stiffened with the ice, that every movement was a pain. They did not even pity them; for, in short, what had they lost by dying? what had they left behind them? They suffered so much; they were still so far from France; so much divested of feelings of country by the surrounding aspect, and by misery, that every dear illusion was broken, and hope almost destroyed. The greater number, therefore, were become careless of dying, from necessity, from the habit of seeing it, and from fashion, sometimes even treating it contemptuously; but more frequently, on seeing these unfortunates stretched out, and immediately stiffened, contenting themselves with the thought that they had no more wishes, that they were at rest, that their sufferings were terminated? And, in fact, death, in a situation quiet, certain, and uniform, may be always a strange event, a frightful contrast, a terrible revolution; but in this tumult, and violent and continual movement of a life of constant action, danger, and suffering, it appeared nothing more than a transition, a slight change, an additional removal, and which excited little alarm.

Such were the last *days* of the grand army. Its last *nights* were still more frightful; those whom they surprised marching together, far from every habitation, halted on the borders of the woods; there they lighted their fires, before which they remained the whole night, erect and motionless like spectres. They seemed as if they could never have enough of the heat; they kept so close to it as to burn their clothes, as well as the frozen parts of their body, which the fire decomposed. The most dreadful pain then compelled them to stretch themselves, and the next day they attempted in vain to rise.

In the mean time, such as the winter had almost wholly spared, and who still retained some portion of courage, prepared their melancholy meal. It consisted, ever since they had left Smolensk, of some slices of horse-flesh broiled, and some rye-meal diluted into a *bouillie* with snow-water, or kneaded into muffins, which they seasoned, for want of salt, with the powder of their cartridges.

The sight of these fires was constantly attracting fresh spectres, who were driven back by the first comers. These poor wretches wandered about from one bivouac to another, until they were struck by the frost and despair together, and gave themselves up for lost. They then laid themselves down upon the snow, behind their more fortunate comrades, and there expired. Many of them, destitute of the means and the strength necessary to cut down the lofty fir trees, made vain attempts to set fire to them at the trunk: but death speedily surprised them around these trees in every sort of attitude.

Under the vast pent-houses which are erected by the sides of the high road in some parts of the way, scenes of still greater horror were witnessed. Officers and soldiers all rushed precipitately into them, and crowded together in heaps. There, like so many cattle, they squeezed against each other round the fires, and as the living could not remove the dead from the circle, they laid themselves down upon them, there to expire in their turn, and serve as a bed of death to some fresh victims. In a short time additional crowds of stragglers presented themselves, and being unable to penetrate into these asylums of suffering, they completely besieged them.

It frequently happened that they demolished their walls, which were formed of dry wood, in order to feed their fires; at other times, repulsed and disheartened, they were contented to use them as shelters to their bivouacs, the flames of which very soon communicated to these habitations, and the soldiers whom they contained, already half dead with the cold, were completely killed by the fire. Such of us as these places of shelter preserved, found next day our comrades lying frozen and in heaps around their extinguished fires. To escape from these catacombs, a horrible effort was required to enable them to climb over the heaps of these poor wretches, many of whom were still breathing.

At Youpranoüi, the same village where the emperor only missed by an hour being taken by the Russian partisan Seslawin, the soldiers burnt the houses completely as they stood, merely to warm themselves for a few minutes. The light of these fires attracted some of those miserable wretches, whom the excessive severity of the cold and their sufferings had rendered delirious; they ran to them like madmen, and gnashing their teeth and laughing like demons; they threw themselves into these furnaces, where they perished in the most horrible convulsions. Their famished companions regarded them undismayed; there were even some who drew out these bodies, disfigured and broiled by the flames,—and it is but too true, that they ventured to pollute their mouths with this loathsome food!

This was the same army which had been formed from the most civilised nation in Europe; that army, formerly so brilliant, which was victorious over men to its last moment, and whose name still reigned in so many conquered capitals. Its strongest and bravest warriors, who had recently been proudly traversing so many scenes of their victories, had lost their noble countenance; covered with rags, their feet naked and torn, supporting themselves on branches of fir tree, they dragged themselves along; all the strength and perseverance which they had hitherto put forth in order to conquer, they now made use of to flee.

Then it was, that, like superstitious nations, we also had our prognostications, and heard talk of prophecies. Some pretended that a comet had enlightened our passage across the Berezina with its ill-omened fire; it is true that they added, "that doubtless these stars did not foretell the great events of this world, but that they might certainly contribute to modify them; at least, if we admitted their material influence upon our globe, and all the consequences which that influence may exercise upon the human mind, so far as it is dependent on the matter which it animates."

There were others who quoted ancient predictions, which, they said, "had announced for that period an invasion of the Tartars as far as the banks of the Seine. And, behold! they were already at liberty to pass over the overthrown French army, and in a fair way to accomplish that prediction."

Some again there were, who reminded each other of the awful and destructive storm which had signalised our entrance on the Russian territory. "Then it was Heaven itself that spoke! Behold the calamity which it predicted! Nature had made an effort to prevent this catastrophe! Why had we been obstinately deaf to her voice?" So much did this simultaneous fall of four hundred thousand men (an event which was not in fact more extraordinary than the host of epidemical disorders and of revolutions which are constantly ravaging the globe) appear to them an extraordinary and unique event, which must have occupied all the powers of heaven and earth; so much is our understanding led to bring home every thing to itself; as if Providence, in compassion to our weakness, and from the fear of its annihilating itself at the prospect of eternity, had so ordered it, that every man, a mere point in space, should act and feel as if he himself was the centre of immensity.

CHAPTER II

WILNA

THE army was in this last state of physical and moral distress, when its first fugitives reached Wilna. Wilna! their magazine, their depôt, the first rich and inhabited city which they had met with since their entrance into Russia. Its name alone, and its proximity, still supported the courage of a few.

On the 9th of December, the greatest part of these poor soldiers at last arrived within sight of that capital. Instantly, some dragging themselves along, others rushing forward, they all precipitated themselves headlong into its suburbs, pushing obstinately before them, and crowding together so fast, that they formed but one mass of men, horses, and chariots, motionless, and deprived of the power of movement.

The clearing away of this crowd by a narrow passage became almost impossible. Those who came behind, guided by a stupid instinct, added to the incumbrance, without the least idea of entering the city by the other entrances, of which there were several. But there was such complete disorganisation, that during the whole of that fatal day, not a single staff-officer made his appearance to direct these men to them.

For the space of ten hours, with the cold at 27 and even at 28 degrees, thousands of soldiers who fancied themselves in safety, died either from cold or suffocation, just as had happened at the gates of Smolensk, and at the bridges across the Berezina. Sixty thousand men had crossed that river, and twenty thousand recruits had since joined them; of these eighty thousand, half had already perished, the greater part within the last four days, between Malodeczno and Wilna.

The capital of Lithuania was still ignorant of our disasters, when, all at once, forty thousand famished soldiers filled it with groans and lamentations. At this unexpected sight, its inhabitants became alarmed, and shut their doors. Deplorable then was it to see these troops of wretched wanderers in the streets, some furious and others desperate, threatening or entreating, endeavouring to break open the doors of the houses and the magazines, or dragging themselves to the hospitals. Everywhere they were repulsed; at the magazines, from most unseasonable formalities, as, from the dissolution of the corps and the mixture of the soldiers, all regular distribution had become impossible.

There had been collected there sufficient flour and bread to last for forty days, and butcher's meat for thirty-six days, for one hundred thousand men. Not a single commander ventured to step forward and give orders for distributing these provisions to all that came for them. The administrators who had them in charge were afraid of being made responsible for them; and the others dreaded the excesses to which the famished soldiers would give themselves up, when every thing was at their discretion. These administrators besides were ignorant of our desperate situation, and when there was scarcely time for pillage, had they been so inclined, our unfortunate comrades were left for several hours to die of hunger at the very doors of these immense magazines of provisions, all of which fell into the enemy's hands the following day.

At the barracks and the hospitals they were equally repulsed, but not by the living, for there death held sway supreme. The few who still breathed complained that for a long time they had been without beds, even without straw, and almost deserted. The courts, the passages, and even the apartments, were filled with heaps of dead bodies; they were so many charnel houses of infection.

At last, the exertions of several of the commanders, such as Eugene and Davoust, the compassion of the Lithuanians, and the avarice of the Jews, opened some places of refuge.[1] Nothing could be more remarkable than the astonishment which these unfortunate men displayed at finding themselves once more in inhabited houses. How delicious did a loaf of leavened bread appear to them, and how inexpressible the pleasure of eating it seated! and afterwards, with what admiration were they struck at seeing a scanty battalion still under arms, in regular order, and uniformly dressed! They seemed to have returned from the very extremities of the earth; so much had the violence and continuity of their sufferings torn and cast them from all their habits, so deep had been the abyss from which they had escaped!

But scarcely had they begun to taste these sweets, when the cannon of the Russians commenced thundering over their heads and upon the city. These threatening sounds, the shouts of the officers, the drums beating to arms, and the wailings and clamour of an additional multitude of unfortunates, which had just arrived, filled Wilna with fresh confusion. It was the vanguard of Kutusoff and Tchaplitz, commanded by O'Rourke, Landskoy, and Seslawin, that had attacked Loison's division, which was protecting the city, as well as the retreat of a column of dismounted cavalry, on its way to Olita, by way of Novoï-Troky.

At first an attempt was made to resist. De Wrede and his Bavarians had also just rejoined the army by Naroc-Zwiransky and Niamentchin. They were pursued by Wittgenstein, who from Kamen and Vileika hung upon our right flank, at the same time that Kutusoff and Tchitchakoff were pursuing us. De Wrede had not two thousand men left under his command. As to Loison's division and the garrison of Wilna, which had come to meet us as far as Smorgoni, and render us assistance, the cold had reduced them from fifteen thousand men to three thousand in the space of three days.

De Wrede defended Wilna on the side of Rukoni; he was obliged to fall back after a gallant resistance. Loison and his division, on his side, which was nearer to Wilna, kept the enemy in check. They had succeeded in making a Neapolitan division take arms, and even to go out of the city, but the muskets actually slipped from the hands of these men transplanted from a burning climate to a region of ice. In less than an hour they all returned disarmed, and the best part of them maimed.

At the same time, the *générale* was ineffectually beaten in the streets; the old guard itself, now reduced to a few platoons, remained dispersed. Every one thought much more of disputing his life with famine and the cold than with the enemy. But when the cry of "Here are the Cossacks," was heard, (which for a long time had been the only signal which the greater number obeyed,) it echoed immediately throughout the whole city, and the rout again began.

De Wrede presented himself unexpectedly before the king of Naples. He said, "the enemy were close at his heels! the Bavarians had been driven back into Wilna, which they could no longer defend." At the same time, the noise of the tumult reached the king's ear. Murat was astonished: fancying himself no longer master of the army, he lost all command of himself. He instantly quitted his palace on foot, and was seen forcing his way through the crowd. He seemed to be afraid of a skirmish, in the midst of a crowd similar to that of the day before. He halted, however, at the last house in the suburbs, from whence he despatched his orders, and where he waited for daylight and the army, leaving Ney in charge of the rest.

Wilna might have been defended for twenty-four hours longer, and many men might have been saved. This fatal city retained nearly twenty thousand, including three hundred officers and seven generals. Most of them had been wounded by the winter more than by the enemy, who had the merit of the triumph. Several others were still in good health, to all appearance at least, but their moral strength was completely exhausted. After courageously battling with so many difficulties, they lost heart when they were near the port, at the prospect of four days' march. They had at last found themselves once more in a civilised city, and sooner than make up their minds to return to the desert, they placed themselves at the mercy of Fortune; she treated them cruelly.

It is true that the Lithuanians, although we had compromised them so much, and were now abandoning them, received into their houses and succoured several; but the Jews, whom we had protected, repelled the others. They did even more; the sight of so many sufferers excited their cupidity. Had their detestable avarice been contented with speculating upon our miseries, and selling us, some feeble succours for their weight in gold, history would scorn to sully her pages with the disgusting detail; but they enticed our unhappy wounded men into their houses, stripped them, and afterwards, on seeing the Russians, threw the naked bodies of these dying victims from the doors and windows of their houses into the streets, and there unmercifully left them to perish of cold; these vile barbarians even made a merit in the eyes of the Russians of torturing them there. Such horrible crimes as these must be denounced to the present and to future ages. Now that our hands are become impotent, it is probable that our indignation against these monsters may be their sole punishment in this world; but a day will come, when the assassins will again meet their victims, and there, certainly, divine justice will avenge us!

On the 10th of December, Ney, who had again voluntarily taken upon himself the command of the rear-guard, left that city, which was immediately after inundated by the Cossacks of Platoff, who massacred all the poor wretches whom the Jews threw in their way. In the midst of this butchery, there suddenly appeared a piquet of thirty French, coming from the bridge of the Vilia, where they had been left and forgotten. At sight of this fresh prey, thousands of Russian horsemen came hurrying up, besetting them with loud cries, and assailing them on all sides.

But the officer commanding this piquet had already drawn up his soldiers in a circle. Without hesitation, he ordered them

to fire, and then, making them present bayonets, proceeded at
the *pas de charge*. In an instant all fled before him; he remained
in possession of the city; but, without feeling more surprise
about the cowardice of the Cossacks than he had done at
their attack, he took advantage of the moment, turned sharply
round, and succeeded in rejoining the rear-guard without loss.

The latter was engaged with Kutusoff's vanguard, which it
was endeavouring to drive back; for another catastrophe, which
it vainly attempted to cover, detained it at a short distance from
Wilna.

There, as well as at Moscow, Napoleon had given no regular
order for retreat:[2] he was anxious that our defeat should have
no forerunner, but that it should proclaim itself, and take our
allies and their ministers by surprise, and that, taking advantage
of their first astonishment, we might be able to pass through
those nations before they were prepared to join the Russians
and overpower us.

This was the reason why the Lithuanians, strangers, and every
one at Wilna, even to the minister himself, had been deceived.
They did not believe our disaster until they saw it; and in that,
the almost superstitious belief of Europe in the infallibility of
the genius of Napoleon was of use to him against his allies. But
the same confidence had buried his own officers in a profound
security; at Wilna, as well as at Moscow, not one of them was
prepared for a movement of any description.

This city contained a large proportion of the baggage of the
army, and of its treasures, its provisions, a crowd of enormous
wagons, loaded with the emperor's equipage, a large quantity
of artillery, and a great number of wounded men. Our retreat
had come upon them like an unexpected storm, almost like a
thunderbolt. Some were terrified and thrown into confusion,
while consternation kept others motionless. Orders, men,
horses, and carriages, were running about in all directions,
crossing and overturning each other.

In the midst of this tumult, several of the commanders
pushed forward out of the city, towards Kowno, with all the

troops they could contrive to muster; but at the distance of a
league from the latter place this heavy and frightened column
encountered the height and the defile of Ponari.

During our conquering march, this woody hillock had only
appeared to our hussars a fortunate accident of the ground, from
which they could discover the whole plain of Wilna, and take a
survey of their enemies. Its rough but short declivity had then
scarcely been remarked. During a regular retreat it would have
presented an excellent position for turning round and stopping
the enemy: but in a disorderly flight, where every thing that
might be of service became injurious, where in our precipitation
and disorder every thing was turned against ourselves, this hill
and its defile became an insurmountable obstacle, a wall of ice,
against which all our efforts were powerless. It detained every
thing, baggage, treasure, and wounded. The evil was sufficiently
great in this long series of disasters to form an epoch.

Here, in fact, it was, that money, honour, and all remains of
discipline and strength were completely lost. After fifteen hours
of fruitless efforts, when the drivers and the soldiers of the escort
saw the king of Naples and the whole columns of fugitives
passing them by the sides of the hill; when they turned their
eyes at the noise of the cannon and musketry which was coming
nearer them every instant, and they saw Ney himself retreating
with three thousand men (the remains of De Wrede's corps
and Loison's division); when at last, turning their eyes back to
themselves, they saw the hill completely covered with cannon
and carriages, broken or overturned, men and horses fallen to
the ground, and expiring one upon the other,—then it was, that
they gave up all idea of saving any thing, and determined only
to anticipate the enemy by becoming plunderers themselves.

One of the covered wagons of treasure, which burst open of
itself, served as a signal: every one rushed to the others: they
were immediately broken, and the most valuable effects taken
from them. The soldiers of the rear-guard, who were passing
at the time of this disorder, threw away their arms to join in
the plunder; they were so eagerly engaged in it as neither to

hear nor to pay attention to the whistling of the balls and the howling of the Cossacks in pursuit of them.[3]

It is even said that the Cossacks got mixed among them without being observed. For some minutes, French and Tartars, friends and foes, were confounded in the same greediness. French and Russians, forgetting they were at war, were seen pillaging together the same treasure-wagons. Ten millions of gold and silver then disappeared.

But amidst all these horrors, there were noble acts of devotion. Some there were, who abandoned every thing to save some of the unfortunate wounded by carrying them on their shoulders; several others, being unable to extricate their half-frozen comrades from this medley, lost their lives in defending them from the attacks of their countrymen, and the blows of their enemies.

On the most exposed part of the hill, an officer of the emperor, colonel the count de Turenne, repulsed the Cossacks, and in defiance of their cries of rage and their fire, he distributed before their eyes the private treasure of Napoleon to the guards whom he found within his reach. These brave men, fighting with one hand and collecting the spoils of their leader with the other, succeeded in saving them. Long afterwards, when they were out of all danger, each man faithfully restored the depôt which had been entrusted to him. Not a single piece of money was lost.

1. Officers had been placed at the gates of Wilna, to point out to the soldiers of the various corps the convents and other edifices, which had been assigned to them as barracks, and where they were to rally and receive their rations. But the soldiers chose rather to wander through the town and enter the houses.—*Ed.*

2. This is contradicted by various instructions, which Napoleon ordered Berthier to address to the generals.—*Ed.*

3. "The real fact is this," says general Gourgaud, "a director of the post-office informed marshal Ney that for want of horses, he had

been obliged to abandon his wagon, which contained some money belonging to the state. The marshal asked whether, at least, he had shared the money among the unfortunate soldiers who swarmed on the road. A negative being returned, Ney expressed his regret that the money should have been left for the enemy. On the morrow he quitted Wilna with the rear-guard, and, when he came to the foot of the mountain of Ponari, he saw a long file of treasure-wagons brought to a stand there. As the enemy followed us so closely, that Ney saw it was impossible to save them, he ordered the chests to be opened, and the money to be given to whoever would take it."—*Ed.*

CHAPTER IV

RETREAT TO
AND DEFENCE OF KOWNO

THIS catastrophe at Ponari was the more disgraceful as it was easy to foresee, and equally easy to prevent it; for the hill could have been turned by its sides. The fragments which we abandoned, however, were at least of some use in arresting the pursuit of the Cossacks. While these were busy in collecting their prey, Ney, at the head of a few hundred French and Bavarians, supported the retreat as far as Evé. As this was his last effort, we must not omit the description of his method of retreat which he had followed ever since he left Viazma, on the 3rd of November, during thirty-seven days, and thirty-seven nights.

Every day, at five o'clock in the evening, he took his position, stopped the Russians, allowed his soldiers to eat and take sortie rest, and resumed his march at ten o'clock. During the whole of the night, he pushed the mass of the stragglers before him, by dint of cries, of entreaties, and of blows. At daybreak, which was about seven o'clock, he halted, again took position, and rested under arms and on guard until ten o'clock; the enemy then made his appearance, and he was compelled to fight until the evening, gaining as much or as little ground in the rear as possible. That depended at first on the general order of march, and at a later period upon circumstances.

For a long time this rear-guard did not consist of more than two thousand, then of one thousand, afterwards about five hundred, and finally of sixty men; and yet Berthier, either designedly or from mere routine, made no change in his instructions. These were always addressed to the commander of a corps of thirty-five thousand men; in them he coolly detailed all the different positions, which were to be taken up and guarded until the next day, by divisions and regiments which no longer existed. And every night, when, in consequence of Ney's urgent warnings, he was obliged to go and awake the king of Naples, and compel him to resume his march, he testified the same astonishment.

In this manner did Ney support the retreat from Viazma to Evé, and a few wersts beyond it. There, according to his usual custom, he had stopped the Russians, and was giving the first hours of the night to rest, when, about ten o'clock, he and De Wrede perceived that they had been left alone. Their soldiers had deserted them, as well as their arms, which they saw shining and piled together close to their abandoned fires.

Fortunately the intensity of the cold, which had just completed the discouragement of our people, had also benumbed their enemies. Ney overtook his column with some difficulty; it was now only a band of fugitives, which a handful of Cossacks chased before them, without attempting either to take or to kill them; either from compassion, for one gets tired of every thing in time, or that the enormity of our misery had terrified even the Russians themselves, and they believed themselves sufficiently revenged, for many of them behaved generously; or, finally, that they were satiated and overloaded with booty. It might also be, that in the darkness they did not perceive that they had only to do with unarmed men.

Winter, that terrible ally of the Muscovites, had sold them his assistance dearly. Their disorder pursued our disorder. We often saw prisoners who had escaped several times from their frozen hands and looks. They had at first marched in the middle of their straggling column without being noticed by it. There were some of them, who, taking advantage of a favourable moment, ventured to attack the Russian soldiers when separated, and strip them of their provisions, their uniforms, and even their arms, with which they covered themselves. Under this disguise, they mingled with their conquerors; and such was the disorganisation, the stupid carelessness, and the numbness into which their army had fallen, that these prisoners marched for a whole month in the midst of them without being recognised. The hundred and twenty thousand men of Kutusoff's army were then reduced to thirty-five thousand. Of Wittgenstein's fifty thousand, scarcely fifteen thousand remained. Wilson asserts, that of a reinforcement of ten thousand men, sent from the interior of Russia with all the precautions which they know how to take against the winter, not more than seventeen hundred arrived at Wilna. But a head of a column was quite sufficient against our disarmed soldiers. Ney attempted in vain to rally a few of them, and he who had hitherto been almost the only one whose commands had been obeyed in the rout, was now compelled to follow it.

He arrived along with it at Kowno, which was the last town of the Russian empire. Finally, on the 13th of December, after marching forty-six days under a terrible yoke, they once more came in sight of a friendly country. Instantly, without halting or looking behind them, the greater part plunged into, and dispersed themselves, in the forests of Prussian Poland. Some there were, however, who, on their arrival on the allied bank of the Niemen, turned round; there, when they cast a look on that land of suffering from which they were escaping, when they found themselves on the same spot, whence five months previously their countless eagles had taken their victorious flight, it is said that tears flowed from their eyes, and that they uttered exclamations of grief.

"This then was the bank which they had studded with their bayonets! this the allied country which had disappeared only five months before, under the steps of an immense united army, and seemed to them then to be metamorphosed into moving hills and valleys of men and horses! These were the same valleys, from which, under the rays of a burning sun, poured forth the three long columns of dragoons and cuirassiers, resembling three rivers of glittering iron and brass. And now, men, arms, eagles, horses, the sun itself, and even this frontier river, which they had crossed replete with ardour and hope, all have disappeared. The Niemen is now only a long mass of flakes of ice, caught and chained to each other by the increasing severity of the winter. Instead of the three French bridges, brought from a distance of five hundred leagues, and thrown across it with such audacious promptitude, a Russian bridge is alone standing. Finally, in the room of these innumerable warriors, of their four hundred thousand comrades, who had been so often their partners in victory, and who had dashed forward with such joy and pride into the territory of Russia, they saw issuing from these pale and frozen deserts, only a thousand infantry and horsemen still under arms, nine cannon, and twenty thousand miserable wretches covered with rags, with downcast looks, hollow eyes, earthy and livid complexions, long beards matted with the frost; some disputing in silence the narrow passage of the bridge, which, in spite of their small number, was not sufficient to the eagerness of their flight; others fleeing dispersed over the asperities of the river, labouring and dragging themselves from one point of ice to another; and this was the whole grand army! Besides, many of these fugitives were recruits who had just joined it!"

Two kings, one prince, eight marshals, followed by a few officers, generals on foot, dispersed, and without any attendants; finally, a few hundred men of the old guard, still armed, were its remains; they alone represented it.

Or rather, I should say, it still breathed completely and entirely in marshal Ney. Comrades! allies! enemies! here I invoke your testimony: let us pay the homage which is due to the memory of an unfortunate hero: and the facts will be sufficient.

All were flying, and Murat himself, traversing Kowno as he had done Wilna, first gave, and then withdrew the order to rally at Tilsit, and subsequently fixed upon Gumbinnen. Ney then entered Kowno, accompanied only by his aides-de-camp, for all besides had given way, or fallen around him. From the time of his leaving Viazma, this was the fourth rear-guard which had been worn out and melted in his hands. But winter and famine, still more than the Russians, had destroyed them. For the fourth time he remained alone before the enemy, and still unshaken, he sought for a fifth rear-guard.

At Kowno the marshal found a company of artillery, three hundred German soldiers who formed its garrison, and general Marchand with four hundred men; of these he took the command. He first walked over the town to reconnoitre its position, and to rally some additional forces, but he found only some sick and wounded, who were endeavouring, in tears, to follow our retreat. For the eighth time since we left Moscow, we were obliged to abandon these *en masse* in their hospitals, as they had been abandoned singly along the whole march, on all our fields of battle; and at all our bivouacs.

Several thousand soldiers covered the market place and the neighbouring streets; but they were laid out stiff before the liquor-shops which they had broken open, and where they drank the cup of death, from which they fancied they were to inhale fresh life. These were the only succours which Murat had left him; Ney found himself left alone in Russia, with seven hundred foreign recruits. At Kowno, as it had been after the disasters of Viazma, of Smolensk, of the Berezina, and of Wilna, it was to him that the honour of our arms and all the peril of the last steps of our retreat were again confided.

On the 14th, at day-break, the Russians commenced their attack. One of their columns made a hasty advance from the Wilna road, while another crossed the Niemen on the ice above the town, landed on the Prussian territory, and, proud of being the first to cross its frontier, marched to the bridge of Kowno, to close that outlet upon Ney, and completely cut off his retreat.

The first firing was heard at the Wilna gate; Ney ran thither, with a view to drive away Platoff's artillery with his own; but he found his cannon had been already spiked, and that his artillerymen had fled! Enraged, he darted forward, and elevating his sword, would have killed the officer who commanded them, had it not been for his aide-de-camp, who warded off the blow, and enabled this miserable fellow to make his escape.

Ney then summoned his infantry, but only one of the two feeble battalions of which it was composed had taken up arms; it consisted of the three hundred Germans of the garrison. He drew them up, encouraged them, and as the enemy was approaching, was just about to give them the order to fire, when a Russian cannon ball, grazing the pallisade, came and broke the thigh of their commanding officer. He fell, and without the least hesitation, finding that his wound was mortal, he coolly drew out his pistols and blew out his brains before his troop. Terrified at this act of despair, his soldiers became completely scared; all of them at once threw down their arms, and fled in disorder.

Ney, abandoned by all, neither deserted himself nor his post. After vain efforts to detain these fugitives, he collected their muskets, which were still loaded, became once more a common soldier, and with only four others, kept facing thousands of the Russians. His audacity stopped them; it made some of his artillerymen ashamed, who imitated their marshal; it gave time to his aide Heymès, and to general Gerard, to embody thirty soldiers, bring forward two or three light pieces, and to generals Ledru and Marchand to collect the only battalion which remained.

But at that moment the second attack of the Russians commenced on the other side of the Niemen, and near the bridge of Kowno; it was then half-past two o'clock. Ney sent Ledru, Marchand, and their four hundred men forward to retake and secure that passage. As to himself, without giving way, or disquieting himself farther as to what was passing in his rear, he kept on fighting at the head of his thirty men, and maintained himself until night at the Wilna gate. He then traversed the town and crossed the Niemen, constantly fighting, retreating, but never flying, marching after all the others, supporting to the last moment the honour of our arms, and for the hundredth time during the last forty days and forty nights, putting his life and liberty in jeopardy to save a few more Frenchmen. Finally, he was the last of the grand army who quitted that fatal Russia, exhibiting to the world the impotence of fortune against great courage, and proving that with heroes every thing turns to glory, even the greatest disasters.

It was eight o'clock at night when he reached the allied bank. Then it was, that seeing the completion of the catastrophe, Marchand repulsed to the entrance of the bridge, and the road of Wilkowisky, which Murat had taken, completely covered with the enemy's troops, he darted off to the right, plunged into the woods, and disappeared.

CHAPTER V

FIRST SYMPTOMS
OF MURAT'S DEFECTION

WHEN Murat reached Gumbinnen, he was exceedingly surprised to find Ney already there, and to find, that since it had left Kowno, the army was marching without a rear-guard. Fortunately the pursuit of the Russians, after they had re-conquered their own territory, became slackened. They seemed to hesitate on the Prussian frontier, not knowing whether they should enter it as allies or as enemies. Murat took advantage of their uncertainty, to halt a few days at Gumbinnen, and to direct the remains of the different corps to the towns on the borders of the Vistula.

Previous to this dislocation of the army, he assembled the commanders of it. I know not what evil genius it was that inspired him at this council. One would fain believe that it was the embarrassment he felt before these warriors for his precipitate flight, and spite against the emperor, who had left him with the responsibility of it: or it might be shame at appearing again, vanquished, in the midst of the nations whom our victories had most oppressed; but as his language bore a much more mischievous character, which his subsequent actions did not belie, and as they were the first symptoms of his defection, history must not pass over them in silence.

This warrior, who had been elevated to the throne solely by the right of victory, now returned discomfited. From the first step he took upon vanquished territory, he fancied he felt it everywhere trembling under his feet, and that his crown was tottering on his head. A thousand times during the campaign, he had exposed himself to the greatest dangers; but he, who, as a king, had as little fear of death as the meanest soldier of the vanguard, could not bear the apprehension of living without a crown. Behold him then, in the midst of the commanders, whom his brother had placed under his direction, accusing that brother's ambition, which he had shared, in order to free himself from the responsibility which its gratification had involved.

He exclaimed, "that it was no longer possible to serve such a madman! that there was no safety in supporting his cause; that no monarch in Europe could now place any reliance on his word, or in the treaties concluded with him. He himself was in despair for having rejected the propositions of the English; had it not been for that, he would still be a great monarch, such as the emperor of Austria and the king of Prussia."

Davoust abruptly cut him short. "The king of Prussia, the emperor of Austria," said he to him, "are monarchs by the grace of God, of time, and the custom of nations. But as to you, you are only a king by the grace of Napoleon, and of the blood of Frenchmen; you cannot remain so but through Napoleon, and by continuing united to France. You are blinded by the blackest ingratitude!" And he declared to him that he would immediately denounce his treachery to his emperor; the other marshals remained silent. They made allowance for the violence of the king's grief, and attributed solely to his inconsiderate heat the expressions which the hatred and suspicious character of Davoust had but too clearly comprehended.

Murat was put entirely out of countenance; he felt himself guilty. Thus was stifled the first spark of treachery, which at a later period was destined to ruin France. It is with regret that history commemorates it, as repentance and misfortune have atoned for the crime.

We were soon obliged to carry our humiliation to Königsberg. The grand army, which, during the last twenty years, had shown itself successively triumphant in all the capitals of Europe, now, for the first time, re-appeared mutilated, disarmed, and fugitive, in one of those which had been most humiliated by its glory. Its population crowded on our passage to count our wounds, and to estimate, by the extent of our disasters, that of the hopes they might venture to entertain; we were compelled to feast their greedy looks with our miseries, to pass under the yoke of their hope, and while dragging our misfortunes through the midst of their odious joy, to march under the insupportable weight of hated calamity.

The feeble remnant of the grand army did not bend under this burden. Its shadow, already almost dethroned, still exhibited itself imposing; it preserved its royal air; although vanquished by the elements, it kept up, in the presence of men, its victorious and commanding attitude.

On their side, the Germans, either from slowness or fear, received us docilely; their hatred restrained itself under an appearance of coolness; and as they scarcely ever act from themselves, they were obliged to relieve our miseries, during the time that they were looking for a signal. Königsberg was soon unable to contain them. Winter, which had followed us thither, deserted us there all at once; in one night the thermometer rose twenty degrees.

This sudden change was fatal to us. A great number of soldiers and generals, whom the tension of the atmosphere had hitherto supported by a continued irritation, sunk and fell into decomposition. Lariboissière, general-in-chief of the artillery, fell a sacrifice; Eblé, the pride of the army, followed him. Every day and every hour, our consternation was increased by fresh deaths.

In the midst of this general mourning, an insurrection, and a letter from Macdonald, contributed to convert all these sorrows into despair. The sick could no longer cherish the expectation of dying free; the friend was either compelled to desert his expiring friend, the brother his brother, or to drag them in that state to Elbing. The insurrection was only alarming as a symptom; it was put down; but the intelligence transmitted by Macdonald was decisive.

CHAPTER VI

MACDONALD AND THE PRUSSIAN ARMY

ON the side where that marshal commanded the whole of the war had been only a rapid march from Tilsit to Mittau, a display of force from the mouth of the Aa to Dünabourg, and finally, a long defensive position in front of Riga; the composition of that army being almost entirely Prussian, its position and Napoleon's orders so willed it.

It was a piece of great daring in the emperor to entrust his left wing, as well as his right and his retreat, to Prussians and Austrians. It was observed, that at the same time he had dispersed the Poles throughout the whole army; many persons thought that it would have been preferable to collect in one point the zeal of the latter, and to have divided the hatred of the former. But we every where required natives as interpreters, scouts, or guides, and felt the value of their audacious ardour on the true points of attack. As to the Prussians and Austrians, it is probable that they would not have allowed themselves to be dispersed. On the left, Macdonald, with seven thousand Bavarians, Westphalians, and Poles, mixed with twenty-two thousand Prussians, appeared sufficient to answer for the latter, as well as for the Russians.

In the advance march, there had been at first nothing to do, but to drive the Russian posts before them, and to carry off some magazines. Afterwards there were a few skirmishes between the Aa and Riga. The Prussians, after a rather warm affair, took Eckau from the Russian general Lewis; after which both sides remained quiet for twenty days. Macdonald employed that time in taking possession of Dünaburg, and in getting the heavy artillery brought to Mittau, which was necessary for the siege of Riga.

On the intelligence of his approach, on the 23rd of August, the commander-in-chief at Riga made all his troops march out of the place in three columns. The two weakest were to make two false attacks; the first by proceeding along the coast of the Baltic sea, and the second directly on Mittau; the third, which was the strongest, and commanded by Lewis, was at the same time to retake Eckau, drive back the Prussians as far as the Aa, cross that river, and either capture or destroy the park of artillery.

The plan succeeded as far as beyond the Aa, when Grawert, supported latterly by Kleist, repulsed Lewis, and following the Russians closely as far as Eckau, defeated them there entirely. Lewis fled in disorder as far as the Dwina, which he re-crossed by fording it, leaving behind a great number of prisoners.

Thus far Macdonald was satisfied. It is even said, that at Smolensk Napoleon thought of elevating Yorck to the dignity of a marshal of the empire, at the same time that at Vienna he caused Schwartzenberg to be named field-marshal. The claims of these two commanders to the honour were by no means equal.

In both wings, disagreeable symptoms were manifested; with the Austrians, it was among the officers that they were fermenting; their general kept them firm in their alliance with us; he even apprised us of their bad disposition, and pointed out the means of preventing the contagion from spreading among the other allied troops which were mixed with his.

The case was quite the contrary with our left wing; the Prussian army marched without the least after-thought, at the very time that its general was conspiring against us. On the right wing, therefore, during the time of combat, it was the leader who drew his troops after him in spite of themselves; while, on the left wing, the troops pushed forward their commander, almost in spite of himself.

Among the latter, the officers, the soldiers, and Grawert himself, a loyal old warrior who had no political feelings, entered frankly into the war. They fought like lions on all occasions when their commander left them at liberty to do so; they expressed themselves, anxious to wash out, in the eyes of the French, the shame of their defeat in 1806, to re-conquer our esteem, to vanquish in the presence of their conquerors, to prove that their defeat was only attributable to their government, and that they were worthy of a better fate.

Yorck had higher views. He belonged to the society of the *Friends of Virtue*, whose principle was hatred of the French, and whose object was their complete expulsion from Germany. But Napoleon was still victorious, and the Prussian afraid to commit himself. Besides, the justice, the mildness, and the military reputation of Macdonald had completely gained the affection of his troops. They said "they had never been so happy as when under the command of a Frenchman." In fact, as they were united with the conquerors, and shared the rights of conquest with them, they had allowed themselves to be seduced by the all-powerful attraction of being on the side of the victor.

Every thing contributed to it. Their administration was directed by an intendant and agents taken from their own army. They lived in abundance. It was on that very point, however, that the quarrel between Macdonald and Yorck began, and that the hatred of the latter found an opening to diffuse itself.

First of all, some complaints were made in the country against their administration. Shortly after, a French administrator arrived, and either from rivalry or a spirit of justice, he accused the Prussian intendant of exhausting the country by enormous requisitions of cattle. "He sent them," it was said, "into Prussia, which had been exhausted by our passage; the army was deprived of them, and a dearth would very soon he felt in it."

By his account, Yorck was perfectly aware of the manœuvre. Macdonald believed the accusation, dismissed the accused person, and confided the administration to the accuser: Yorck, filled with spite, from that moment thought of nothing but revenge.

Napoleon was then at Moscow. The Prussian was on the watch; he joyfully foresaw the consequences of that rash enterprise, and it appears as if he yielded to the temptation of taking advantage of it, and of getting the start of fortune. On the 29th of September, the Russian general learned that Yorck had recovered Mittau; and either from having received reinforcements, (two divisions had actually just arrived from Finland,) or from confidence of another kind, he adventured himself as far as that city, which he retook, and was preparing to push his advantage. The grand park of the besiegers' artillery was about to be carried off; Yorck, if we are to believe those who were witnesses, had exposed it, he remained motionless—he betrayed it.

It is said that the chief of his staff felt indignant at this treachery; we are assured that he represented to his general in the warmest terms, that he would ruin himself, and destroy the honour of the Prussian arms; and that, finally, Yorck, moved by his representations, allowed Kleist to put himself in movement. His approach was quite sufficient. But on this occasion, although there was a regular battle, there were scarcely four hundred men put *hors du combat* on both sides. As soon as this petty warfare was over, each army tranquilly resumed its former quarters.

CHAPTER VII

GROWING DISAFFECTION
IN PRUSSIA

ON the receipt of this intelligence, Macdonald became uneasy, and very much incensed; he hurried from his right wing, where perhaps he had remained too long at a distance from the Prussians. The surprise of Mittau, the danger which his park of artillery had run of being captured, Yorck's obstinacy in refusing to pursue the enemy, and the secret details which reached him from the interior of Yorck's head-quarters, were all sufficiently alarming. But the more ground there was for suspicion, the more it was necessary to dissemble; for as the Prussian army was entirely guiltless of the designs of its leader, and had fought readily, and as the enemy had given way, appearances had been preserved, and it would have been wise policy in Macdonald if he had appeared satisfied.

He did quite the contrary. His quick disposition, or his loyalty, were unable to dissemble; he broke out into reproaches against the Prussian general, at the very moment when his troops, satisfied with their victory, were only looking for praise and rewards. Yorck artfully contrived to make his soldiers, whose expectations had been frustrated, participators in the disgust of a humiliation which had been reserved solely for himself.

We find in Macdonald's letters the real causes of his dissatisfaction. He wrote to Yorck, "that it was shameful that his posts should be continually attacked, and that in return he had never once harrassed the enemy; that ever since he had been in sight of them, he had done no more than repel attacks, and in no one instance had ever acted on the offensive, although his officers and troops were filled with the best dispositions." This last remark was very true, for in general it was remarkable to see the ardour of all these Germans for a cause completely foreign to them, and which might to them even appear hostile.

They all rivalled each other in eagerness to rush into the midst of danger, in order to acquire the esteem of the grand army, and an eulogium from Napoleon. Their princes preferred the plain silver star of French honour to their richest orders. At that time the genius of Napoleon still appeared to have dazzled or subdued every one. Equally munificent to reward, as prompt and terrible to punish, he appeared like one of those great centres of nature, the dispenser of all good. In many of the Germans, there was united with this feeling that of a respectful admiration for a life which was so completely stamped with the marvellous, which so much affects them.

But their admiration was a consequence of victory, and our fatal retreat had already commenced; already from the north to the south of Europe, the Russian cries of vengeance replied to those of Spain. They crossed and echoed each other in the countries of Germany, which still remained under the yoke; these two great fires, lighted up at the two extremities of Europe, were gradually extending towards its centre, where they were like the dawn of a new day; they covered sparks which were fanned by hearts burning with patriotic hatred, and exalted to fanaticism by mystic rites. Gradually, as our disaster approached to Germany, there was heard rising from her bosom an indistinct rumour, a general but still trembling, uncertain and confused murmur.

The students of the universities, bred up with ideas of independence, inspired by their ancient constitutions, which secure them so many privileges, full of exalted recollections of the ancient and chivalrous glory of Germany, and for her sake jealous of all foreign glory, had always been our enemies. Total strangers to all political calculations, they had never bent themselves under our victory. Since it had become pale, a similar spirit had caught the politicians and even the military. The association of the *Friends of Virtue* gave this insurrection the appearance of an extensive plot; some chiefs did certainly conspire, but there was no conspiracy; it was a spontaneous movement, a common and universal sensation.

Alexander skilfully increased this disposition by his proclamations, by his addresses to the Germans, and by the distinction which he made in the treatment of their prisoners. As to the monarchs of Europe, he and Bernadotte were as yet the only ones who marched at the head of their people. All the others, restrained by policy or feelings of honour, allowed themselves to be anticipated by their subjects.

This infection even penetrated to the grand army; after the passage of the Berezina, Napoleon had been informed of it. Communications had been observed to be going on between the Bavarian, Saxon, and Austrian generals. On the left, Yorck's bad disposition increased, and communicated itself to a part of his troops; all the enemies of France had united, and Macdonald was astonished at having to repel the perfidious insinuations of an aide-de-camp of Moreau. The impression made by our victories was still, however, so deep in all the Germans, they had been so powerfully kept under, that they required a considerable time to rouse themselves.

On the 15th of November, Macdonald, seeing that the left of the Russian line had extended itself too far from Riga, between him and the Dwina, made some feigned attacks on their whole front, and pushed a real one against their centre, which he broke through rapidly as far as the river, near Dahlenkirchen. The whole left of the Russians, Lewis, and five thousand men, found themselves cut off from their retreat, and thrown back on the Dwina. Lewis vainly sought for an outlet; he found his enemy every where, and lost at first two battalions and a squadron. He would have infallibly been taken with his whole force, had he been pressed closer, but he was allowed sufficient space and time to take breath; as the cold increased, and the country offered no means of escape, he ventured to trust himself to the weak ice which had begun to cover the river. He made his troops lay a bed of straw and boards over it, in that manner crossed the Dwina at two points between Friedrichstadt and Lindan, and re-entered Riga at the very moment his comrades had begun to despair of his preservation.

The day after this engagement, Macdonald was informed of the retreat of Napoleon on Smolensk, but not of the disorganisation of the army. A few days after, some sinister reports brought him the news of the capture of Minsk. He began to be alarmed, when, on the 4th of December, a letter from Maret, magnifying the victory of the Berezina, announced to him the capture of nine thousand Russians, nine standards, and twelve cannon. The admiral, according to this letter, was reduced to thirteen thousand men.

On the 3rd of December the Russians were again repulsed in one of their sallies from Riga, by the Prussians. Yorck, either from prudence or conscience, restrained himself. Macdonald had become reconciled to him. On the 19th of December, fourteen days after the departure of Napoleon, eight days after the capture of Wilna by Kutusoff, in short when Macdonald commenced his retreat, the Prussian army was still faithful.

CHAPTER VIII

THE PRUSSIAN ARMY DESERTS

IT was from Wilna, on the 9th of December, that orders were transmitted to Macdonald, of which a Prussian officer was the bearer, directing him to retreat slowly upon Tilsit. No care was taken to send these instructions by different channels. They did not even think of employing Lithuanians to carry a message of that importance. In this manner the last army, the only one which remained unbroken, was exposed to the risk of destruction. An order, which was written at the distance of only four days' journey from Macdonald, lingered so long on the road, that it was nine days in reaching him.

The marshal directed his retreat on Tilsit, by passing between Telzs and Szawlia. Yorck, with the greatest part of the Prussians, forming his rear-guard, marched at a day's distance from him, in contact with the Russians, and left entirely to themselves. By some this was regarded as a great error on the part of Macdonald; but the majority did not venture to decide, alleging that in a situation so delicate, confidence and suspicion were alike dangerous.

The latter also said that the French marshal did every thing which prudence required of him, by retaining with him one of Yorck's divisions; the other, which was commanded by Massenbach, was under the direction of the French general Bachelu, and formed the vanguard. The Prussian army was thus separated into two corps, Macdonald in the middle, and the one seemed to be a guarantee to him for the other.

At first every thing went on well, although the danger was every where, in the front, in the rear, and on the flanks; for the grand army of Kutusoff had already pushed forward three vanguards, on the retreat of the duke of Tarentum. Macdonald encountered the first at Kelm, the second at Piklupenen, and the third at Tilsit. The zeal of the black hussars and the Prussian dragoons appeared to increase. The Russian hussars of Ysum were sabred and overthrown at Kelm. On the 27th of December, at the close of a ten hours' march, these Prussians came in sight of Piklupenen and the Russian brigade of Laskow; without stopping to take breath, they charged, threw it into disorder, and cut off two of its battalions; next day they retook Tilsit from the Russian commander Tettenborn.

A letter from Berthier, dated at Antonowo, on 14th of December, reached Macdonald several days before, in which he was informed that the army no longer existed, and that it was necessary that he should arrive speedily on the Pregel, in order to cover Königsberg, and to be able to retreat upon Elbing and Marienberg. This news the marshal concealed from the Prussians. Hitherto the cold and the forced marches had produced no complaints from them; there was no symptom of discontent exhibited by these allies; brandy and provisions were not deficient.

But on the 28th, when general Bachelu extended to the right, towards Regnitz, in order to drive away the Russians, who had taken refuge there, after their expulsion from Tilsit, the Prussian officers began to complain that their troops were fatigued; their vanguard marched unwillingly and carelessly, allowed itself to be surprised, and was thrown into disorder. Bachelu, however, restored the fortune of the day, and entered Regnitz.

During this time, Macdonald, who had arrived at Tilsit, was waiting for Yorck and the rest of the Prussian army, which did not make its appearance. On the 29th, the officers, and the orders which he sent them, were vainly multiplied; no news of Yorck transpired. On the 30th, Macdonald's anxiety was redoubled; it was fully exhibited in one of his letters of that day's date, in which, however, he did not yet venture to appear suspicious of a defection. He wrote "that he could not understand the reason of this delay; that he had sent a number of officers and emissaries with orders to Yorck to rejoin him, but that he had received no answer. In consequence, when the enemy was advancing against him, he was compelled to suspend his retreat; for he could not make up his mind to desert this corps, to retreat without Yorck and yet this delay was ruinous." This letter concluded thus:—"I am lost in conjectures. If I retreat, what would the emperor say? what would be said by France, by the army, by Europe? Would it not be an indelible stain on the 10th corps, voluntarily to abandon a part of its troops, and without being compelled to do it otherwise than by prudence! Oh, no; whatever may be the result, I am resigned, and willingly devote myself as a victim, provided I am the only one:" and he concluded by wishing the French general "that sleep which his melancholy situation had long denied him."

On the same day, he recalled Bachelu, and the Prussian cavalry, which was still at Regnitz, to Tilsit. It was night when Bachelu received the order; he wished to execute it immediately, but the Prussian colonels refused; and they covered their refusal under different pretexts. "The roads," they said, "were not passable. They were not accustomed to make their men march in such dreadful weather, and at so late an hour! They were responsible to their king for their regiments." The French general was astonished, commanded them to be silent, and ordered them to obey; his firmness subdued them, they obeyed, but slowly. A Russian general had stolen into their ranks, and urged them to deliver up this Frenchman, who was alone in the midst of those who commanded them; but the Prussians, although fully prepared to abandon Bachelu, could not resolve to betray him: at last they began their march.

At Regnitz, at eight o'clock at night, they had refused to mount their horses; at Tilsit, where they arrived at two in the morning, they refused to alight from them. At five o'clock in the morning, however, they had all gone to their quarters, and as order appeared to be restored among them, the general went to take some rest. But the obedience had been entirely feigned, for no sooner did the Prussians find themselves unobserved, than they resumed their arms, went out with Massenbach at their head, and escaped from Tilsit in silence, and by favour of the night. The first dawn of the last day of the year 1812, informed Macdonald that the Prussian army had deserted him.

It was Yorck, who, instead of rejoining him, deprived him of Massenbach, whom he had just recalled. His own defection, which had commenced on the 26th of December, was just consummated. On the 30th of December a convention between Yorck and the Russian general Diebitsch was concluded at Taurogen. "The Prussian troops were to be cantoned on their own frontiers, and remain neutral during two months, even in the event of this armistice being disapproved of by their own government. At the end of that time, the roads should be open to them to rejoin the French troop should their sovereign persist in ordering them to do so."

Yorck, but more particularly Massenbach, either from fear of the Polish division to which they were united, or from respect for Macdonald, showed some delicacy in their defection. They wrote to the marshal. Yorck announced to him the convention he had just concluded, which he coloured with specious pretexts. "He had been reduced to it by fatigue and necessity; but," he added, "that whatever judgment the world might form of his conduct, he was not at all uneasy about; that his duty to his troops, and the most mature reflection, had dictated it to him; that finally, whatever might be the appearances, he was actuated by the purest motives."

Massenbach excused himself for his clandestine departure. "He had wished to spare himself a sensation which his heart felt too painfully. He was afraid, lest the sentiments of respect and esteem which he should preserve to the end of his life for Macdonald, should have prevented him from doing his duty."

Macdonald saw all at once his force reduced from twenty-nine thousand to nine thousand, but in the state of anxiety in which he had been living for the last two days, any termination to it was a relief.

CHAPTER IX

MACDONALD RETREATS

THUS commenced the defection of our allies. I shall not venture to set myself up as a judge of the morality of this event; posterity will decide upon it. As a contemporaneous historian, however, I conceive myself bound not only to state the facts, but also the impression they have left, and such as it still remains, in the minds of the principal leaders of the two corps of the allied army, either as actors or sufferers.

The Prussians only waited for an opportunity to break our alliance, which was forced upon them; when the moment arrived, they embraced it. Not only, however, did they refuse to betray Macdonald, but they did not even wish to quit him, until they had, as it may be said, drawn him out of Russia, and placed him in safety. On his side, when Macdonald became sensible that he was abandoned, but without having positive proofs of it, he obstinately remained at Tilsit, at the mercy of the Prussians, sooner than give them a motive of defection, by too speedy a retreat.

The Prussians did not abuse this noble conduct. There was defection on their part, but no treachery; which in this age, and after the evils they had endured, may still appear meritorious; they did not join themselves with the Russians. When they arrived on their own frontier, they could not resign themselves to aid their conqueror in defending their native soil against those who came in the character of their deliverers, and who were so; they became neutral, and this was not, I repeat, until Macdonald, disengaged from Russia and the Russians, had his retreat free.

This marshal continued it from Königsburg, by Labiau and Tente. His rear was protected by Mortier, and Heudelet's division, whose troops, newly arrived, still occupied Insterburg, and kept Tchitchakoff in check. On the 3rd of January he effected his junction with Mortier, and covered Königsberg.

It was, however, a happy circumstance for Yorck's reputation, that Macdonald, thus weakened, and whose retreat his defection had interrupted, was enabled to rejoin the grand army. The inconceivable slowness of Wittgenstein's march saved that marshal: the Russian general, however, overtook him at Labiau and Tente; and there, but for the efforts of Bachelu and his brigade, the valour of the Polish colonel Kameski, captain Ostrowski, and the Bavarian major Mayer, the corps of Macdonald, thus deserted, would have been broken or destroyed; in that case Yorck would appear to have betrayed him, and history would, with justice, have stigmatised him with the name of traitor. Six hundred French, Bavarians, and Poles, remained dead on these two fields of battle; their blood accuses the Prussians for not having provided, by an additional article, for the safe retreat of the leader whom they had deserted.

The king of Prussia disavowed Yorck's conduct. He dismissed him, appointed Kleist to succeed him in the command, ordered the latter to arrest his late commander, and send him, as well as Massenbach, to Berlin, there to undergo their trial. But these generals preserved their command in spite of him; the Prussian army did not consider their monarch at liberty; this opinion was founded on the presence of Augereau and some French troops at Berlin.

Frederick, however, was perfectly aware of the annihilation of our army. At Smorgoni, Narbonne refused to accept the mission to that monarch, until Napoleon gave him authority to make the most unreserved communication. He, Augereau, and several others, have declared that Frederick was not merely restrained by his position in the midst of the remains of the grand army, and by the dread of Napoleon's re-appearance at the head of a fresh one, but also by his plighted faith; for every thing is of a mixed character in the moral as well as the physical world, and even in the most trifling of our actions there is a variety of different motives. But finally, his good faith yielded to necessity, and his dread to a greater dread. He saw himself, it was said, threatened with a species of forfeiture by his people and by our enemies.

It should be remarked that the Prussian nation, which drew its sovereign toward Yorck, only ventured to rise successively, as the Russians came in sight, and by degrees, as our feeble remains quitted their territory. A single fact, which took place during the retreat, will paint the dispositions of the people, and show how much, notwithstanding the hatred they bore us, they were curbed under the ascendency of our victories.

When Davoust was recalled to France he passed, with only two attendants, through the town of X——. The Russians were daily expected there; its population were incensed at the sight of these last Frenchmen. Murmurs, mutual excitations, and finally outcries, rapidly succeeded each other; the most violent speedily surrounded the carriage of the marshal, and were already about to unharness the horses, when Davoust made his appearance, rushed upon the most insolent of these insurgents, dragged him behind his carriage, and made his servants fasten him to it. Frightened at this action, the people stopped short, seized with motionless consternation, and then quietly and silently opened a passage for the marshal, who passed through the midst of them, carrying off his prisoner.

CHAPTER X

DEFECTION OF THE AUSTRIANS

IN this sudden manner did our left wing fall. On our right wing, on the side of the Austrians, whom a well cemented alliance retained, a phlegmatic people, governed despotically by an united aristocracy, there was no sudden explosion to be apprehended. This wing detached itself from us insensibly, and with the formalities required by its political position.

On the 10th of December, Schwartzenberg was at Slonim, presenting successively vanguards towards Minsk, Novogrodeck, and Bielitza. He was still persuaded that the Russians were beaten and fleeing before Napoleon, when he was informed at the same moment of the emperor's departure, and of the destruction of the grand army, but in so vague a manner that he was for some time without any direction.

In his embarrassment he addressed himself to the French ambassador at Warsaw. The answer of that minister authorised him "not to sacrifice another man." In consequence, he retreated on the 14th of December from Slonim towards Bialystock. The instructions which reached him from Murat in the middle of this movement were conformable to it.

About the 21st of December, an order from Alexander suspended hostilities on that point, and as the interest of the Russians agreed with that of the Austrians, there was very soon a mutual understanding. A moveable armistice, which was approved by Murat, was immediately concluded. The Russian general and Schwartzenberg were to manœuvre on each other, the Russian on the offensive, and the Austrian on the defensive, but without coming to blows.

Regnier's corps, now reduced to ten thousand men, was not included in the arrangement; but Schwartzenberg, while he yielded to circumstances, persevered in his loyalty. He regularly gave an account of every thing to the commander of the army; he covered the whole front of the French line with his Austrian troops, and preserved it. This prince was not at all complaisant towards the enemy; he believed him not upon his bare word; at every position he was about to yield, he would actually satisfy himself with his own eyes, that he only yielded it to a superior force, ready to combat him. In this manner he arrived upon the Bug and the Narew, from Nur to Ostrolenka where the war terminated.

He was in this manner covering Warsaw, when, on the 22nd of January, he received instructions from his government to abandon the Grand-duchy, to separate his retreat from that of Regnier, and re-enter Gallicia. To these instructions he only yielded a tardy obedience: he resisted the pressing solicitations and threatening manœuvres of Miloradowitch until the 25th of January: even then, he effected his retreat upon Warsaw so slowly, that the hospitals and a great part of the magazines were enabled to be evacuated. Finally, he obtained more favourable capitulation for the Warsavians than they could venture to expect. He did more; although that city was to have been delivered up on the 5th, he only yielded it on the 8th, and thus gave Regnier the start of three days upon the Russians.

Regnier was afterwards, it is true, overtaken and surprised at Kalisch, but that was in consequence of halting too long to protect the flight of some Polish depôts. In the first disorder occasioned by this unexpected attack, a Saxon brigade was separated from the French corps, retreated on Schwartzenberg, and was well received by him; Austria allowed it to pass through her territory, and restored it to the grand army, when it was assembled near Dresden.

On the 1st of January, 1813, however, at Königsberg, where Murat then was, the desertion of the Prussians and the intrigues forming by Austria were not known, when suddenly Macdonald's despatch, and an insurrection of the people of Königsberg, gave information of the beginning of a defection, of which it was impossible to foresee the consequences. The consternation was excessive. The seditious movement was at first only kept down by representations, which Ney very soon changed into threats. Murat hastened his departure for Elbing. Konigsberg was encumbered with ten thousand sick and wounded, most of whom were abandoned to the generosity of their enemies. Some of them had no reason to complain of it; but prisoners who escaped, declared that many of their unfortunate companions were massacred and thrown out of the windows into the streets; that an hospital which contained several hundred sick was set fire to; and they accused the inhabitants of committing these horrid deeds.

On another side, at Wilna, more than sixteen thousand of our prisoners had already perished. The convent of St. Basil contained the greatest number; from the 10th to the 23rd of December they had only received some biscuits; but not a stick of wood nor a drop of water had been given them. The snow collected in the courts, which were covered with dead bodies, quenched the burning thirst of the survivors. They threw out of the windows such of the dead bodies as could not be kept in the passages, on the staircases, or among the heaps of corpses which were collected in all the apartments. The additional prisoners that were every moment discovered were thrown into this horrible place.

The arrival of the emperor Alexander and his brother at last put a stop to these abominations. They had lasted for thirteen days, and if a few hundreds escaped out of the twenty thousand of our unfortunate comrades who were made prisoners, it was to these two princes they owed their preservation. But a most violent epidemic had already arisen from the poisonous exhalations of so many corpses; it passed from the vanquished to the victors, and fully avenged us. The Russians, however, were living in plenty; our magazines at Smorgoni and Wilna had not been destroyed, and they must have found besides immense quantities of provisions in the pursuit of our routed army.

But Wittgenstein, who had been detached to attack Macdonald, descended the Niemen; Tchitchakoff and Platoff pursued Murat towards Kowno, Wilkowiski, and Insterburg; shortly after, the admiral was sent towards Thorn. Finally, on the 9th of January, Alexander and Kutusoff arrived on the Niemen at Merecz. There, as he was about to cross his own frontier, the Russian emperor addressed a proclamation to his troops, completely filled with images, comparisons, and eulogiums, which the winter had much better deserved than his army.

CHAPTER XI

DEFECTION OF MURAT

IT was not until the 22nd of January, and the following days, that the Russians reached the Vistula. During this tardy march, from the 3rd to the 11th of January, Murat remained at Elbing. In this situation of extremity that monarch was wavering from one plan to another, at the mercy of the elements which were fermenting around him; sometimes they raised his hopes to the highest pitch, at others they sunk him into an abyss of disquietude.

He had taken flight from Königsberg in a complete state of discouragement, when the suspension of the march of the Russians, and the junction of Macdonald with Heudelet and Cavaignac, which doubled his forces, suddenly inflamed him with vain hopes. He who had the day before believed that all was lost, wished to resume the offensive and begin immediately; for he was one of those dispositions who are making fresh resolutions every instant. On that day he determined to push forward, and the next to flee as far as Posen.

This last determination, however, was not taken without reason. The rallying of the army on the Vistula had been completely illusory; the old guard had not altogether more than five hundred effective men; the young guard scarcely any; the first corps, eighteen hundred; the second, one thousand; the third, sixteen hundred; the fourth, seventeen hundred; added to which, most of these soldiers, the remains of six hundred thousand men, could scarcely handle their arms.[1]

In this state of impotence, with the two wings of the army already detached from us, Austria and Prussia failing us together, Poland became a snare which might close around us. On the other hand, Napoleon, who never consented to any cession, was anxious that Dantzic should be defended; it became necessary, therefore, to throw into it all that could keep the field.

Besides, if the truth must be told, when Murat talked at Elbing of reconstituting the army, and was even dreaming of victories, he found that most of the commanders were themselves worn out and disgusted. Misfortune, which leads to fear every thing, and to believe readily all that one fears, had penetrated into their hearts. Several of them were already uneasy about their rank and their grades, about the estates which they had acquired in the conquered countries, and the greater part only sighed to re-cross the Rhine.

As to the recruits who arrived, they were a mixture of men from several of the German nations. In order to join us they had passed through the Prussian states, from whence arose the exhalation of so much hatred. As they approached, they encountered our discouragement and our long train of disorder; when they entered into line, far from being put into companies with, and supported by old soldiers, they found themselves left alone, to fight with every kind of scourge, to support a cause which was abandoned by those most interested in its success; the consequence was, that at the very first bivouac, most of these Germans disbanded themselves. At sight of the disasters of the army returning from Moscow, the tried soldiers of Macdonald were themselves shaken. Notwithstanding, this corps d'armée, and the completely fresh division of Heudelet, preserved their unity. All these remains were speedily collected into Dantzic; thirty-five thousand soldiers, from seventeen different nations, were shut up in it. The remainder, in small numbers, did not begin rallying until they got to Posen and upon the Oder.

Hitherto it was hardly possible for the king of Naples to regulate our flight any better; but at the moment he passed through Marienwerder on his way to Posen, a letter from Naples again unsettled all his resolutions. The impression which it made upon him was so violent, that by degrees as he read it, the bile mixed itself with his blood so rapidly, that he was found a few minutes after with a complete jaundice.

It appeared that an act of government, which the queen had taken upon herself, had wounded him in one of his strongest passions. He was not at all jealous of that princess, notwithstanding her charms, but furiously so of his royal authority; and it was particularly of the queen, as sister of the emperor, that he was suspicious.

Persons were astonished at seeing this prince, who had hitherto appeared to sacrifice every thing to glory in arms, suffering himself to be mastered all at once by a less noble passion; but they forgot that, with certain characters, there must be always a ruling passion.

Besides, it was still the same ambition under different forms, and always entering completely into each of them; for such are passionate characters. At that moment his jealousy of his authority triumphed over his love of glory; it made him proceed rapidly to Posen, where, shortly after his arrival, he disappeared, and abandoned us.

This defection took place on the 16th of January, twenty-three days before Schwartzenberg detached himself from the French army, of which Prince Eugene took the command.

Alexander arrested the march of his troops at Kalisch.[2] There the violent and continued war, which had followed us all the way from Moscow, slackened: it became only, until the spring, a war of fits, slow and intermittent. The strength of the evil appeared to be exhausted; but it was merely that of the combatants; a still greater struggle was preparing, and this halt was not a time allowed to make peace, but merely given to the premeditation of slaughter.

1. M. de Segur has omitted the 5th corps (which consisted of 20,000 men), and the 6th, 7th, 9th and 10th.—*Ed.*

2. The loss sustained by the Russians, in this winter campaign, was inferior only to that of the French. At the battle of Krasnoi, Kutusoff had 100,000 men under arms; by the time that he arrived at Wilna they had dwindled to 35,000. Some companies had not a single man, and a great number of battalions could not muster more than 50 men.—*Ed.*

CHAPTER XII

CONCLUSION

THUS did the star of the North triumph over that of Napoleon. Is it then the fate of the South to be vanquished by the North? Cannot that subdue it in its turn? Is it against nature that that aggression should be successful? and is the frightful result of our invasion a fresh proof of it?

Certainly the human race does not march in that direction; its inclination is towards the south, it turns its back to the north; the sun attracts its regards, its wishes, and its steps. We cannot with impunity turn back this great current of men; the attempt to make them return, to repel them, and confine them within their frozen regions, is a gigantic enterprise. The Romans exhausted themselves by it. Charlemagne, although he rose when one of these great invasions was drawing to a termination, could only check it for a short time; the rest of the torrent, driven back to the east of the empire, penetrated it through the north, and completed the inundation.

A thousand years have since elapsed; the nations of the north have required time to recover from that great migration, and to acquire the knowledge which is now indispensable to a conquering nation. During that interval, it was not without reason that the Hanse Towns opposed the introduction of the warlike arts into the immense camp of the Scandinavians.

The event has justified their fears. Scarcely had the science of modern war penetrated among them, when Russian armies were seen on the Elbe, and shortly after in Italy; they then came to reconnoitre these countries; some day they will come and settle in them.

During the last century, either from philanthropy or vanity, Europe was eager in contributing to civilise these men of the north, of whom Peter had already made formidable warriors. She acted wisely, in so far as she diminished for herself the danger of relapsing into fresh barbarism; if we allow that a second relapse into the darkness of the middle ages is possible, war having become so scientific, that mind predominates in it, so that success in it requires a degree of instruction, which nations that still remain barbarous can only acquire by civilisation.

But, in hastening the civilisation of these Normans, Europe has probably hastened the epoch of their next invasion. For let no one believe that their pompous cities, their exotic and forced luxury, will be able to retain them; that by polishing them, they will be kept stationary, or rendered less formidable. The luxury and effeminacy which are enjoyed in spite of a barbarous climate can only be the privilege of a few. The masses, which are incessantly increasing by an administration becoming gradually more enlightened, will continue sufferers by their climate, barbarous like that, and always more and more envious; and the invasion of the south by the north, recommenced by Catherine II., will continue.

Who is there that can fancy that the great struggle between the North and the South is at an end? Is it not, in its full grandeur, the war of privation against enjoyment, the eternal war of the poor against the rich, that which devours the interior of every empire?

Comrades, whatever was the motive of our expedition, this was the point which made it of importance to Europe. Its object was to wrest Poland from Russia; its result would have been to throw the danger of a fresh invasion of the men of the north at a greater distance, to weaken the torrent, and oppose a new barrier to it; and was there ever a man, or a combination of circumstances, so well calculated to ensure the success of so great an enterprise?

After fifteen hundred years of victories, the revolution of the fourth century, that of the kings and nobles against the people, was, in its turn, vanquished by the revolution of the nineteenth century, that of the people against the nobles and kings. Napoleon was born of this conflagration; he obtained such complete power over it, that it seemed as if that great convulsion had only been that of the bringing into the world one man. He commanded the revolution as if he had been the genius of that terrible element. At his voice she became tranquil. Ashamed of her excesses, she admired herself in him, and precipitating herself into his glory, she united Europe under his sceptre, and obedient Europe rose at his call to drive back Russia within her ancient limits. It seemed as if the North was in its turn about to be vanquished, even among its own ices.

And yet this great man, in these great circumstances in his favour, could not subdue nature! In this powerful effort to re-ascend that rapid declivity, so many forces failed him! After reaching these icy regions of Europe he was precipitated from their very summit. The North, victorious over the South in its defensive war, as it had been in the middle ages in its offensive one, now believes itself invulnerable and irresistible.

Comrades, believe it not! Ye might have triumphed over that soil and these spaces, that climate, and that rough and gigantic nature, as ye had conquered its soldiers.

But some errors were punished by great calamities! I have related both the one and the other. On that ocean of evils I have erected a melancholy beacon of gloomy and blood-red light; and if my feeble hand has been insufficient for the painful task, at least I have exhibited our floating wrecks, in order that those who come after us may see the peril and avoid it.

Comrades, my task is finished; it is now for you to bear your testimony to the truth of the picture. Its colours will no doubt appear pale to your eyes and to your hearts, which are still full of these great recollections. But which of you is ignorant that an action is always more eloquent than its description; and that if great historians are produced by great men, the first are still more rare than the last?

THE END